GARY T. MARX received his doctorate from the University of California at Berkeley, where he taught in the Department of Sociology and was a Research Associate at the Survey Research Center. He is presently an Assistant Professor in the Department of Social Relations at Harvard University and a Research Associate at the M.I.T.–Harvard Joint Center for Urban Studies. He lives in Cambridge, Massachusetts, with his wife and two children.

PROTEST

AND

PREJUDICE

PROTEST AND PREJUDICE

A Study of Belief in the Black Community

By GARY T. MARX

HARPER & ROW, PUBLISHERS

NEW YORK, EVANSTON, AND LONDON

Volume Three in a series based on
the University of California Five-Year Study of Anti-Semitism
in the United States,
being conducted by the Survey Research Center
Charles Y. Glock, Program Coordinator,
under a grant from the Anti-Defamation League of B'nai B'rith

FIRST EDITION

LIBRARY OF CONGRESS CATALOG CARD NUMBER: 67-22531

I-R

*To those oppressed because of their racial,
religious, or ethnic identity in the hope
that they will become more militant and more
tolerant and thus transcend evils so long
and cruelly perpetrated by man on man*

Contents

Tables

Foreword
by Bayard Rustin

This study by Gary T. Marx of Negro thought and attitudes—as well as the aspirations of our movement—tells it like it is, which is not the way many friends and enemies of the Negro struggle think it is. Its first virtue is that it does not look at the Negro community as simply a monolithic mass of apathy or militancy, but, in pointing out its complexity, takes full account of the variety of social and economic strata and opinions within it. This is in sharp contradiction to one aspect of white chauvinism which holds strongly to the stereotype of a "Big Black" opinion.

At the height of the civil rights struggle, one remembers that even as esteemed a journal as *The New York Times,* whose civil rights reporting was generally commendable, declared on occasions that "militants" were replacing the "old moderate" leadership of the movement. Such prognoses notwithstanding, the Negro leadership, and especially such thoughtful leaders as A. Philip Randolph, Roy Wilkins, Whitney Young and Dr. Martin Luther King, retained, as this study shows, the overwhelming support of the Negro communities, and are still in positions of leadership. As an act of charity, we can easily forget the number of "militants" who at one time or another have been crowned kings of the Negro movement by the mass media. Less humorous, but of no more substance, was the discovery by the New York press of the "Blood Brothers," a group of young Negroes supposedly bent on murdering and raping the white race. This, at the time, was a sensational "discovery," but the "Blood Brothers" proved to be without flesh or substance and to have a spiritual existence only in the minds of the reporter and a few policemen. Of the same order was the mass media's periodic discovery of enormous upsurges of Black Muslimism, something as fearsome as the "yellow peril." The building of these myths did considerable damage to Negro-white relationships; and also led some would-be civil rights leaders, with no real base of support in the Negro

community, to issue inflammatory statements on race relations for the
sheer sake of personal publicity. Through such publicity they hoped to
gain at least one supporter in the Negro community and perhaps a little
bit of that money from those white philanthropists who had been frightened
by their blood-curdling cries and portentous slogans. These great battles of
the press release left most of the Negro movement and community completely cold and disturbed, but presumably many papers were sold outside
of Harlem.

A lot of this foolishness could have been avoided had the mass media
maintained the same devotion to truth, the same care in its interviewing,
and the same high standards in compiling and analyzing information that
one finds in the study at hand. Black Americans are not so exotic as to
prevent the mass media from making a profound understanding of their
human aspirations. The ability to do this is clearly demonstrated by Mr.
Marx's study; he has not only sympathy with, but also considerable background knowledge and experience in the writing of Negro history. In addition, the clear, good writing one finds here is more than is usually
encountered in opinion polls and sociological tracts.

This study, meant to deal with Negro anti-Semitism, is part of a larger
one on anti-Semitism in the United States. It is to the credit of its author
and its sponsor, the Anti-Defamation League, that they recognized that one
cannot understand Negro prejudice against Jews unless one understands
something about Negro attitudes, life, and reactions to white prejudice.
Rather than isolating Negro anti-Semitic attitudes, the study concentrates
on examining the social and economic deprivations that lie at the roots of
much irrational hatred and prejudice. To its credit also, the study did not
attempt to apologize for some of the shadier operations of some Jewish
businessmen in the ghetto (which, of course, are no different from the
chiseling and price gouging practiced by non-Jewish, white, and Negro
businessmen in the ghettoes throughout the U.S.A.). It recognizes that
Negro resentment of these practices is justified, but also points out some of
the irrational hostility some Negroes have toward Jews who are not guilty
of exploiting them. And, most important, rather than merely deploring unjust attitudes and practices on both sides, the study attempts to understand
them in the context of ghetto conditions and life so that a real solution can
be sought.

The discovery by these investigations that there is less anti-Semitism in
the Negro community than there is in the broader white community is something that most people don't realize. I am thinking particularly of a television
show which not long ago featured three Negro "militants" who were supposed to be expressing the typical hatred that Negroes felt toward Jews. They
denounced Jews roundly for a variety of offenses to Negroes. One of the
participants even charged a "Jewish-Zionist" conspiracy against black men

and people of color throughout the world. It did not matter to the producer of this program, fishing for sensationalism in troubled waters, that his panelists, although presented as Negro spokesmen, had no real following in the Negro community. Even if they represented any thinking at all it was that of a thin stratum of the Negro *petite bourgeoisie* with the kind of severe status deprivation upon which anti-Semitism feeds. This book makes it clear that Negroes, if anything, are less intolerant than whites. (Negroes, in fact, do not share the traditional anti-Semitic biases. They do not revile Judaism as a religion. On the contrary, Martin Luther King is called "Moses." Malcolm X always exhorted Negroes to behave as the Jews did, by which he meant get an education, buy stores, etc. His remarks were anti-Jewish perhaps, but certainly he did not think the Jews were an inferior people.) But, unfortunately, it will reach a much smaller audience than the television program that did such great harm to the relationships between Negroes and Jews.

We cannot and must not tolerate any Negro anti-Semitism as we cannot and must not tolerate any anti-Negro prejudices in the Jewish community. Many respected Negro and Jewish leaders have spoken out against such bigotry, and recently James Baldwin and Ossie Davis resigned from the Board of a Negro magazine that gave its pages over to a vicious anti-Jewish article. But more meaningful than appeals for brotherhood and denunciations of prejudice is the recognition that unfair business practices and some forms of anti-Semitism are endemic to the ghetto. Ghetto thinking by Negroes who live there and Jews who work there is a product of the social and economic deprivations that exist in its confines. And those that live outside its borders are also victims of the illusions and prejudices common to that larger ghetto. It is the ghetto, the social and economic walls between the races, that must be destroyed if real tolerance and brotherhood are to exist. This is the approach of Professor Marx's study, and one of the reasons it is worthy of consideration by both Negroes and whites.

Beyond this, it provides interesting information and thoughtful conclusions about the Negro movement and the whole problem of racism and exploitation. As this study throws much light on the dynamics of social struggle and probes the deeper motives and aspirations in the Negro community, many myths fall by the wayside.

For instance: Ghetto life, rather than heightening the desire to struggle, decreases militancy, since it limits awareness of the possibility for change. Thus, the integrated character of the Freedom movement, instead of dampening militancy among Negroes, may encourage it. Similarly, membership in major civil rights organizations like the NAACP was found to be a key index of constructive militancy. A sense of relative deprivation, and not grinding oppression, was found to be a major stimulus to civil rights concern. Thus, greater militancy was found not among those most economically depressed, but among steadily employed industrial workers and middle-class elements earning between $4,000 and $6,000 a year. Concrete victories and reforms won by the movement, rather than pacifying and absorbing Negroes into the establishment, as some would-be revolutionaries had argued, inspired them to greater militancy and greater demands for basic social change.

The facts of this study help to puncture another myth held in common by both white moderates and Black Muslims: the pull-yourself-up-by-your-own-bootstraps school of thinking, which holds that a major cause of poverty and social misery in the Negro community is the lack of Negro self-help organizations. What the study shows is that Negroes have at least as many voluntary associations as other ethnic groups, and concludes that the cause of the Negroes' plight is the ghettos' lack of economic wherewithal and not the lack of good intentions or adequate organization. The blame for Negro apathy (much exaggerated, as this study shows) is put right where it belongs: on the American social structure which victimizes the Negro.

Also worthy of consideration is some of the information in this study on Negro reactions to the riots that flared up in a number of ghettos across the country. Although a minority in the Negro community thought the violence did some good, given the large-scale indifference to Negro demands shown by the white community, Negroes in areas where the riots took place, particularly in Harlem, had the greatest doubts about its usefulness.

Another interesting finding was that Black Muslim sympathizers were more likely to be recent migrants who couldn't get jobs or find their bearings amidst the confusion of ghetto and northern industrial life. Despite the misleading mass media reports, the study correctly concludes: "The 'rising tide' of black nationalism was unduly misleading; strong and consistent support for the Muslims was an infinitesimal ripple in the Negro community." Then and now, the overwhelming majority of Negroes were committed to integration: Not separatism, but integration in its profoundest sense; not tokenism, but equal opportunity and a fair share of the good things in life that other Americans enjoy. A number of us in the civil rights movement had always held this to be true, but amidst all the sound and fury we were often ignored.

But the exaggerated conception in the press of the size of the Black Muslims should not make us sanguine. The frustration and anger resulting from "a dream deferred" is growing in the Negro community, particularly in the racial and economic underclass America has created. Still, as the noted historian C. Vann Woodward pointed out, "It is clear that among the great majority of leaders and followers of the Negro movement, the racial reserve of patience and responsibility has never failed." The study bears this out and predicts that "as time passes, the proportion of the Negro community which is aroused and militant will increase." The study concludes that the direction the Negro community movement takes—toward thoughtful militancy and more effective political action, or toward angry outbursts and frustration tactics—will be determined by the response of the white majority to the Negroes' just demands. Most Negroes, the study shows, still maintain their commitment to nonviolent social change and willingness to work with men of good will in the white community. But should their hopes for true equality be thwarted and the road to social and economic progress remain closed to the Negro masses, there will certainly be a bitter harvest. Already there are ominous signs of this. With the falling off of white support for the Freedom movement, such thoughtful scholars as C. Vann Woodward have warned of the dangers of a second Reconstruction. "If we are realists we will no longer pretend that the movement for racial justice and Negro rights is sustained by the same foundation of moral assurance, or that it is supported today by the same political conditions, the same interracial accommodations, and such harmony of purpose, and commitment and dedication as recently prevailed."

Thus, today, America is at a crossroads. The civil rights revolution generated the most healthy and constructive creative climate the country has known in decades; it sparked social consciousness and action that benefited all Americans. The compromise with racism that marked the first Reconstruction led to an era of reaction and moral callousness toward human rights from which the country has still not fully been freed. And a second Reconstruction means social retrogression, spawned by racial conflict among white and blacks at the bottom of the economic ladder, that will poison our society with bigotry of all kinds at a time when it needs to move dynamically forward to meet the new social problems generated in the wake of our technological revolution. We must recreate, in a new interracial movement, the high idealism and moral commitment that was reborn in the United States with the civil rights revolution. But this time we cannot build around the effort to get Negroes a cup of coffee at a segregated lunch counter, an integrated seat on a bus or a vote in a lily white electoral process. Considerable progress has been made in these areas, but we still have not touched the deeper misery of the black and white poor. The great "coalition of conscience"—that alliance of Negro, labor, liberal and religious groups that offers the best hope for a truly great society—must be restructured to confront the more basic socioeconomic problems of our society and meet the needs of both black and white Americans. To complete the unfinished democratic revolution of our time, we need a program with the social vision of A. Philip Randolph's $185 billion Freedom Budget, which goes to the social and economic roots of bigotry, proposes to tear down the ghettos and slums and replace them with decent integrated communities, and can unite the Negro and white poor as well as all men of good will in the task of a just and equitable reconstruction.

This study delineates the problem, now we must get on with the solution.

Preface

This book—the third volume in the series *Patterns of American Prejudice*—is part of the University of California Five-Year Study of Anti-Semitism in the United States, sponsored by the Anti-Defamation League of B'nai B'rith and conducted by the Survey Research Center of the University of California at Berkeley.[1] Despite the title of the research project, the present volume is not primarily concerned with Negro attitudes toward Jews.

During the initial planning of the five-year program, begun in 1961, no special study of Negroes was contemplated. Rather, investigation of anti-Semitism among Negroes was to have been part of a general assessment of anti-Semitism to be based on interviews with a national sample of American adults. The national study was planned for the fall of 1964.

Before the national study was launched, the fateful summer of 1964 intervened. Negro riots flared up in a number of cities, including New York. Rumors and reports were current that anti-Semitism among Negroes was rampant, that the riots were specifically directed against Jewish shopkeepers, that anti-Semitism was burgeoning along with Negro resentment and the civil rights struggle. In view of these rumors and reports, and the events of the summer of 1964, it became increasingly apparent that so-called Negro anti-Semitism could no longer be studied apart from Negro attitudes toward their own situation, the whites, the community, and the civil rights movement.

This new perspective evolved over months of frequent conversation between participants in the general project and Mr. Oscar Cohen, the ADL's program director. The ADL, originally founded as a Jewish defense

[1] The first two volumes in the series, published by Harper & Row in 1966, are *Christian Beliefs and Anti-Semitism*, by Charles Y. Glock and Rodney Stark, and *The Apathetic Majority: A Study Based on Public Responses to the Eichmann Trial*, by Charles Y. Glock, Gertrude J. Selznick, and Joe L. Spaeth. Further volumes include a study of politics and anti-Semitism, a study of the formation of intergroup attitudes and friendship patterns among school youth, and a national study of the extent and sources of anti-Semitism.

organization, long ago extended its program to include all aspects of inter-group relations. Its concern about the lack of carefully documented social research on the civil rights struggle equaled my own, and it generously provided funds for an expanded study of the climate of opinion in the Negro American community. The result is *Protest and Prejudice*.

The interviews on which this study is based were conducted in late 1964. Since that time, important changes have taken place in the civil rights struggle: the death of Malcolm X; Watts; the shooting of James Meredith during his march in Mississippi; the widening split in the civil rights movement over the slogan of black power and its implications. No doubt some shifts in opinion in the Negro community have also taken place. However, while dramatic events may have profound implications for the organized civil rights struggle, they may have little effect on the attitudes of the masses of Negroes, particularly in the short run. In spite of changes on the civil rights scene, a nationwide inquiry by *Newsweek* magazine reported in their August 22, 1966, issue shows results very similar to those of the present study, carried out two years earlier, and of another *Newsweek* survey carried out in 1963. Subsequent data from Gallup polls and the UCLA study on Watts are also comparable, as are three recent and as yet unpublished studies of the attitudes of Negro youth. Although new issues have developed and attitudes toward old issues have shifted slightly, the dominant thrust of black opinion seems to have remained about the same during the last few years. However, even if changes in Negro opinion had been more pronounced than these surveys indicate, this would not seriously detract from the present inquiry. The main concern of this study is not so much with attitudes toward single issues as with the basic orientations of Negroes to the civil rights struggle and toward whites. Those relatively uninterested in the struggle in 1964 are probably still among the apathetic today, just as those militant three years ago are probably militant today. Furthermore, the factors that shaped Negro responses to the civil rights struggle in 1964 are doubtless as relevant today as they were two years ago (just as many are relevant to understanding militancy under slavery).

Our data suggest that many people hold an overly sensational image of the Negro mood. To be sure there is deep anger and frustration, as well as varying degrees of suspicion and resentment of whites. Yet, there is still optimism about the possibility of change within the system. Most Negroes favor integration in principle, are loyal to the United States, are opposed to indiscriminate violence, and are not consistently antiwhite or anti-Semitic. These facts aside, rather than endless discussion about the nature of so-called Negro extremism,[2] attention might better be focused on changing the general social conditions that have given rise to virulent hatreds

[2] See footnote 12, Chapter 5.

and extreme attitudes on the part of a small but no doubt increasing minority of the black community.

With respect to my own values, I have been involved in the civil rights struggle and am concerned with the issues of which this book treats. The effect of my personal concerns on the analysis of the data has, I hope, been minimal. However, someone with a different commitment might have written a different book.

I am grateful to Charles Y. Glock for his guidance and for the opportunity to pursue this inquiry as I saw fit. Gertrude J. Selznick and Rodney Stark carefully went over the entire manuscript and made many helpful improvements in the prose, as well as offering useful substantive comments. Nathan Glazer, Stephen Steinberg, Robert Blauner, Donald Noel, and Seymour Levantman offered useful criticisms. Wendy Shuken and Toni Brown helped with the data processing and with clerical and editorial tasks. I am particularly indebted to the ADL and their program director, Mr. Cohen, for making this study possible. Finally, I am grateful to my wife Phyllis for her editorial assistance and for Joshua, who joined us shortly before work on this project was completed.

Berkeley, California   G. T. M.
October 1, 1966

Introduction:
Protest and Prejudice

> The whole history of the progress of human liberty shows that all con-
> cessions yet made to her august claims have been born of earnest strug-
> gle . . . if there is no struggle there is no progress. . . . This struggle may
> be a moral one or it may be a physical one . . . but it must be a struggle.
> —*Frederick Douglass*

The response of the oppressed to oppression is not uniform. Sometimes
oppression produces docility; at other times it is violently resisted. One
may contrast the many centuries of placidity of the Indian untouchables
with the enduring rebelliousness of the Caribbean slaves. Oppression has
varied consequences, from the "white is right" attitude of the loyal Southern retainer, to the vibrant militancy of young civil rights workers.

Despite variation within oppressed groups, ours is clearly a time of widespread protest. Throughout the world, the struggle against discrimination
and subjugation is probably more in evidence now than at any other time
in human history. Africans in Rhodesia, Pakistanis in England, Australian
aborigines, American Indians, Eskimos, and even homosexuals, are demanding justice.

More than half a century ago, W. E. B. Du Bois wrote that "the problem of the Twentieth Century is the problem of the color line." Since
that time, overpopulation and atomic annihilation have emerged as global
concerns. Yet his judgment remains true today. Protest on behalf of self-
determination and for an end to racial, religious, and national subjugation, and tension arising from these conflicts, is a defining characteristic of
our time.

Protest and revolt are apt to catch the imagination and win the sympathy of the observer with an aroused social conscience. The social revolutions being born of protest promise a better world, free at least of one kind

of historic exploitation. Ironically, however, they harbor a potential for new hatreds. Out of misery and just grievances can come the desire for revenge and categorical hatred of the oppressors.

This book is concerned with both these themes: with the reaction of Negro Americans to their oppression and quest for justice; and with the hostility of Negro Americans toward whites and the extent to which protest is linked to this hostility.

In response to a reporter's question about the antecedents of the Watts revolt, a young Negro said, "Man, it started four hundred years ago." Various types of protest have gone on continually since Negro slaves first jumped ship over three centuries ago. The historical record reveals numerous attacks on slave owners, arson, other property damage, legal efforts to secure manumission, flight, and occasionally armed rebellion and revolt. Protest was also expressed in less direct ways: not only in the subtle forms of folklore, humor, and song, but in suicide, self-maiming, work slowdowns, pretended illness, and petty thievery.

For centuries, serious obstacles stood in the way of effective protest by the masses of black people.[1] Recent decades have seen the emergence of a sizable Negro middle class, the decreasing isolation of Negroes from American society, large concentrations of Negroes in urban centers, an increase in their economic power, and a more favorable national and international milieu. With these changes, effective, organized protest has become both possible and visible.

Current racial protest has many aspects and requires analysis from many points of view. Recently there have been studies of particular civil rights organizations such as CORE (the Congress of Racial Equality), SNCC (the Student Non-Violent Coordinating Committee), and the Black Nationalists, as well as general studies of the characteristics of the Negro American community and its leadership. A neglected area of major significance has been the response of the Negro community as a whole to the civil rights struggle.

From earliest times, commentators have been interested in the social and psychological roots of social movements. Herodotus reports that of those Persian tribes whom Cyrus persuaded to revolt some were "nomads" and others were engaged in "husbandry," but all were "a poor people with a proud spirit." With the advent of modern research techniques it has become possible to document empirically the characteristics of those who give their support to various movements for political and social change.

The first part of this study is concerned with describing various Negro responses to the civil rights struggle and evaluating their prevalence. How

[1] The slave system in the United States evolved in such a way as to inhibit protest. Compared with Brazil, for example, there was a relative absence of Negro institutions, and the power of the slave owner was greater, as was the isolation of slaves from each other and from society generally (Stanley M. Elkins, *Slavery*, New York, Grosset and Dunlap, 1963, pp. 81–139).

many Negroes seem untouched and uninterested in the civil rights struggle? How many appear highly concerned? Finally, how many, in their despair with racial injustice, have become receptive to means and ends outside the framework of traditional democratic values? After delineating these three major civil rights orientations, we shall then identify some of the social, demographic, and psychological factors that help to explain them.

Prejudice has been one of the subjects most studied by American social science. However, while the prejudices of the dominant group have been analyzed in thousands of research projects, the other side of intergroup relations has rarely been approached. The fact that Negro hostility toward whites may be more understandable and to an important extent a result of the practices of white society does not minimize the importance of studying it. Understanding the prejudices held by minority groups is relevant for several reasons. From the standpoint of social science, it is important to know how the prejudices of submerged groups compare with those of dominant groups and whether the same theories can account for both. However, given the increase in racial tension and conflict, there are now vital practical reasons for understanding the intergroup attitudes of Negroes as well as whites. If white attitudes revealed in the word "nigger" have implications for racial conflict, so do Negro attitudes symbolized by the word "whitey."[2]

It is most unfortunate that the revelation of Negro hostility toward whites in some cases may serve to justify anti-Negro feelings and even make some whites feel self-righteous, and that it can focus attention away from the failings of white society onto the supposed imperfections of those victimized by that society. Yet it is important to realize that among some Negroes hatred is prevalent. Without adequate understanding of this, as well as of other aspects of what exists of urban working class Negro culture, ameliorative programs and efforts at improving Negro-white relations would seem to be severely limited in their chances for success.

The second part of this study is thus concerned with Negro attitudes toward whites. It seeks to ascertain just how widespread hostility toward whites is, where it is located, and what factors are most useful in understanding it. It also examines Negro attitudes toward one white group in particular, the Jews.

A study of Negro attitudes toward Jews is, in one respect, a study of American attitudes in one subgroup of the population. However, certain

---

[2] While racial prejudice from any standpoint is unfortunate, the following quotation from Malcolm X about the hostility of many Negroes seems particularly relevant in the above context: ". . . it's a reaction that was produced by the society; and I think that it is the society that produced this that should be attacked, not the reaction that develops among the people who are the victims of that negative society" (Malcolm X, with the assistance of Alex Haley, *The Autobiography of Malcolm X*, New York, Grove Press, 1965, p. 425).

difficulties arise in understanding and interpreting Negro hostility toward Jews that do not arise in the case of other groups. Particularly in urban areas, the shopkeepers, peddlers, and salesmen with whom Negroes come into contact are disproportionately likely to be Jews, earning a living in the ghetto on the periphery of the American economy. In some respects, then, these two minority groups are in a unique relationship. Has this unique relationship affected Negro attitudes toward Jews? Is anti-Semitism merely a specialized kind of antiwhite feeling? Is it true that Jews have in fact been singled out as the white group particularly hated by Negroes? To the white American, Jews are a minority group. To the Negro, Jews may be seen as part of the dominant, exploitative white majority.

The more perceptive and realistic social analysts have realized that conflict goes hand in hand with the eradication of the color line. Still, there remains the open and highly, significant question of the extent to which an aroused Negro community, demanding its Constitutional rights, and being to some extent aware of the crippling consequences of its participation in what Malcolm X has called "the American Nightmare" (others have called it "the American Dream"), need become caught up in the blind hatred and categorical negative thinking that tends to characterize the dominant group. The violent protests of these sympathetic to the KKK and White Citizens Councils against efforts at desegregation clearly involve the most virulent hatred of Negroes. To what extent is the protest of Negroes against enforced segregation and inferior status related to antiwhite attitudes? This book was conceived in the hope that the Negro American community can become ever more militant (in the sense defined in Chapter 1), and yet remain relatively tolerant. The compatibility of militancy and tolerance, and the likelihood of their occurrence, are considered in the final section of the book. There, response to the civil rights struggle is examined in light of attitudes toward whites.

The interviews on which this study is based were conducted in October, 1964, at a time when civil rights interest seemed to have reached a peak. Congress had just passed the most comprehensive civil rights act in one hundred years; Negro rioting in Northern cities and the brutal murder of three young civil rights workers in Mississippi were constantly in the news.

In all, 1,119 interviews were conducted with Negro adults. These were obtained from several different samples. The first, the metropolitan sample, consists of 492 persons and is representative of Negroes living in metropolitan areas of the nation outside the South. To obtain the sample, metropolitan areas outside the South were randomly sampled. From these sampled areas, Negro respondents were selected through modified probability procedures.

In addition to the metropolitan sample, four urban centers were chosen for special study and a representative sample of Negroes selected from each.

These cities were Chicago, New York, Atlanta, and Birmingham. These four were chosen because they are among the most important urban centers of Negro population, and differ in region, history, and present Negro-white relations. It was hoped that differences in the climate of Negro opinion among these four urban centers, and between them and the general metropolitan sample, might yield insights.

At many points in the analysis, respondents from the metropolitan sample and from the four cities are combined to provide more cases for analysis. This procedure is warranted on empirical grounds since in most cases relations found in the combined sample hold in each of the subsamples.

Occasionally data will be drawn from a representative cross-sectional sample of the adult American population when comparisons between white and Negroes are pertinent. The national sample was interviewed during the same period as the five special Negro samples that are the basis of this report. Data from the national study of anti-Semitism will be reported in a forthcoming volume in this series.

Interviewing and sampling were done by the National Opinion Research Center at the University of Chicago. NORC has conducted national surveys for several decades and its methods are widely respected.[3]

The actual interviews lasted from an hour to an hour and a half. The original research design called for all interviews to be conducted by Negro interviewers. This was possible for almost nine out of ten respondents. For the non-Southern metropolitan area sample Negro interviewers sometimes were unavailable (for example, in Waterbury, Connecticut, and Hamilton, Ohio) and experienced white poll takers were used instead. This did not bias the results to any significant degree. Where analysis suggested that the race of the interviewer had a biasing effect on expressed attitudes toward whites, those interviewed by whites were excluded from consideration.[4]

The first chapter describes the climate of opinion on a number of civil rights issues as it existed in late 1964, and develops a measure of civil rights militancy. Chapters 2–4 are concerned with the social and psycho-

[3] Further information on technical details of NORC sampling procedure may be found in the forthcoming national study of anti-Semitism by Gertrude J. Selznick and Stephen Steinberg.

[4] Using Negro interviewers does not eliminate all sources of bias. One of the ways of making out as a workingclass Negro in America is to be suspicious of outsiders, even if they are black, and hence some respondents may have been hesitant to give their true feelings.

In addition, the interviewer, whether Negro or white, was usually higher in social position than the respondent. In some cases this may have inhibited expressions of militancy.

A further problem lies in obtaining a sample which is representative of certain segments of the Negro community, in particular unattached younger males. Even the U. S. Census seems to undersample this group. Given the unique experience and perspective of many in this group it is possible that they are somewhat more militant and antiwhite than our sample indicates.

logical contexts of militancy and the effect of religion on protest. Chapter 5 examines black nationalism of the type manifested by the Muslims. Chapter 6 begins the second part of the book; it analyzes some of the unique factors in the Negro-Jewish relationship and compares attitudes toward Jewish whites with attitudes toward non-Jewish whites. Chapter 7 considers general antiwhite feelings and their relation to anti-Semitism, as well as some social and psychological factors associated with hostility toward whites. Chapter 8 examines the connection between responses to the civil rights struggle and attitudes toward whites and the future of Negro protest.

PROTEST
AND
PREJUDICE

"Well I'll Tell It Like It Is": The Climate of Opinion on Civil Rights Issues

> I don't believe in participating in politics. My church don't vote—they just depends on the plans of God.
>
> —*Housewife, South Bend, Indiana*

> Freedom's name is mighty sweet:
> Soon one day we're gonna meet
>
> —*Freedom song*

> We need less demonstrations and more shooting of the white man. Mass black violence must be organized.
>
> —*Sanitation department worker, New York City*

To begin to understand the civil rights struggle one must know what is in the hearts and minds of those whose struggle it is. Before seeking explanations for Negro responses to the civil rights struggle it is important to have an idea of what kinds of attitudes characterized the black population in late 1964. It will then be possible to build more complex measures of civil rights concern.

For all of the attention that civil rights receives in the mass media and from academicians, it is remarkable that so little is known about the mood within the Negro community as a whole.[1] A flood of articles, books, and newspaper statements tell us what Negroes "really" feel. But they rarely

[1] For example, *Daedalus,* a publication of the American Academy of Arts and Sciences, recently devoted two issues to the Negro American (Fall 1965 and Winter 1966). These issues contain a large number of articles; yet few tell us anything about the feelings and attitudes of Negroes other than on an impressionistic basis. An article about the white American's attitudes toward civil rights is even presented, but nothing about Negro attitudes.

offer systematic evidence for their assertions about the Negro mood. Indeed, there are often good reasons to suspect their accuracy. Many of the statements about the mood of the Negro in America or the increasing attraction of black nationalism, or even widespread hostility toward police, have been made by civil rights leaders. Their primary and legitimate concern is with the mobilization of opinion, not with a quantitatively accurate assessment of it. Characterizations of Negro sentiment by novelists and essayists are also sometimes suspect. While they frequently offer profound insights into the quality of Negro life, their generalizations may be unwarranted. This may be especially true with respect to attitudes on particular issues. Lacking systematic evidence, everyone is reduced to making informed guesses.

The recent outbreak of riots offers convincing evidence to the uncritical that all Negroes are militantly antiwhite and ripe for rebellion and violence. Yet these uprisings have actively involved only a small percentage of Negro Americans. Because of the prominence of rioters in depictions of the Negro mood in the mass media, it is particularly urgent to seek a reliable portrait of the actual outlook of a representative sample.

Only *Newsweek* magazine, in surveys conducted in 1963 and 1966, has attempted to portray the actual mood of the black population. Unfortunately, these data were not subjected to systematic analysis, except of a cursory and superficial kind, and were presented in a journalistic context. In addition, the data reported did not treat attitudes toward whites in any detail.

Our concern in this chapter is primarily to describe the over-all climate of opinion in the black community with regard to their present situations and the civil rights movement. In late 1964, how did Negroes feel about discrimination, segregation, the police, various civil rights leaders? How sympathetically did they listen to the nationalist aspirations of the Muslims? How widespread was anger and impatience?

Statistical reports and sociological treatises seem barren and remote even when they deal with the most poignant of human problems. To avoid this dehumanization of what is so pre-eminently a human problem, verbatim remarks made by respondents will be woven into this account. By this means we hope to preserve a concrete sense of the personal and intimate meaning of the Negro's struggle. But ultimately, cold statistics are what we need to know.

Words such as "Negro" encourage generalizing, and through categorical thinking many white Americans regard the black community as an undifferentiated mass. In actuality, there is not one mood of the Negro American, but many. For convenience, the phrase "Negro mood" was used above, but this should not obscure the fact that our intent is to seek out differences in this mood. In later chapters differing moods will be submitted to intensive analysis. Since there are differences as well as similarities in the situation of Northern and Southern Negroes, and since region of the country is one possible source of variation in mood, data will be presented separately for each of the five major areas sampled (non-Southern metropolitan areas, New York, Chicago, Atlanta, and Birmingham).

Progress?

Whether or not Negroes have collectively made much progress in recent years is a complex question; the answer depends in part on region of the country and the particular institution under consideration. If we judge by the passage of formal laws such as the Civil Rights Bill and the Voter Registration Act or by changes in self-image, then undoubtedly Negroes have made tremendous progress in recent years. However, if we judge by the implementation of these laws and concrete changes in the average person's total life situation, then there is serious question as to just how much progress has been made. Negroes still earn only about half as much as whites and, contrary to the trend of the recent past, the income differential between the masses of whites and Negroes seems to be increasing.[2] The economy has failed to expand rapidly enough to provide jobs for the ever-increasing number of unskilled youth. At the same time, many older unskilled people are being thrown out of jobs which were secure ten years ago, but are now being automated. Since the unskilled are disproportionately Negro, this has served to increase the Negro-white differential. Similarly, while there has been some slight desegregation of schools in the South (2 per cent of Negro pupils in eleven Southern states, which formerly had completely segregated school systems, now attend school with whites)[3] de facto segregation in the North has actually increased.

Thus the facts of progress are contradictory. But what do Negroes believe about progress? The interview included six questions dealing with the progress that has (or has not) been made and with future expectations of progress. While objective observers find it difficult to agree on whether or not progress is actually being made, particularly outside the South, our respondents showed much unanimity of opinion. When asked,

[2] Daniel P. Moynihan, "Employment, Income, and the Negro Family," *Daedalus,* Fall 1965, p. 755. In the same issue Rashi Fein notes that although both Negroes and whites show improvement in education, health, and welfare, white progress has been so much faster than Negro progress that the differential between them is greater than a generation ago ("An Economic and Social Profile of the Negro American," *Daedalus,* Fall 1965).

For a more optimistic long-range view see Arnold M. Rose, "The American Negro Problem in the Context of Social Change," *Annals of the American Academy of Political and Social Science,* January 1965.

[3] G. Franklin Edwards, "Community and Class Realities: The Ordeal of Change," *Daedalus,* Winter 1966, p. 18.

"Do you think things are getting better or worse for Negroes in this country?" *approximately eight out of ten respondents said "better"* (Table 1). The fact that changes have been more pronounced in the South than in the North is reflected in the higher percentage of Southerners than non-Southerners who think things are getting better. Yet, even in New York, seven out of ten felt that things were getting better.

Table 1.   NEGRO PROGRESS

Reply to: "Do you think that in general things are getting better or getting worse for Negroes in this country?"

	Metro[a]	N.Y.[a]	Chic.[a]	Atl.[a]	Birm.[a]
Better	81%	70%	76%	85%	89%
Worse	11	15	12	8	7
Same	5	11	9	4	1
Don't know	3	4	4	3	3
Total	100%	100%	100%	100%	100%
Number of respondents	(492)[b]	(190)[b]	(133)[b]	(198)	(200)

[a] Metro area = Non-Southern metropolitan area sample; N. Y. = New York City sample; Chic. = Chicago, Illinois, sample; Atl. = Atlanta, Georgia, sample; Birm. = Birmingham, Alabama, sample. In subsequent tables where the number of cases remains approximately the same as is indicated in this table, the number of cases will not be reported.

[b] The original New York City sample consisted of 146 cases and the Chicago sample of 79 cases. However, here and in subsequent tables where a breakdown by region is shown, those interviews from the metropolitan area sample which occurred in New York (44 cases) and in Chicago (54 cases) have been reported in both the metropolitan area sample and the New York and Chicago samples.

Most of those who indicated why they felt things were getting better mentioned changes in the Negro's economic situation and an increase in dignity. Others felt that things had been so bad in this country that any change (no matter how slight) had to be for the better. However, very few respondents mentioned a reduction of the prejudice held by whites as the basis for their belief in progress. Some sample comments:

Things are getting better because Negroes are no longer afraid of the white man. They used to shiver when he came around.

—Retired porter, New York City

They are getting better jobs because they are getting more education, so there are more opportunities for the young people than we had.

—Retired cafeteria worker, Los Angeles

We are getting better jobs and whites respect us more.

—Fireman, Pittsburgh

More job opportunities are opening up for Negroes, better education, and more skilled labor.

—Janitor with two full-time jobs, Detroit

They have to get better; they can't get worse.

—Housewife, Compton, California

There has been much progress. The Negro has progressed faster in a given period than any other people throughout the world.

—TV repairman, Springfield Gardens, N.Y.

Those who felt things were getting worse were also likely to refer to the economic situation, in this case the difficulty of finding employment. Their comments probably reflect the increasing difficulty which the unskilled and semiskilled face in finding work. Excluding housewives and the retired, roughly 15 per cent in each sample reported they were unemployed or laid off, and an additional 10 per cent were only working part time.

Jobs are getting scarce for Negroes except the ones that are in show business or sports. If they can do something better than somebody else then they are okay. If they are just poor Negroes they are out of luck and ain't nobody going to give them a job.

—Nurse's aide, Hamilton, Ohio

If things were getting better young people should get their share of the jobs, but this isn't happening. My children have not been successful in getting jobs.

—Housewife, Chicago

No improvement that is meaningful, too many tokens.

—Linotype operator, New York City

I say things are getting worse if four hundred years after being brought here as slaves and freed some time ago a civil rights bill still has to be passed in order to give us our rights. The white man tries to brainwash us into thinking things are getting better.

—Retired worker, Los Angeles

Another question asked whether things were improving more rapidly in the North or in the South. The majority of those who felt that a difference existed chose the South as the area of most rapid improvement (Table 2). Southern Negroes were considerably more likely to say the South rather than the North, but even Northern Negroes tended to choose the South over the North. Despite differences between the deep South, where Birmingham is located, and the relatively more progressive upper South, of which Atlanta is a part, there is little difference in responses from Birmingham and Atlanta.

It is interesting to note that, in New York and Chicago, the South is not chosen much more often than the North, and that, in the metropolitan sample, the South is actually chosen slightly less frequently than the North. This pattern appears in spite of the relatively greater and more visible

Table 2. REGIONAL SPEED OF PROGRESS

Reply to: "Where would you say things are improving faster for Negroes—
in the South, in the North, or isn't there any difference?"

	Metro	N.Y.	Chic.	Atl.	Birm.
South	37%	40%	42%	59%	55%
North	40	34	32	14	20
No difference	18	21	21	17	16
Don't know	5	5	5	10	9
Total	100%	100%	100%	100%	100%

changes that have taken place in the South. As the next question suggests, for many, but certainly not for all, the North is still perceived as the promised land in spite of its unemployment and ghetto life.

Reasons for Northern Negroes choosing the South were varied. Some respondents pointed out that in the South any improvement is a big improvement. Others, however, recognized the leading role of the Southern civil rights struggle.

Well, I'll tell it like it is. They are like slaves in the South so anything they get is better.

—*Housewife, Buffalo*

In the South they never had nothing so whatever they get now it's better.

—*Janitor, Buffalo*

More opportunities are opening for Negroes in the South so that now there is not the waste of education and talents of Negroes. It used to be there was no use for a Negro to have and education because all doors were closed to him. Now they are opening, and he knows he has a better chance than his parents had to be a real citizen.

—*Engineer, Los Angeles*

It is improving faster in the South. Those people are fighting for their rights down there more than we are up here.

—*Housewife, Pittsburgh*

In the South they are putting up a harder battle than we are in the North. They are accomplishing things such as seating in public places, riding anywhere on the bus, things in other words they have never done before and things we have always had in the North. The people in the North are not moving as fast. They are integrating schools in the South. We still have segregation in many schools in the North and we are doing less about it.

—*Domestic worker, Detroit*

In spite of thinking that things are improving more rapidly in the South than in the North, when asked, "Do you think Negroes are better off in the South, in the North, or isn't there any difference?" the overwhelming majority of non-Southerners chose *the North* (Table 3). Although there may be a tendency for people to like the areas they live in, Northerners were much more likely to favor the North than were Southerners to favor the South. This is not surprising, for the gains being made by Southerners are largely on such matters as the right to vote and the use of public facilities which have been generally open to Northern Negroes for a long time.

Table 3.   REGIONAL DIFFERENCES IN LIVING CONDITIONS

Reply to: "Do you think Negroes are better off in the South, in the North, or isn't there any difference?"

	Metro	N.Y.	Chic.	Atl.	Birm.
South	8%	14%	11%	32%	20%
North	60	57	55	23	35
No difference	27	25	27	36	33
Don't know	5	4	7	9	12
Total	100%	100%	100%	100%	100%

Thus, in the metropolitan area sample, 60 per cent chose the North as the place where Negroes are best off while only 8 per cent chose the South. On this question, dealing with where Negroes are better off, a sharp difference between Birmingham and Atlanta emerges. Among Negroes in Birmingham only 20 per cent chose the South while 35 per cent preferred conditions in the North. In Atlanta, the percentages are almost exactly reversed: 32 per cent felt that Negroes are better off in the South while only 23 per cent chose the North.

Those who felt Negroes were better off in the North generally referred to economic differences and less discrimination.

I guess it's because the Negroes have got more money in the North and more of them has gone to school and they know how to talk and act. Them Negroes in the South don't know how to do nothing but work on a farm and be kicked around.

—Assembly line worker, Hamilton, Ohio

It's a little bit easier in the North . . . you have a better choice of restaurants, rest rooms, . . . down South you have to get back of the bus. They won't serve you and you can't use rest rooms.

—Housewife, Buffalo

In the North people make more money.

—Domestic worker, Atlanta

I believe they are better off in the North . . . the schools or restaurants. You go where you want to as long as you have money. . . . You don't have to use the white man's back entrance.

—Unemployed worker, Cleveland

I believe they are better in the North. They should start walking away from the South if they could all get here. Just hitchhike any way to get away from the South.

—*Housewife, Detroit*

Nevertheless, depending on the sample, between one-third and one-fourth felt there was no difference between the two areas. For a few this was a positive response to the great progress that has recently been made in the South. As a worker from Birmingham put it:

It used to be better in the North, but since progress is being made in the South so rapidly, things seem to be about the same.

—*Worker, Birmingham*

However, for the majority it seemed to be a rejection of "mere appearances" in the North—a belief that behind the facade of Northern tolerance lies discrimination and prejudice fully as bad as the open bigotry of the South. For this group the view of the North as the "promised land" clearly does not hold and there is agreement with Malcolm X that everything south of the Canadian border is South.

You are a Negro no matter where you go.

—*Laundry worker, Hamilton, Ohio*

There is the same amount of prejudice but they just don't show it as openly. In my job whites pretend we are the best of friends. Then when they were trying to pass the law on sales of homes to anybody my coworkers were among the first to go down and protest.

—*Practical nurse, Detroit*

I can't get a job here or down South so what's the difference?

—*Unemployed truck driver, Brooklyn*

It's done in the dark here but in the South it's done in the light. If a colored person wants to be something to better themselves in the South they just say "no." But here when they try to be something they say not enough education.

—*Factory worker, Chicago*

It is a false illusion. In the South a Negro knows his place; in the North he thinks he is accepted, but there are many places he can not go and activities he cannot take part in and a Negro coming from the South to the North is often disillusioned.

—*Engineer, Los Angeles*

Those who felt Negroes were better off in the South referred to the hypocrisy of the North and to the fact that at least in the South white people were more honest about their feelings. In addition, many respondents referred to things having nothing to do with Negro-white relations, for example, the simplicity of life in the rural South.

It's better off in the South—you know your place in the South. In the North they try to fool you, make you think you are welcome to everything like they are when you really are not.

—*Truck driver, Birmingham*

In the North people make more money, but the living is easier in the South.

—*Domestic worker, Atlanta*

This climate is better for them. Negroes are 100 times better in the South. Colored people throw off more heat.

—*Newspaper worker, Atlanta*

In the South you are better off since you can raise vegetables and have a garden.

—*Domestic worker, Atlanta*

It's better in the South because most own their own homes and it's not as congested as in Northern cities.

—*Youth worker, New York City*

We have just seen that the vast majority of Negroes in these samples do think that things are getting better. It is widely believed, however, that the Negro community despairs at the slow pace of change. The more radical civil rights leaders depict the federal government as, at best, a reluctant partner in the struggle to share in the American promise. It is virtually an article of faith among many activists that the government acts only at the last possible moment, and then only to avoid widespread bloodshed and unfavorable international publicity.

Table 4.   SATISFACTION WITH FEDERAL SUPPORT OF INTEGRATION

Reply to: "In your opinion, is the government in Washington pushing integration too slow, too fast, or about right?"

	Metro	N.Y.	Chic.	Atl.	Birm.
Too slow	34%	51%	38%	31%	24%
Too fast	2	2	3	2	1
About right	59	39	55	63	72
Don't know	5	8	4	4	5
Total	100%	100%	100%	100%	100%

Consequently, one would have expected our respondents overwhelmingly to complain of the slow speed of civil rights improvement. Yet, when asked, "In your opinion is the government in Washington pushing integration too slow, too fast, or about right?" *a majority, except in New York, expressed satisfaction with the speed at which the federal government is pushing integration* (Table 4). The percentage saying "about right" goes from a low of 39 per cent for those in New York to 72 per cent for those in Birmingham.

This table and respondents' comments suggest that a large segment of the Negro community is satisfied with the speed at which progress is being made and is not as impatient as is generally believed or as the occurrence of riots would imply. However, it is probable that satisfaction with the speed of civil rights change is not quite as widespread as this question indicates, for two reasons. First, many respondents may feel things are moving much too slowly but place the blame on local and state authorities rather than the federal government. Secondly, if the question had asked about concrete changes in the Negro's economic and housing conditions, rather than about integration, more discontent might have been expressed. Integration, as such, may not be the burning issue among American Negroes. The right to sit next to a white man in a restaurant may be irrelevant to those who have no money for restaurants. Furthermore, even though Negroes say the present speed of integration is about right, they differ greatly from whites in their view: Whites think integration is going too fast. In response to a similar question asked by Gallup in November 1963, 73 per cent of white Southerners and 45 per cent of white Northerners said the government is pushing integration "too fast." Only 2 per cent of the Negroes in our samples shared this view.

The majority of Negroes who felt integration was being pushed at about the right speed took a long-term view of human progress. They felt that human institutions cannot be changed overnight, and many expressed fears that excess speed would cause setbacks.

About right. You see, God didn't make the world in one day so this segregation can't be solved in one day.

—*Maid, Birmingham*

They can't afford to go too fast because the people, especially the ones in the South just ain't ready to give in. They have to take it easy like.

—*Factory worker, Hamilton, Ohio*

You can't hurry God. He has a certain time for this to take place. I don't know about Washington.

—*Retired clerk, Atlanta*

You can't do it overnight. It has to be gradually worked in. Too fast you'll have a civil war.

—*Painter, Los Angeles*

First things first. They have to do things as they come to them. It took God six days to create this world, and man can't do any better. It takes time.

—*Housewife, Detroit*

If pushed too fast too many deaths would result and thereby race relations will go down and more hate groups will arise.

—*Housewife, Birmingham*

Only about 6 per cent of those in the various samples felt either that things were going too fast or said they did not know. These few respondents tended to be of two types. Some were black nationalists who did not want to integrate for reasons of their own, such as a machinist in New York City who said, "I don't go for integration so I'd rather not answer. I wish integration wasn't pushed at all. I don't want to mingle with the white man." The others were simply apathetic; many were traditional "Uncle Toms." Such persons were not interested in integration for reasons which reveal the destruction that prejudice has wrought to their sense of dignity. As a Chicago domestic worker said, "I don't know. I have got enough sense to stay in my place."

Those who felt things were going too slowly often referred to the fact that it has already taken four hundred years and complained of the lack of enforcement of existing civil rights laws.

In the South where whites are not applying the civil rights law all the way, the government is not doing enough. . . . I would like for them to really enforce the law. The government has passed the civil rights bill. Now it is up to them to force people to accept it in a democratic way, of course.

Jazz musician, Brooklyn

I think it's too slow. Four hundred years, and it's much too slow. They could get together up there in Washington, D. C. I don't see what could be holding them back. All we want is some decent jobs like the white man.

—Janitor, Cleveland

I can't see where the government is "pushing" at all.

—Unemployed clerical worker, Chicago

Too slow. I think we have a lot of promises, and very little is being done about it.

—Public utilities worker, Altanta

Two questions were asked about expectations for the future. These indicate considerable optimism among the majority of Negroes. To some extent, both questions are related to Muslim ideology. However, as will be

Table 5. EXPECTATION THAT WHITES WILL FULLY ACCEPT NEGROES

Reply to: "The day will come when Negroes will be fully accepted by whites."

	Metro	N.Y.	Chic.	Atl.	Birm.
Agree	70%	72%	77%	77%	74%
Disagree	24	19	20	17	20
Don't know	6	9	3	6	6
Total	100%	100%	100%	100%	100%

clear shortly, few respondents seem to have recognized this fact and most did not respond on the basis of black nationalism.

In each sample, more than seven out of ten respondents agreed that "The day will come when Negroes will be fully accepted by whites" (Table 5). Unfortunately, respondents were not asked how soon they thought this day would come. However, probably more respondents would have agreed with a retired clerk in New York City who said, "Some day but not in our times. This business can't go on this way forever," than with the Atlanta ditch digger who said, "It's coming now."[4]

Of the approximately one in five who rejected this hope for future acceptance, none echoed the extreme view of Marcus Garvey, who claimed, "All white men are klansmen at heart." However, some who held no hope of eventual acceptance by whites seemed to share the black nationalist sentiment that prejudice is permanent and separation the only answer. An unemployed worker in New York said, "The day will come only if Negroes have their own government," and a housewife in Los Angeles indicated, "No, that day will never come." But such views were not widespread. In addition, a few respondents were offended by the question and ventured to say, as did a housewife in Gary, Indiana, "The real question is how many Negroes are willing to accept whites."

Table 6.   EXPECTATION THAT NEGROES WILL ACHIEVE WORLD LEADERSHIP

Reply to: "Negroes some day are going to rise to the leadership of the world."

	Metro	N.Y.	Chic.	Atl.	Birm.
Agree	59%	69%	68%	78%	83%
Disagree	23	17	17	14	9
Don't know	18	14	15	8	8
Total	100%	100%	100%	100%	100%

A large majority in each sample also agreed with the statement, "Negroes some day are going to rise to the leadership of the world" (Table 6). This statement is also related to the ideology of the Muslims, who stress that, as God's chosen people, Negroes are destined to take the leadership of the world away from the corrupt and decadent white man. However, it appears that the widespread agreement with this item has very little to do with the

[4] The bold optimism revealed in the one statement and the implied optimism in the other are both perhaps not very realistic. Full acceptance often comes hard, or may never come even for groups whose "difference" is not immediately visible. Centuries-old prejudice against the Eta in Japan, the Harijans in India, and the Jews in the West still exists. It might even be argued that old prejudices rarely die but just get tucked away until societies face major crises or someone's daughter wants to marry one of the minority. Perhaps some respondents were indicating their hopes about the future rather than their convictions about what the future will actually be.

specific ideology of the Muslims. Rather it seems an indication of a positive self-image and an identification with Africa, for none of those who agreed with this question mentioned anything even remotely related to the elaborate ideology of the rise and fall of the white man offered by the Muslims. Instead, comments offered were often similar to those of a railroad clerk in Mount Vernon, New York, who said, "Yes, because of the African countries." The percentage of "don't know" responses for this question is much higher than for most of the other questions considered, suggesting that the item is not very salient for many people, not being something they are immediately concerned with.

Civil Rights Demonstrations

While in many areas slow and steady progress was made after the Supreme Court decision in 1954, significant gains really began under the pressure of more direct Negro protest. The massive campaigns of nonviolent civil disobedience led to important changes in the traditional social patterns of the South, and forcefully brought the Negro's case before the public.

Table 7.   VALUE OF CIVIL RIGHTS DEMONSTRATIONS

Reply to: "What would you say about the civil rights demonstrations over the last few years—that they have helped Negroes a great deal, helped a little, hurt a little, or a great deal?"

	Metro	N.Y.	Chic.	Atl.	Birm.
Helped a great deal	48%	42%	67%	73%	63%
Helped a little	36	42	22	18	27
Hurt a little	7	5	4	5	3
Hurt a great deal	4	6	2	2	1
Don't know	5	5	5	2	6
Total	100%	100%	100%	100%	100%

In late 1964, Negroes in our samples differed over whether demonstrations had helped "a great deal" or only "a little," but they were nearly unanimous in thinking they had helped (Table 7). The proportion who said that demonstrations had hurt Negroes never exceeded 11 per cent in any of the samples. At that time, demonstrations had occurred primarily in the South and had primarily a Southern impact. It is understandable, therefore, that Southern Negroes were more inclined to see them as having helped "a great deal." Thus, while 48 per cent in the national sample, and 42 per cent in New York thought the demonstrations had helped a great deal, 73 per cent in Atlanta and 63 per cent in Birmingham thought so.

Those who felt the demonstrations had been very helpful generally stressed their value in capturing public attention and in showing that Negroes meant business. They failed to cite the power Negroes were able to muster in their struggle. Those who felt that demonstrations had been only somewhat helpful, often stressed that only token advances had been made.

It keeps the whites knowing we are around. If we make noise they've got to listen.

—Welder, Buffalo

They have focused the eyes of the world on the Negro problem.

—Construction worker, New York City

Without demonstrations people would have never recognized the Negro injustices and the poor way they have been treated.

—Janitor, Detroit

We would probably still be without many of the rights and privileges we have now if it had not been for the demonstrations.

—Factory worker, Birmingham

The passive demonstrations helped everyone a great deal. Negroes' living conditions are so foreign to most whites that they did not realize what Negroes were asking.

—Aircraft industry worker, Los Angeles

Demonstrations have helped a little but the masses are still suffering.

—Cleaner and presser, New York City

Some of those who felt that demonstrations had been harmful associated them with riots. Others offered religious objections, or did not believe in the end toward which they were directed. Still others felt progress could be achieved only by calm discussion. It must be remembered, however, that these responses make up only a very small fraction of the total.

I don't approve of demonstrations. I think demonstrations should be confined to having organizational meetings and talking things over and coming to decisions.

—Retired tailor, Brooklyn

The demonstrations hurt a great deal because a lot of people got hurt and killed and they didn't change nobody's mind down there [in the South]. . . . God is the creator of everything. We don't know why we all dark skinned. We should try to put forth the effort to do what God wants and not question.

—Housewife, South Bend

The demonstrations were the worst thing that happened to the Negro. Martin Luther King knows nothing about the Negro. . . . His father was wealthy, and he never was among the lowly people. It is silly to have these ragged children demonstrate when they must go to white people for a job.

—Worker, Atlanta

I'm for civil rights, that is the truth. But there are some things in civil rights that *I won't stand for—for instance picketing. Well, I'm not against demonstrations. I would like to see demonstrations in the right way. Like stating our cause* rather than lying on the ground. [Italics supplied.]
—*Domestic worker, Brooklyn*

Bayard Rustin and Whitney Young, among others, have suggested that the time has come for something beyond demonstrations, that what is now needed is a new phase in the civil rights struggle. While demonstrations were tremendously useful, their day as the main instrument in the civil rights struggle has passed. It is suggested that now energy must be focused on less dramatic activities such as job training, education, and community organization. With this in mind respondents were asked whether they would like to see more or fewer demonstrations. The virtual unanimity of opinion on the helpfulness of demonstrations was not matched by a unanimous desire for additional demonstrations. In fact, opinion was more evenly divided on this question than on any yet reported; only about one-half wanted more demonstrations (Table 8). The least support for continuing demonstrations

Table 8. DESIRE TO CONTINUE CIVIL RIGHTS DEMONSTRATIONS

Reply to: "Would you like to see more demonstrations or less demonstrations?"

	Metro	N.Y.	Chic.	Atl.	Birm.
More	47%	53%	53%	56%	39%
Less	41	40	38	32	52
Same	6	3	4	4	3
Don't know	6	4	5	8	6
Total	100%	100%	100%	100%	100%

was in Birmingham, where 52 per cent wanted fewer demonstrations while only 39 per cent wanted more. Perhaps this is a reaction to the police dogs, cattle prods, bombings, and general police brutality associated with the Birmingham demonstrations of 1963.

Many of those who wanted fewer demonstrations felt that the government should enforce civil rights laws and that Negroes should become more concerned with self-help. Others were more likely to refer to the violence and disorder which they associated with demonstrations.

Since the civil rights bill has been passed, let the local and national government enforce them.
—*Janitor, Birmingham*

Parents have to get behind their children and prepare them for the opportunities that are ahead.
—*Housewife, Detroit*

So much murder has come out of these demonstrations. A lot of people have died since the demonstrations.

—68-year-old domestic worker, Atlanta

So many folks get hurt doing them things that I can't see where more will help us.

—Housewife, Bessemer, Alabama

No more, too much fear and tensions.

—Elderly widow, Birmingham

Less demonstrations. Now I think we are past that stage.

—Office worker, New York City

With God helping to fight our battle, I believe we can do with less demonstrations.

—Salvage worker, Cleveland

The statement of a maid in Birmingham was typical of those who wanted more demonstrations: "Demonstrations have helped a great deal, and things have improved quite a bit. If they continue to improve I'd like to see more."

A similar question involved religion as an alternative to direct action. Opinion was somewhat divided on the statement, "Negroes should spend more time praying and less time demonstrating" (Table 9). A majority of

Table 9.   PRAYER VS. DEMONSTRATIONS

Reply to: "Negroes should spend more time praying and less time demonstrating."

	Metro	N.Y.	Chic.	Atl.	Birm.
Agree	32%	26%	38%	58%	58%
Disagree	61	65	55	34	36
Don't know	7	9	7	8	6
Total	100%	100%	100%	100%	100%

those in Birmingham and Atlanta (58 per cent) agreed with this statement. In the North, 38 per cent of those in Chicago, 32 per cent of the metropolitan area sample, and only 26 per cent of those in New York agreed. This regional pattern, in addition to indicating differences in militancy, may also reflect the greater religious fervor of the South. In a later chapter the connection between religiosity and militancy will be explored in some detail.

Those who wanted less time spent praying tended to stress the importance of secular activity and were often critical of what they perceived the traditional role of religion to be.

Pray less. You know when we pray down South we still get killed. I don't think God intended for us to get down on our knees and let somebody stab you in the back.

—Laundry worker, Brooklyn

It doesn't mean anything how much you pray. You have to get out and fight for what you want to get.

—Clothing salesman, New York City

Gosh, Negroes have spent seventy-five years on their knees. It's time they did something else.

—Domestic worker, Cleveland

The comments of those who wanted more praying indicated either a complete lack of interest in political and social change or the belief that prayer is one means of bringing about social change.

I don't believe in participating in politics. My Church don't vote—they just depends on the plans of God.

—Housewife, South Bend

I think praying is good. Praying help a lot. Spend more time praying.

—Worker, Bronx

I, as a Jehovah's Witness, cannot express things involving race issues.

—Automobile serviceman, Philadelphia

In my religion we do not approve of anything except living like it says in the Bible. Demonstrations mean calling attention to you, and it's sinful.

—Housewife, Los Angeles

Praying is demonstrating.

—Clergyman, Atlanta

While this study is primarily concerned with expressed attitudes (and assumes that in many situations there is likely to be a fairly strong relation between attitudes and behavior), respondents were also asked about their actual and hypothetical civil rights behavior. The ultimate commitment, as many civil rights leaders have stressed, lies not in simply believing discrimination is wrong or giving money to the cause, but in concrete action on behalf of the struggle—a willingness to lay your body on the line.

Table 10.   MEMBERSHIP IN CIVIL RIGHTS ORGANIZATIONS

	Metro	N.Y.	Chic.	Atl.	Birm.
Respondents who say they belong to a civil rights organization	24%	26%	26%	22%	10%

When asked if they belonged to any civil rights organizations, about one respondent in five indicated membership, and this was usually the NAACP (Table 10). This figure may seem somewhat high, particularly when applied to active members of such organizations. It seems likely that some respondents interpreted this question rather broadly and many may be no more than "two-dollar-a-year" dues-paying members. Respondents were also asked if they would be afraid to take part in a civil rights demonstration. About three out of four indicated that they would not, although some of this group were no doubt hesitant openly to admit their fear.[5] Differences by region are slight (Table 11).

Table 11.   FEAR OF PERSONAL PARTICIPATION IN CIVIL RIGHTS DEMONSTRATIONS

Reply to: "To tell the truth I would be afraid to take part in civil rights demonstrations."

	Metro	N.Y.	Chic.	Atl.	Birm.
Yes, true	26%	26%	22%	26%	29%
No, not true	71	72	74	71	68
Don't know	3	2	4	3	3
Total	100%	100%	100%	100%	100%

Among those who would not be afraid to demonstrate, the comment of a Brooklyn sewing machine operator is typical: "I will do anything to make things better for my child than they were for me." Many also stressed that the demonstration would have to be orderly and without violence. However, for several others nonviolence was a deterrent. A college-educated New Yorker, in a workingclass occupation, said, "I would be afraid to demonstrate only if it was a nonviolent demonstration."

Most of those who indicated that they would be afraid to demonstrate offered religious explanations; the rest were simply apathetic. In indicating her unwillingness to demonstrate, a Detroit housewife said, "I don't go for demonstrations. I believe that God created all men equal and at his appointed time he will give every man his portion. No one can hinder it." And a tailor in Pittsburgh: "I just don't believe in it. I'm not afraid. I wouldn't be afraid to march for Jesus, but even that's not right."

Discrimination and Segregation: "Learn Them Books Together"

It is widely believed, at least in the North, that Negroes are unanimous in their opposition to discrimination and segregation. Southern apologists for racial segregation argue that, on the contrary, Negroes really prefer these historical patterns. The truth depends, in part, upon the issue raised.

The practice of discrimination which has received most widespread at-

[5] However, the first *Newsweek* survey reports that 51 per cent of their nationwide representative sample said they would march in a demonstration if asked, though only 12 per cent said they had actually marched in a demonstration. This survey is reported in William Brink and Louis Harris, *The Negro Revolution in America*, New York, Simon and Schuster, 1964, p. 203.

tention, and been the focus of the greatest legal efforts to bring about change, is school segregation. Next is probably segregation of public facilities. Housing discrimination, one of the most grievous problems for Northern Negroes, has received far less legal and political attention.

Table 12.   DESIRABILITY OF INTEGRATED SCHOOLING

Reply to: "Do you think white children and Negro children should go to the same schools or to separate schools?"

	Metro	N.Y.	Chic.	Atl.	Birm.
Same schools	96%	96%	93%	84%	79%
Separate schools	3	3	6	14	19
Don't know	1	1	1	2	2
Total	100%	100%	100%	100%	100%

Table 13.   SUPPORT OF COMPULSORY NONDISCRIMINATION IN RESTAURANT SERVICE

Reply to: "A restaurant owner should not have to serve Negroes if he doesn't want to."

	Metro	N.Y.	Chic.	Atl.	Birm.
Agree	20%	14%	24%	17%	29%
Disagree	79	85	74	81	68
Don't know	1	1	2	2	3
Total	100%	100%	100%	100%	100%

Table 14.   SUPPORT OF COMPULSORY NONDISCRIMINATION IN REAL ESTATE SALES

Reply to: "An owner of property should not have to sell to Negroes if he doesn't want to."

	Metro	N.Y.	Chic.	Atl.	Birm.
Agree	50%	33%	58%	50%	53%
Disagree	47	64	37	47	43
Don't know	3	3	5	3	4
Total	100%	100%	100%	100%	100%

The passage of laws and government pressure may be unable to eliminate prejudiced attitudes among whites, though this is less true for discriminatory behavior. However, in the white community, legal changes in the patterning of race relations do have an impact, even on attitudes. Ironically, this may hold true in the Negro community as well. The opposition to school segregation and to discrimination in public facilities and housing found in our sample varied according to the attention that has been given them and the legitimacy surrounding them. Like opinion among whites, Negro opinion on civil rights seems greatly fashioned by publicity and agitation, and by conformity to law. Thus, Negroes displayed the most widespread opposition to school segregation and the least to discrimination in housing (Tables 12–14).

Almost all non-Southern respondents felt that Negroes and whites should go to the same schools, and about eight out of ten of Southern respondents felt this way.[6] Those living in Birmingham were the most conservative, with 19 per cent preferring separate schools. However the percentage that would be willing to take legal action against school segregation and would be willing to have their child be the first to desegregate a school is no doubt much smaller.

In rejecting segregated schools, respondents referred to the oneness of mankind or drew on the Supreme Court edict that separate schools were inherently unequal.

There should never be a separating of peoples. That's not God's arrangement; that is man's arrangement to separate people.

—Worker, Philadelphia

No such thing as separate but equal. Anytime they are separate, they separate and different.

—Postal clerk, Philadelphia

Equal but separate schools just don't exist.

—Engineer, Los Angeles

Learn them books together is what I say.

—Retired railroad worker, Alabama (whose father was a slave)

Same schools 'cause we made out of one blood.

—Domestic worker, Birmingham

I don't see any difference. Back in us foreparents' time they went together. That's how they got their learning.

—Housewife, Chicago

Those few people who were against school integration were either traditional Uncle Toms, such as a charwoman in Atlanta who said, "It doesn't look right for them to be together," or were influenced, perhaps, by black

[6] In this regard, it is interesting to note that in an NORC survey done in November 1963, 62 per cent of a nationwide sample of whites felt that Negro and white students should go to the same schools. When broken down by region 73 per cent of those in the North felt this way as against only 31 per cent of those in the South. It also appears that Southern whites underestimate Negro feeling toward integrated schools. Only a third of Southern whites agreed that "most Negroes felt strongly about the right to send children to the same schools as whites." Yet it has just been observed that fully eight out of ten Southern Negroes favor integrated schools (P. Sheatsley, "White Attitudes Toward the Negro," *Daedalus,* Winter 1966, p. 219).

nationalist ideology; for example, a worker in New York City who said, "I don't like integration. The so-called Negro will never be able to live in peace with the white man."

Almost as much opposition to discrimination emerged in response to a question which asked about service in restaurants. Approximately eight out often rejected the statement that "a restaurant owner should not have to serve Negroes if he doesn't want to." This is not surprising, given the widespread attention that efforts to desegregate lunch counters and other public facilities have received. Those in Birmingham again appear as the most conservative, with New York and Atlanta showing the most opposition to discrimination.

Somewhat more conservatism was shown in response to the statement "An owner of property should not have to sell to Negroes if he doesn't want to." Only slightly more than four respondents in ten rejected this statement, except for New York where more than six in ten rejected it. However, the wording of the statement may have led to some misinterpretation and an unduly conservative response. That is, the question may carry with it the idea that owners *have* to sell to Negroes in preference to whites. If the question had asked, "Should an owner of property have the right to refuse to sell to an otherwise qualified person simply because he is a Negro?" the percentage sanctioning discrimination would perhaps have been much smaller.

Table 15.   NEGRO MERIT AND TIMING OF ACHIEVEMENT OF CIVIL RIGHTS

Reply to: "Before Negroes are given equal rights, they have to show that they deserve them."

	Metro	N.Y.	Chic.	Atl.	Birm.
Agree	42%	33%	49%	64%	45%
Disagree	55	67	48	34	53
Don't know	3	0	3	2	2
Total	100%	100%	100%	100%	100%

In opposing discrimination in restaurants and in the sale of property most respondents who offered comments referred to the immorality and illegality of discrimination and felt that as members of the American public they should have the same opportunities to spend their money as white Americans have. Many of those who felt that discrimination should be permitted quickly took the offensive and added, as did an unemployed nurse in Hollis, New York, "I don't want to deal with people who don't want to deal with me."

Respondents were also asked to agree or disagree with a standard line of racial moderation: "Before Negroes are given equal rights, they have to show that they deserve them" (Table 15). Acceptance of this statement was somewhat more widespread than might be expected. Those in New York again appear as the most militant (only one out of three accepted it), while Atlanta (where two out of three accepted it) replaced Birmingham as the least militant. Just why there should be such widespread acceptance of this statement is hard to say. In all probability, many did not interpret "equal rights" to mean "equal *civil* rights," and answered from the perspective of the achieved-status system characteristic of American society.

Acceptance of this statement by Negroes demonstrates the degree to which they are embedded in American culture. Like many whites, many Negroes believe in the American myth of rugged individualism: The man of true merit can surmount all adversity and succeed entirely through his own resources. This extreme notion of free will, which attributes failure as well as success entirely to individual merit, remains widespread in modern America.

Those who accepted this statement generally referred to what they perceived to be some negative characteristic of the Negro group. Thus a garment worker in New York indicated, "Yes, most won't take a job if you give it to them"; and a Chicago housewife stated, "Definitely must show. They are so lazy"; while an Atlanta housewife indicated, "We do have a few shortcomings that have to be cleaned up."

Those who rejected this statement stressed the fact that, as citizens, they had the same inalienable rights as whites. Thus a salesman in New York said, "Negroes have been in this country as long as whites and built it as much as the whites, and they shouldn't have to prove anything"; while a Detroit practical nurse said, "He deserves his rights as a man. When he was born, he was born equal." A Brooklyn housewife angrily stated, "We don't have to show them nothing. It's a good thing a white person didn't ask that question. I'd put him out right away."

But regardless of attitudes toward integration and Negro rights, how widespread is the belief that Negroes are kept from getting ahead by job discrimination? Unfortunately, respondents were asked this question in a roundabout way, and hence our measure is a limited one.

Table 16. ATTITUDES TOWARD PRESENT-DAY OPPORTUNITIES FOR
NEGRO ADVANCEMENT

Reply to: "Negroes who want to work hard can get ahead just as easily
as anyone else."

	Metro	N.Y.	Chic.	Atl.	Birm.
Agree	63%	52%	65%	72%	68%
Disagree	36	47	35	25	31
Don't know	1	1	0	3	1
Total	100%	100%	100%	100%	100%

Agreement with the statement "Negroes who want to work hard can get ahead just as easily as anyone else" was highest in the South, where seven out of ten agreed, while in the metropolitan and Chicago samples about six out of ten and in New York about five out of ten agreed (Table 16). The high level of acceptance of this American cliché is perhaps surprising. If a more direct statement had been used such as "Negroes no longer face discrimination when it comes to employment whether in hiring or once on the job," it seems certain that fewer than six out of ten would have agreed.

Civil Rights Groups and Leaders

At the time this inquiry was carried out, many observers believed that one of the trends in the civil rights struggle was the increasing sympathy of the masses of Negroes for groups such as the Muslims. Some observers suggested that relatively large segments of the black community had withdrawn allegiance from the conventional civil rights groups in favor of the Muslims. Our data offer little support for such an assertion.

Table 17.   COMMENDATION OF CIVIL RIGHTS ORGANIZATION

Reply to: "Which one of the following groups do you think is doing the most at the present time to help Negroes?[a]"

	Metro	N.Y.	Chic.	Atl.	Birm.
NAACP	79%	70%	84%	87%	92%
CORE	11	12	6	2	3
Muslims	3	8	3	0	1
None	2	6	2	1	0
Don't know	6	5	7	10	5
Total	101%[a]	101%[a]	102%[a]	100%	101%[a]

[a] For Tables 17–20 percentages may add up to more than 100 because some individuals mentioned more than one group.

Respondents were given a list of three organizations, the NAACP, CORE, and the Muslims, and asked which group they felt was doing the most at the present time to help Negroes. They were also asked if they disliked or disapproved of any of these groups. Similar questions were asked about the following individuals: Malcolm X, James Farmer, Martin Luther King, and Roy Wilkins. Tables 17–20 show attitudes toward these groups and individuals.

There was very little diversity of opinion on these questions. In the South about nine out of ten felt the NAACP was doing the most to help Negroes while in the other samples about eight out of ten felt this way

(Table 17).[7] The group chosen next most frequently was CORE; and finally, outside of New York, between 0 and 3 per cent chose the Muslims. Even in New York this figure was only 8 per cent. When asked which leader has done the most to help Negroes, again about nine out of ten in each sample chose Martin Luther King (Table 18).

Table 18.   COMMENDATION OF CIVIL RIGHTS LEADER

Reply to: "Which person on the card do you think has done most to help Negroes?"

	Metro	N.Y.	Chic.	Atl.	Birm.
Malcolm X	1%	5%	1%	0%	0%
James Farmer	1	1	0	0	1
Martin Luther King	88	85	92	93	95
Roy Wilkins	6	4	3	5	1
None	0	1	0	1	1
Don't know	4	4	4	1	2
Total	100%	100%	100%	100%	100%

Thus, in response to the rhetorical question posed by Claude Brown, author of *Manchild in the Promised Land*, a best-selling autobiography about Harlem street life: "Who the hell is Martin Luther King in Harlem? You mean that old Southern preacher who is always going around talking about peace? Non-violence?"[8] one might answer, "Oh he's only that Nobel Peace Prize winner whom four out of five of Harlem's people would probably choose as having done the most to help Negroes."

When the other side of this question is considered, seeing which groups are disliked or disapproved of, the results are equally consistent (Table 19). Literally the only group disliked was the Muslims, and from 44 per cent of

[7] The pattern observed here is similar to that noted previously. An NAACP executive, in noting that for many years the NAACP was the only consistent force fighting the Negro battles, states, "In view of the significant legal victories that marked these battles, it is not surprising that in every national sample of Negroes polled, 90 per cent or better have expressed their confidence in the aims and actions of the Association. No other group has ever come close to this figure" (J. A. Morsell, "The National Association for the Advancement of Colored People and Its Strategy," *Annals of the American Academy of Political and Social Science*, January 1965, p. 98). Virtually the entire sample reported having heard of the NAACP, but 12 per cent were not familiar with the Muslims, and 27 per cent were not familiar with CORE.

[8] As quoted in *New Republic*, October 16, 1965. In response to a similar finding from a *New York Times* poll done in that city which indicated that three-fourths of the black population chose Martin Luther King as "doing the best for Negroes" as against only 6 per cent who chose Malcolm X, the latter stated ". . . some of history's greatest leaders never were recognized until they were safely in the ground!" (Malcolm X, with the assistance of Alex Haley, *The Autobiography of Malcolm X*, New York, Grove Press, 1965, p. 419). Malcolm X is again prophetic as there can be little doubt that he commands much greater respect today than when he was alive.

Table 19. DISAPPROVED CIVIL RIGHTS ORGANIZATIONS

Reply to: "Are there any groups on the card you don't like or disapprove of?"

	Metro	N.Y.	Chic.	Atl.	Birm.
NAACP	1%	6%	1%	1%	1%
CORE	2	5	2	1	1
Muslims	57	51	52	45	44
None	30	37	42	32	39
Don't know	10	5	5	22	16
Total	100%	104%a	102%a	101%a	101%a

a See Table 17.

those in Birmingham to 57 per cent of those in the nationwide sample indicated disapproval. Outside of New York, where a combined total of 5 per cent indicated dislike of the NAACP or CORE, less than 1 per cent of those in the other four samples indicated dislike or disapproval of these civil rights groups. If just those who indicated dislike for one of the three groups are considered then 98 per cent chose the Muslims! A similar finding emerges when attitude toward individual leaders is observed (Table 20). In Table 20, only Malcolm X aroused appreciable disfavor among Negroes;

Table 20. DISAPPROVED CIVIL RIGHTS LEADERS

Reply to "Are there any persons on the card you don't like or disapprove of?"

	Metro	N.Y.	Chic.	Atl.	Birm.
Malcolm X	48%	55%	41%	36%	41%
James Farmer	1	3	1	2	0
Martin Luther King	1	1	1	0	0
Roy Wilkins	1	2	1	1	1
None	24	24	35	24	33
Don't know	26	17	21	38	27
Total	101%a	102%a	100%	101%a	102%a

a See Table 17.

nearly half disapproved of him. Indeed looking at only that half of the combined sample who indicated dislike or disapproval for one of the four leaders, *97 per cent chose Malcolm X* as most disliked. Such a very strong finding clearly indicates that, whatever dislike Negroes feel toward groups working in their behalf, this is almost exclusively directed toward the Muslims, not toward the conventional groups. This is, of course, not to say that poorer slum dwellers necessarily feel that conventional groups such as the NAACP represent or speak for them. These data tell us nothing about the underlying class resentment which may be felt toward these groups or the extent to which their philosophy of nonviolence is accepted. This latter question will be examined in a later section.

It should be noted that the data shown in these tables are for the Negro community as a whole. Within particular subgroups such as younger, relatively uneducated Northern males, support for Malcolm X and the Muslims was slightly more pronounced. However, even among this group the percentage thinking that Malcolm X was the leader, and the Muslims the group, doing the most to help Negroes increases to only 4 and 7 per cent, respectively.

Another Country and Allegiance to the United States

A vital element of all Negro protest is the quest for dignity. At the time of our study, among the Black Muslims, unlike other groups, it was being argued that dignity is best pursued within the framework of an all-black so-

Table 21.   DESIRABILITY OF ESTABLISHING A NEGRO NATION

Reply to: "It would be a good idea to give American Negroes their own country and let them set up their own nation."

	Metro	N.Y.	Chic.	Atl.	Birm.
Agree	17%	16%	25%	26%	20%
Disagree	79	79	71	68	75
Don't know	4	5	4	6	5
Total	100%	100%	100%	100%	100%

ciety. Long ago Marcus Garvey, a forerunner of today's black nationalists, was asking, "Where is the black man's government? Where is his King and his Kingdom?"[9] The Black Muslims have continued to ask this question. Their stress on "a separate state or territory of our own" distinguishes them from many other black nationalist groups. Those interviewed were asked to agree or disagree with the statement "It would be a good idea to give American Negroes their own country and let them set up their own nation" (Table 21).[10] Slightly fewer than eight out of ten disagreed with the statement. Differences between regions were slight, but those in the South and in

[9] As quoted in E. D. Cronon, *Black Moses,* Madison, University of Wisconsin Press, 1955, p. 16.
[10] Other studies have found somewhat less support for this idea. Thus a 1964 national survey reports 6 per cent think it would be a good idea to have a Negro society that is completely separate from whites, while 7 per cent said "it depends." Brink and Harris, *op. cit.,* p. 119. A July 27, 1964, *New York Times* survey of New York City Negroes reports 4 per cent favor setting up a separate state or states in this country or in Africa, with 9 per cent "not sure."

Chicago were slightly more likely to be favorable than were those elsewhere.

Most respondents regarded a Negro nation not only as politically unfeasible, but as undesirable. Those questioned thought of themselves as Americans whose relatives had worked and died fighting for and building this country. Some were angered by the question and attributed it to white racists, apparently being unaware that a Negro group favored it as well.

This is the only country they've ever had. They fought and bled and died for it. Stay here.

—*Retired bank office worker, Cleveland*

We built up this one.

—*Electrician's assistant, New York City*

We should be able to live where we want to.

—*Longshoreman, Brooklyn*

I personally disagree with that. It could not be done. What country? I don't know of any country but this one. It doesn't belong to the white man alone.

—*Elevator operator, Los Angeles*

I feel the Muslims are teaching the wrong thing and the way we should live or have a country to ourselves when our forefathers tilled and worked hard that we might share our heritage, and I feel they are wrong in saying we should be separated.

—*Steelworker, Chicago*

We were in Africa and they fetched us out. Now we can stay here if we want to.

—*Domestic worker, Atlanta*

Those who favored a separate Negro nation felt as did a textile worker in New York City, who said, "I don't like integration. We (the so-called Negroes) will never be able to live in peace with the white man in this country"; or an unemployed Brooklyn truckdriver, who said, "Every nationality has its own country but the Negro has no place to really call his own . . . they need a flag to fight for; it's just a matter of pride."

One of the many controversies that Marcus Garvey was involved in with the respectable Negro leadership of his day was the question of whether or not Negroes should fight for this country in World War I. He stated: "The first dying that is to be done by the black man in the future will be done to make himself free. [After this is done] if we have any charity to bestow, we may die for the white man but as for me I think I have stopped dying for him."[11]

A similar emphasis may be found in the program of today's Muslims.[12]

[11] *Ibid.*, p. 66.
[12] Each issue of the Muslims' newspaper, *Muhammad Speaks,* includes as one of "the 12 things which the Muslims believe" a statement against fighting for the United States.

Some Muslims are now in jail for failing to cooperate with the draft. A refusal to fight for one's country (except for those with a philosophically grounded pacificism) would seem to be one of the ultimate indications of rejection and alienation from society. To measure the depth of this estrangement, and to see how much potential support existed for this position, those interviewed were asked if in the event of a war they would feel this country was worth fighting for. As can be seen in Table 22 there was more unanimity of opinion on this question than on almost any other; almost nine out of ten said they felt this country was worth fighting for. New York with 15 per cent, Chicago with 14 per cent, and the metropolitan area sample with 11 per cent had higher percentages responding negatively than did Atlanta with 8 per cent and Birmingham with 7 per cent.

Table 22. IS AMERICA WORTH FIGHTING FOR?

Reply to: "If the United States got into a war today, would you personally feel this country was worth fighting for, or not?

	Metro	N.Y.	Chic.	Atl.	Birm.
Yes	87%	83%	86%	90%	91%
No	11	15	14	8	7
Don't know	2	2	0	2	2
Total	100%	100%	100%	100%	100%

While almost 90 per cent of the sample indicated they felt the United States was worth fighting for, subjects differed markedly in the intensity of their response and many qualified their answers. But it seemed that, for the majority of these respondents, the question of refusing to fight, if called upon, had never entered their minds. They were Americans with the attitude that, if the government calls upon you to do something, why of course you do it; it's the law, whether it be obtaining a driver's license or fighting in a war. For others the question was answered affirmatively, not out of any great allegiance or love for country, but from the belief that the United States, with all its problems, was still much better than any other country. Others, however, while agreeing to the question, offered stronger qualifications; they would fight but only because they realized that an attack on the United States would be an attack on their homes and their famiiles, or, they would fight but only because they would be forced to.

Who you going to fight for—some other country?

—*Construction worker, Philadelphia*

I served in World War II. This is my country. I would do it again. This is the only country I ever knew.

—*Heavy equipment operator, Pittsburgh*

Yes, I would fight. This is home.

—*Housewife, Atlanta*

This is where I live so it is natural I would think it's worth fighting for.

—*Domestic worker, Detroit*

We have problems here, true. I think they are slowly straightening themselves out. We also might have worse problems in another country.

—*Janitor, Detroit*

I have to say yes because I have seen countries worse than this, like South Africa.

—*Bakery worker, Bronx*

It's not so much for the country. It's mostly for the individual, the family. They have no choice.

—*Housewife, Philadelphia*

Yes—fight only for the colored, not for the whites.

—*Housewife, Atlanta*

I wouldn't have any choice if I was called to war, but I can't help feeling that since I can't buy a sandwich or a cup of coffee in a white restaurant down South because my face is not white, I just might not if I had my choice.

—*Construction worker, Brooklyn*

In the responses of the few who felt the country would not be worth fighting for a depth of anger and despair far beyond that held by the average Negro could be seen. The unwillingness of some to fight would exist only until "we get our rights," but others made no such qualifications.

I really don't see why colored people should fight; when they signed the Constitution they signed that for white people.

—*Housewife, Philadelphia*

Not under a second-class citizenship. Hell no!

—*Investigator for Veteran's Administration, Chicago*

I don't think colored people have anything to fight for but their civil rights.

—*Worker, Chicago*

I don't know what I would be fighting for until I have my freedom.

—*Welfare worker, Bronx*

Well, I hate to say it but we have been kicked about so long until we wouldn't feel much like fighting for the U.S. again.

—*Janitress, Cleveland*

For myself I am not so sure, but I have children and I think things will improve in their life.

—*Auto mechanic, Compton, California*

Riots and Violence

The interviews took place in October, 1964; the previous summer had witnessed a number of riots. Respondents were queried about these riots and the efficacy of violence in general. The data show that in 1964, a substantial number felt that riots and violence do some good (Tables 23–24).

Opinion was about evenly divided on whether or not riots do the Negro cause some good, and about a third rejected the statement "Violence will never help Negroes get equal rights." Least support for the efficacy of riots was found in New York (four out of ten), while the most widespread support was in Atlanta (six out of ten).

Table 23. VALUE OF RIOTS

Reply to: "Some people say that no good can ever come from riots like those that happened in Harlem this past summer. Other people say that such riots do some good because they make whites pay attention to the problems of Negroes. Which comes closest to what you feel?"

	Metro	N.Y.	Chic.	Atl.	Birm.
No good can ever come from riots	52%	57%	38%	26%	39%
Riots do some good	41	39	55	63	52
Don't know	7	4	7	11	9
Total	100%	100%	100%	100%	100%

Table 24. VALUE OF VIOLENCE

Reply to: "Violence will never help Negroes get equal rights."

	Metro	N.Y.	Chic.	Atl.	Birm.
Agree	64%	68%	64%	57%	58%
Disagree	29	27	32	39	35
Don't know	7	5	4	4	7
Total	100%	100%	100%	100%	100%

On the question of whether or not violence can help the Negro cause the greatest opposition to violence was again found in New York, while the greatest support came from Negroes in Atlanta and Birmingham.

These findings are interesting in light of statements such as the following by Claude Brown: "Non-violence? . . . Nobody wants to hear that nonsense in Harlem. Harlem is not a passive community. People are violent."[13] Brown's portrait is no doubt accurate for his circle of acquaintances. But

[13] As quoted in the *New Republic,* October 16, 1965.

the data in Tables 23 and 24 suggest he is as wrong in his portrayal of the opinion of the man-in-the-Harlem-Street on this matter as he was in denying the massive popularity of Martin Luther King. Harlem may be a violent community, but those who live in New York City *are more likely to oppose riots and violence than are Negroes living anywhere else in the United States.*

Many respondents who agreed that riots and violence can do some good believed that such actions force attention to the problem and make whites realize that the Negro is willing to go into the streets to obtain justice. Some felt that violence was the only thing that the violent white man could understand.

However, the motifs of revenge, given so much attention in the press during the recent riots, and glorification of violence preached by some black nationalists rarely appear. Negroes by and large do not seem to want to get even; they want equality. This fact emerges again when attitudes toward whites are considered in a later chapter.

I'm against violence but riots do good. Some of them don't understand anything else but an eye for an eye.

—Retired domestic worker, Atlanta

People get scared in riots. So we get action and the government tries to find out why we riot. White people are afraid of getting hurt.

Welder, Buffalo

They have to get out there and show these people we mean business. If we set back like our foreparents we will never get anywhere.

—Housewife, Detroit

If the white man knows that the Negro will fight, he will get his rights.

—Hotel chambermaid, New York City

Seems nothing impresses people of the wrong done like a riot. I hate it, but it's true. But a lot of people lose their jobs in riot areas.

—Janitress, Atlanta

I don't approve of riots, but when you are oppressed it has got to stop. Sometime you just have to fight back. I know that some of these riots started out peacefully, but the police brutality caused them to get out of hand. It's like training a dog—if you keep tricking him he'll tuck in his tail, but once he bites back you will treat him better.

—Engineer, Los Angeles

Less demonstrations and more shooting of the white man. Mass black violence must be organized.

—Sanitation department worker, New York City

Reverend King has been wonderful in getting the young ones to calm down, but I couldn't stand nobody hitting and kicking on me.

—Housewife, Chicago

Those who opposed riots and violence cited the destruction of life and property, the lack of respect for law and order. They also commonly feared that such acts would generate greater white hostility and create still greater distance between blacks and whites. For a few respondents the rejection of violence was based on the purely pragmatic consideration that Negroes are simply outnumbered.

People only get hurt this way.
—*Auto mechanic, Buffalo*

They rioted in the wrong place. They should have been rioting in Mississippi. They ought to do some rioting down South.
—*Shipping clerk, Chicago*

Riots no good. People get hurt and killed.
—*Housewife, Hollis, N.Y.*

Rioting is just an excuse to be a thief and liar. I feel that when you demonstrate it is for the good, to help someone. You are trying to build a foundation, but when you riot you are destroying the foundation you have not yet built.
—*Office clerk, Brooklyn*

Riots just confuse people and cause blind hatred.
—*Postal clerk, Atlanta*

These riots I believe were caused by Goldwaterites.
—*Retired rural school teacher, Atlanta*

I think the riots was wrong. They stole.
—*Sewing machine operator, New York City*

I feel these riots were put up either by the Muslims, some Communists or KKK was paying for this.
—*Janitor, Detroit*

It can't help because we are outnumbered. In fact with all the people that are against us, we couldn't possibly win any type of battle. We would be beaten before we started.
—*Housewife, Buffalo*

By riots you put a fear in people which takes you further away from them.
—*Electrical worker, Brooklyn*

We have better methods than force.
—*Railway porter, Atlanta*

That one-half the sample said riots do some good and one-third felt that violence can help may indicate what we already know, namely, that the race situation in this country has become unstable and volatile. On the other hand, the results should not be interpreted as indicating a predilection for or a commitment to violence. More likely they reflect a realistic appraisal of the actual situation. The 1965 Los Angeles riots resulted in thirty-five tragic deaths, over a thousand injuries, the loss of many jobs, and perhaps the defeat of a hospital bond. However, the riots also led to the prompt release of War on Poverty funds that had previously been tied up for months and millions of dollars in government aid to rebuild the area and improve community conditions. A vast amount of national and international attention was focused on Los Angeles, and numerous commissions of inquiry were set up. Prior to this, Los Angeles Negroes had been largely ignored by the local government. The cohesiveness of the black community seems to have increased. Furthermore for some of the participants a sense of dignity and manhood may have been achieved through defiance and violence.

The Southern racial scene shows examples of the cessation of Klan harassment and the reduction of injustice on the part of local authorities as a result of the activities of groups formed for self-defense such as the Deacons for Defense and Justice of Bogalusa, Louisiana. Even when actual violence does not take place, the threat and fear of it are, no doubt, a latent bargaining factor in the seeming victories of civil rights groups deeply committed to nonviolence and love. However, recognition of the role of force and violence in the civil rights struggle clashes radically with the democratic commitments of most civil rights leaders. It is not surprising that the latent role of force and violence has been minimized by civil rights spokesmen.

It must be borne in mind that these questions did not measure whether or not respondents would *personally* participate in such actions or whether they think they should be encouraged.[14] It is possible to think that violence

[14] In this regard it is interesting to note that a study of Watts residents reports that approximately 20 per cent were actively involved in the uprising there. (D. O. Sears, "Riot Activity and Evaluation: An Overview of the Negro Survey," paper prepared for the American Psychological Association Conference, New York, September 1966.)

While the connection between attitudes and behavior in such matters is likely to be particularly tenuous, it is significant that in asking about participation in a hypothetical riot, the *Newsweek* (August 1966) national survey found 15 per cent who indicated that they would participate.

We can also see evidence of the fact that although a majority of the opinionated feel that riots do some good, they are nevertheless negative in their over-all evaluation of such uprisings. Thus in Watts 38 per cent felt that the riot had helped, while 24 per cent that it had hurt; in the *Newsweek* survey these figures with respect to "Watts-style riots" were 34 per cent and 20 per cent. However, when asked how they felt about the riot, by a 2 to 1 margin, Watts residents reported feeling unfavorably, partly because of the number of Negroes killed. When asked what was the most effective method for Negroes to use, 12 per cent mentioned violent protest. In the national *Newsweek* sample those questioned felt by a 2 to 1 margin that Negroes could get more with persuasion than with force, and by a 3 to 1 margin that they could win without violence.

Kenneth Clark reports data on the attitudes of Harlem residents to the 1943 riot there, which are comparable to the data shown in Tables 23 and 24 above. He notes that six out of ten rejected or condoned it. ("Group Violence: A Preliminary Study of the Attitudinal Pattern of Its Acceptance and Rejection: A Study of the 1943 Harlem Riot," *The Journal of Social Psychology*, 1944, p. 321.)

may help and riots do some good without at the same time thinking either should be encouraged. The questionnaire also failed to inquire just how good "some good" is. Many who said riots do some good might well agree that they still do much more harm than good.

Numerous commentators have suggested that the hatred, fear and contempt which many Negroes have for the police are an important cause of riots. The policeman with his monopoly of violence becomes the living embodiment of all the hatred felt toward whites. Indeed, outside of shopkeepers, he may be the only white with whom Negroes come into frequent, face-to-face contact. Resentment toward the police is also often based on the belief that they are involved in the flourishing crime in Negro slums and that they give inadequate protection to citizens of these areas.

Table 25. ATTITUDES TOWARD POLICE

Reply to: "In (name of city or town), how would you say that the police treat Negroes—very well, fairly well, fairly badly or very badly?"

	Metro	N.Y.	Chic.	Atl.	Birm.
Very well	15%	9%	11%	13%	5%
Fairly well	44	47	53	40	26
Fairly badly	13	16	11	21	18
Very badly	13	18	12	18	42
Don't know	15	10	13	8	9
Total	100%	100%	100%	100%	100%

In view of the crucial role of the police in Negro areas, respondents were asked, "In (name of city or town), how would you say that the police treat Negroes—very well, fairly well, fairly badly or very badly?" (Table 25). Only a very small minority in each area said "very well"; the highest figure was 15 per cent, in the metropolitan area sample. Moreover, the percentage saying that police treat Negroes "very badly" was generally slightly higher than the percentage saying "very well."[15] In Birmingham, this difference was extreme: 42 per cent said "very badly" and only 5 per cent "very well."

[15] Some quantitative measure of what "fairly badly" or "very badly" mean may no doubt be inferred from the more specific questions asked in the UCLA study of Watts. Roughly seven out of ten people agreed that the police lack respect or use insulting language, that they roust, frisk, and search people, and that they use unnecessary force. When asked if they personally had had such experiences, 24 per cent, 20 per cent, and 8 per cent, respectively, indicated that they had. When residents were asked if anyone they knew had had such experiences, these figures increased to 42 per cent, 38 per cent, and 32 per cent. Thirty four per cent reported that someone they knew had been beaten up by the police and 37 per cent that the police had stopped and searched the car of someone they knew. (Data graciously supplied by David Sears.) A comparable study of Los Angeles whites would no doubt reveal significantly lower percentages.

Undoubtedly Birmingham stands out because of the visible police brutality during the demonstrations there. When the "very badly" and "fairly badly" categories are combined, six out of ten in Birmingham, four out of ten in Atlanta, three out of ten in New York, and slightly more than two out of ten in Chicago and the metropolitan area sample feel the police treat Negroes badly. The fact that the least hostility is expressed toward the police in Chicago may indicate the fact that Chicago was one of the first cities to integrate and to specially train its police force for racial tension.

The size of the "don't know" category was a little higher here than for most of the other questions. For some this probably genuinely reflected lack of knowledge of police practices. But others may have been unwilling to reveal their strong negative opinions to an unknown interviewer. A foundry worker in Los Angeles in answering "don't know" went on to comment, "Well, I've been in jail a couple of times myself. I'm on probation now so I refuse to commit myself." Thus, the percentage who in fact think police treat Negroes badly is probably somewhat higher than the figures indicate. In any case, however, there is a sizable reservoir of dissatisfaction with the police in Negro communities. Even if police practices were to change overnight, it would still take time for this to be widely recognized.

Unlike respondents' comments reported earlier in this chapter, which often tended to be fairly abstract and based on vague feelings or hunches, questions on police treatment drew many concrete examples stemming from personal experiences. While the question did not specifically inquire about brutality, most of those who felt police treated Negroes badly recounted an experience involving police brutality. For some this did not necessarily mean only physical brutality, but the general lack of respect shown them.

White police don't do the whites like they do the Negroes.

—*Domestic worker, Atlanta*

Two summers ago two police beat a boy into bad health because he didn't understand and couldn't hear them due to an ear operation he had.

—*Housewife, Cleveland*

At no point do they treat them fair because anything that happens, the policemen will approach any person and draw out his pistol. There are some they kill you quick as you look at them.

—*Unemployed baker, New York City*

I saw the police handcuff a little boy. That's no way to teach a child to respect the law . . . wouldn't do that to a white boy.

—*Factory worker, Los Angeles*

Very badly. I have experience. I got beat all over my head.

—*Welder, Cleveland*

I haven't been treated very nice. Some years ago I lived in a predominantly white neighborhood and coming home late from work one night I was stopped by a policeman asking where I was going. I explained home. He replied, "You are a liar. No colored bastards live in this area and I should shoot your ass on the spot." I pleaded and talked with him and asked him to follow me home. He threatened me some more but finally released me to go home.

—*Automobile assembly line worker, Detroit*

They are constantly employing brutality because the Negro is the poorer class of people. From what I've seen and know we are treated awful.

—*Salesman, New York City*

There is a lot of police brutality going on you know. I seen them beat one young boy about seventeen. He almost lost his eye. Then they found out he wasn't the one they wanted.

—*Maintenance worker, Cleveland*

When I was younger and had a fight in school with a white girl, the police threw me around and laughed at the way I talked and made me go to court. Nothing was done to the white girl.

—*Factory worker, Brooklyn*

Police beat up this boy and he was in the right. I guess it was because of his color.

—*Housewife, Seattle*

They had a colored man and they were beating him something terrible. That causes hoodlums.

—*Housewife, Chicago*

In commenting about favorable police treatment some respondents sounded like the most punitive and authoritarian, right-wing, white moralists. Some believed that although the police may occasionally be brutal, some Negroes "have it coming to them" and in the best American tradition have "earned" the treatment they receive at the hands of the police. Some respondents also suggested that Negro policemen were worse than whites.

The police are too easy on Negro hoodlums in our community. The police are a little too weak in Cleveland.

—*Electrical worker, Cleveland*

My husband said white police are better than colored police.

—*Housewife, Atlanta*

I would say they treated a Negro as a human being. They respect you as a man.

—*Bartender, New York City*

I have never had no trouble with the police. Some people deserve what is coming to them.

—*Domestic worker, Brooklyn*

People have got so unruly police have to be rough.

—Disabled truck driver, Atlanta

As long as you live within the law they are your friends. If you go outside the law the color of your skin don't matter. Police gets you.

—Housewife, Buffalo

A white policeman treats you better than a Negro policeman.

—Automobile serviceman, Philadelphia

As far as I know most of the time the Negro bring it on himself, yet he blames the other for it.

—Retired railway porter, Atlanta

Having examined opinion on a wide variety of civil rights issues, what conclusions can be drawn about the climate of opinion in the Negro community in late 1964? One of the interesting things about almost all the questions asked was the very low percentage of "don't know" responses. Attitudinal research into matters of public policy usually finds a large segment of the population who are uninformed, who have little knowledge of public issues, and who answer "don't know." Poorly educated Negroes are of all groups the most likely to be opinionless on most issues. It is thus significant that for most questions in the present study only a minute fraction of the sample responded "don't know." This indicates the salience of civil rights issues to black men and the extent to which the struggle on behalf of equal rights has kindled at least a minimal degree of interest and awareness throughout the entire Negro community.[16]

But what of the nature of this opinion? In late 1964 was the Negro community generally irrational in its anger, suspicious, deeply pessimistic? Did it reject loyalty to the United States and desire its own country and institutions? Had it abandoned its quest for integration and withdrawn support from traditional civil rights groups? From these data the answer is clearly no. The overwhelming majority of those questioned felt that progress is being made and that integration is being pushed by the government at the right speed, and were optimistic about the future. Strong support was also indicated for school integration and desegregation of public facilities. In addition, in 1964 whatever dislike was felt toward Negro civil rights organizations was clearly

---

[16] Another study in this series concerned with public response to the Eichmann trial noted that 34 per cent of the Negro community in Oakland were unaware of the trial. However, consistent with the data shown here, virtually the entire Negro sample was knowledgeable about the Freedom Riders.

About half of those questioned in the 1963 *Newsweek* national survey indicated a willingness to go to jail on behalf of the civil rights struggle (Brink and Harris, *op. cit.,* p. 68). It is difficult to imagine a contemporary issue that would illicit a similar response from the white community.

directed toward the Muslims and not the more conventional groups. The ideas of the Muslims also were overwhelmingly rejected.[17]

Although the present study was carried out in October of 1964 it is significant that the *Newsweek* survey, carried out almost two years later, in August 1966, reached very similar conclusions. This more recent study even revealed an increase in optimism and satisfaction relative to its 1963 survey. In spite of the more obvious manifestations of white backlash, a slight majority felt that white attitudes were changing for the better. Although the black power issue is likely to have important implications, thus far it has not been able to mobilize mass opinion on its behalf. Margins as high as eight to one rejected certain tenets associated by many with black power such as that integration is irrelevant or that Negroes should go it alone without white help. A similar lack of support for the Muslims was again noted. Only about one in twenty-five expressed approval of this group, and almost nine out of ten again indicated that in the event of a war they felt this country was worth fighting for.

An Index of Militancy

So far this chapter has examined the Negro mood in bits and pieces. In order to ask systematic questions, it is necessary to sum these parts into a coherent whole. We shall now reorganize our data to classify respondents in terms of a standard of militancy. This will permit some assessment of the extent to which the general Negro mood is a militant one.

The dictionary defines militancy as a "fighting spirit, attitude, or policy." To be sure, there are many styles of fighting racial injustice and types of militancy. Thus far the most significant in bringing about social change has been that of the organized civil rights movement.

One of the aims of this study was to assess Negro response to the civil rights struggle. To this end we are here concerned with support for the kind of militancy manifested by the conventional civil rights groups in 1964.

The concept of militancy used here is that of *conventional militancy*. At the time of the interviews, the outlook of the conventional civil rights groups and spokesman had a great deal in common. Each of these groups was urgently aware of the extensiveness of discrimination faced by the American black man. All called for an end to discrimination and segregation

---

[17] In absolute terms there were sizable reservoirs of support for these ideas, if not for the organizations which promote them. It was noted that "only" one Negro in ten felt that the United States would not be worth fighting for, and that two in ten felt it would be a good idea to give Negroes their own country. While this is a very small minority of the Negro community taken as a whole, it is still a sizable number of people. If one generalizes from this sample to the population at large, about two million probably feel this country is not worth fighting for and four million agree it would be a good idea to give Negroes their own country.

and demanded the admission of the Negro to the economic and political mainstream of American life. And they wanted these changes quickly— "Freedom Now." In pursuit of this end, participation in peaceful non-violent demonstrations was encouraged. For the purposes of this study, in the next three chapters, we judge militancy by commonly held standards of civil rights activists at the time the interviews were conducted.[18]

The following eight items were used as the test of Negro militancy in 1964; the response scored as militant is indicated for each.

In your opinion, is the government in Washington pushing integration too slow, too fast, or about right? (Too slow.)

Negroes who want to work hard can get ahead just as easily as anyone else. (Disagree.)

Negroes should spend more time praying and less time demonstrating. (Disagree.)

To tell the truth I would be afraid to take part in civil rights demonstrations. (Disagree.)

Would you like to see more demonstrations or less demonstrations? (More.)

A restaurant owner should not have to serve Negroes if he doesn't want to. (Disagree.)

Before Negroes are given equal rights, they have to show that they deserve them. (Disagree.)

An owner of property should not have to sell to Negroes if he doesn't want to. (Disagree.)

These eight items were combined into an Index of Conventional Militancy. Respondents received one point for responding to each question in a militant way. Those who said they had no opinion, or who responded in an unmilitant way, received no score on the item. Scores on the index could range from zero (not a single militant response) to eight (militancy shown on all eight questions).

Scores were combined to produce three categories of respondents: mil-

[18] There were, of course, important differences in the tactics, short-run goals, and sources of support among the NAACP, the Urban League, SCLC (Southern Christian Leadership Conference), CORE, and SNCC. The differences between the last two groups and the others became even more pronounced in the summer of 1966 with the raising of the issue of black power and the questioning of nonviolence and the role of whites in the civil rights struggle. But even in 1966 there is some similarity beneath the divergent rhetorics, particularly if one contrasts these involved and concerned Negroes with those uninvolved and relatively unconcerned.

It should be clearly understood that by militancy here we are not referring to black nationalist or extremist attitudes, although our measure of militancy does not preclude the holding of such attitudes. As will be noted in Chapter 5, the relative lack of support for black nationalism prevented a more elaborate analysis.

itants, moderates, and conservatives. *Militants* were all those who scored six or higher on the index. Persons who scored three, four, or five were classified as *moderates*. Those with scores of two or less were classified as *conservatives*. The average score on the index was 3.7 in the South, slightly above 4.0 in both Chicago and the national sample, and nearly 5 in New York. Since the average respondent in all samples is a moderate, conservative respondents fall below the norm everywhere, while militants exceed it. Before proceeding, it is important to clarify just what it means in terms of responses to concrete questions for an individual to be classified in each of these three categories.

The militant Negro is one who actively opposes discrimination and segregation. He feels barriers now exist which keep Negroes from getting ahead, and is impatient with the speed of social change. He demands his rights *now* and is likely to agree with Martin Luther King that "the oft-repeated clichés, 'the time is not ripe,' 'Negroes are not culturally ready,' are a stench in the nostrils of God."[19] The militant Negro encourages civil rights demonstrations and his concern with the here and now leads him to think that Negroes should spend more time in the secular activity of demonstrating than in the otherworldly one of praying. He also would, or already has, taken part in such demonstrations and is likely to agree with St. Augustine that "those that sit at rest while others take pains [to act] are tender turtles and buy their quiet with disgrace."

On the other hand the conservative seems happy in his place or, rather, the place relegated to him by racism; he is not opposed to discrimination, thinks that Negroes who want to work hard can get ahead as well as anyone else, is content with the speed of social change (or even thinks it is moving too fast), feels that Negroes must show they deserve equal rights before they are given them, desires fewer civil rights demonstrations and would not participate in such demonstrations, and thinks that Negroes should spend more time praying and less time demonstrating. Those scored as moderates fall somewhere in between these two types: They protest some inequities, but accept others.[20]

---

[19] Martin Luther King, "A Challenge to the Churches and Synagogues" in M. Ahmann, ed., *Race: Challenge to Religion,* Chicago, Henry Regnery Company, 1964, p. 168.

[20] This measure is of necessity abstract and general. In particular local situations Negro militancy is not an easily defined homogeneous entity. The concrete demands of "militant" middle-class Negroes may be very different from, and even conflict with, the demands of "militant" workingclass Negroes. Related to class differences in the substantive content of "militancy" are the differences in ideology and approach of groups such as the NAACP and SNCC. In addition, *within* these same organizations there is often bitter factionalism between the "moderates" and "radicals." In spite of this diversity of approach and the difficulty in narrowly defining militancy, at a more general level there is likely to be some basic agreement (such as over the items included in the index).

Combining single items into a composite index has many advantages in measuring social and psychological phenomena. Responses to single questions are never entirely reliable; they can be based on such idiosyncratic factors as misunderstanding the question or interviewer error. By its very nature, an index measures *consistency* of response. On the Index of Militancy, an individual is classified as militant or conservative only if he is consistently so.

Aside from considerations of accurate and reliable measurement, an index of militancy has important descriptive functions. A summary assessment of Negro militancy cannot be arrived at if only single questions are considered; depending on the question asked, militancy varies widely. However, after constructing an index of militancy, one can decide on a single standard of militancy, in this case, at least six militant responses out of eight. It then becomes possible to say that, using this standard, such and such a percentage of Negroes are militant, moderate, or conservative in their civil rights orientation.

It should be emphasized that employing an index can never overcome the relative nature of social and psychological measurement. The concept of militancy used in this study is relative in at least two senses. It is relative to the questions included in the index; furthermore, those termed "militant" are militant not in an absolute sense but only relative to respondents with lower scores. Nevertheless, only an index of militancy allows us to judge, in a rough way, the extent of militancy in the Negro community as militancy is defined in this study.

Kenneth Clark has referred to Harlem as "the fountainhead of Negro protest movements,"[21] and it was seen earlier in this chapter that New York City consistently emerged as the most militant area when single issues, other than the efficacy of riots and violence, were considered. It is not surprising that Negroes in New York City are again much more likely to be militant than those in the other cities sampled (Table 26). In New York City, fully 45 per cent of the sample scored as militant (scores of six, seven, eight). This figure drops to 27 per cent for the Chicago and nationwide samples, to 19 per cent in Birmingham, and to 16 per cent in Atlanta. Differences between Atlanta and Birmingham were slight; while the latter had a slightly higher percentage scoring as militant it also had a slightly higher percentage scoring as conservative. The greater civil rights activity in Birmingham (up to the time of the study) seems to have produced a polarization of opinion—a movement to both ends of the continuum.

For each of the samples (except New York) slightly over half scored as moderate on the Index of Militancy (and for those in New York City this figure is only slightly less—44 per cent). Half the Negro population, in short, seems moderate in the sense that they neither consistently accept

21 *Dark Ghetto*, New York, Harper & Row, 1965, p. 26.

Table 26.   SCORES ON INDEX OF CONVENTIONAL MILITANCY BY REGION

Scores[a]	N.Y.	Chic.	Metro	Atl.	Birm.
0	1%	2%	3%	2%	2%
1	4	5	5	7	12
2	6	11	11	15	15
3	11	20	14	21	17
4	16	21	21	22	20
5	17	14	19	17	15
6	21	15	13	9	11
7	15	10	10	5	7
8	9	2	4	2	1
Total	100%	100%	100%	100%	100%
Number	(190)	(132)	(483)	(194)	(194)
Average score	4.97	4.15	4.30	3.77	3.62
Styles of response to civil rights struggle:					
Conservative (0–2)	11%	18%	19%	24%	29%
Moderate (3–5)	44	55	54	60	52
Militant (6–8)	45	27	27	16	19
Total	100%	100%	100%	100%	100%

[a] Altogether, 23 cases could not be scored either because one or more questions were not asked or because of respondent's refusal to answer.

nor consistently reject statements designed to measure militancy. Since most of the statements in the index are moderate in nature, the moderation so widely expressed in the Negro community appears to be genuine and not a function of our having included items to which only the most radical would have consented.

Although the proportion of Negro moderates is about the same everywhere, the proportions of militants and conservatives vary greatly from place to place. In the South three in ten were scored as conservatives, and two in ten as militants. Outside the South conservatism was lower, militancy higher. Excluding New York City, two out of ten were conservatives and three out of ten were militants. In New York City only one person in ten took a conservative stand on the civil rights struggle, while four in ten were militants.

Thus, when questions concerning riots and violence are excluded, the portrait of New York City Negroes as relatively the most militant seems accurate. The common-sense supposition that "Uncle Tomism" and conservatism on civil rights are most widespread in the South is also supported. However, a moderate stance is the statistically predominant outlook on civil rights protest.

Validity of the Index

Because the sources and consequences of civil rights attitudes are the main concern of subsequent chapters, it is necessary to seek assurance that the Index of Militancy accurately measures what it is intended to measure. By three standard criteria of validity, the index seems fully justified.

First of all, the items making up the index have face validity. With one or possibly two exceptions, every statement bears directly on the current civil rights struggle.

Secondly, the items are internally consistent. First, the items are highly intercorrelated. In addition, response to each is related to score on the index. At any given point on the index the proportion who agreed with any item was higher than at any lower point on the index. In other words, each item made an independent and systematic contribution to respondents' scores. These patterns were the same in all samples. Furthermore, the natural cutting points in the data coincided with the points at which the index was collapsed to form the three categories of militancy, moderation, and conservatism.

External validation is a third criterion for determining whether a measure is a valid one. An index is said to be externally valid when it predicts responses to items that are not a part of the index but are related to the phenomenon the index purports to measure. In Table 27, where scores on the index are considered in relation to a number of items related to militancy, it is clear that the index is in fact externally valid. This table also indicates something about what beliefs and activities characterize people at every point on the index.

Presumably an important indication of militancy is membership in a civil rights organization. Since the notion of conventional militancy was developed largely from observing the statements and actions of conventional civil rights groups, if the measure of militancy is a valid one then it should help to predict membership in organizations such as the NAACP and CORE. In considering Table 27, as one moves up the Index of Conventional Militancy, the percentage reporting membership in a civil rights organization consistently increases from a low of only 4 per cent among those with zero scores on the index, to a high of 40 per cent among those with scores of eight.[22] This table also provides added justification for drawing the line between militancy and moderation at a score of six or more. Among those with a score of five (classified as moderates) only 18 per cent report membership, while for those with a score of six (classified as militants) this figure is 36 per cent, or twice as high. This demonstrates that the index is a useful predictor of behavior as well as of attitudes. Too often in survey

---

[22] It is occasionally suggested that civil rights workers are more conservative than the people they represent. However, in terms of these attitudinal items this certainly is not the case.

Table 27. EXTERNAL VALIDATION OF INDEX OF CONVENTIONAL MILITANCY

Score on Index of Conventional Militancy

	0	1	2	3	4	5	6	7	8
Per cent who:									
Are members of civil rights organization	4%	7%	13%	15%	22%	18%	36%	39%	40%
Voted in 1960[a]	52	53	51	64	59	67	77	78	77
Are certain to vote in 1964	65	57	63	63	71	72	79	83	82
Think police treat Negroes badly	13	26	26	31	34	39	36	44	47
Read one Negro newspaper or more	60	65	70	70	78	85	84	84	84
Identified four civil rights leaders correctly	26	12	29	27	37	45	64	66	64
Think white and Negro children should go to same schools	70	85	83	87	93	94	96	95	100
Think civil rights demonstrations helped	52	76	85	85	87	91	93	96	100

[a] Among those old enough to vote at the time of the election.

reports it can only be assumed that attitudes and behavior are correlated. Here, however, it can be shown that the attitudes measured have important implications for behavior.

If activism increases as militancy does, then one should expect militants to be politically more active in a variety of ways. One form of such action is voting. While for many higher-status individuals voting is taken for granted, among America's poor it often tends to be the exception rather than the rule. Even outside the South, where obvious barriers do not exist, a sizable percentage of black Americans (as well as white Americans) do not vote. The late President Kennedy and many others have put great and perhaps unwarranted faith in the power of the ballot as a means of obtaining racial justice, and much of the civil rights struggle in the last few years has been concerned with voter registration. Civil rights strategists speak of a tactical shift where, as Rustin suggests, what began as a protest movement emphasizing demonstrations is being challenged to translate itself into a political movement. Observing voting behavior ought, then, to be an excellent test of whether the index is measuring willingness to act on behalf of civil rights. Individuals were asked whether they had voted in 1960 and whether they were planning to vote in the November 1964 Presidential election. Of interest here is not how respondents actually cast their ballots, but simply whether or not they voted. Table 27 shows that, as militancy increases, so does the proportion who voted in 1960 and the proportion who say they are "certain to vote" in 1964. Only about half of those low on militancy report voting in 1960 compared with over three-quarters of those high on militancy.[23]

It is also to be expected that, as militancy increases, so does concern over the treatment Negroes receive at the hands of the police; and this, again, is clearly the case. The percentage thinking that the police treat Negroes badly steadily increases from 13 per cent among those with a score of zero on the index up to 47 per cent for those who chose the militant response for all eight questions.

One ought also to expect that as militancy increases so does contact with Negro media and knowledge about civil rights. If the index is a true measure of concern over matters of racial injustice, then those with this concern should be more interested in matters of race and also better informed about the civil rights struggle. While reading Negro newspapers was fairly wide-spread among all respondents, as militancy increases so does the proportion reading one or more of these papers, from 60 per cent among those at the bottom of the index to 84 per cent for those highest in militancy.

Militancy, besides being related to concern for civil rights and to exposure to the Negro media (and indeed, as will be seen later, to other newspapers and magazines as well), is also related to knowledge of matters related to racial protest. As part of a measure of cultural sophistication, respondents were given a list containing the names of prominent Negroes, four of whom were active in the civil rights field. The percentage scoring high on knowledge of these civil rights leaders (identifying all four correctly) goes from a low of 26 and 12 per cent for those with scores of zero and one up to 64 per cent for those with scores of eight. One of the characteristics of the militant individual, then, is having significantly more knowledge about civil rights.

The low level of knowledge among those low on militancy as well as some of their comments indicate that the bulk of our so-called conservatives, rather than holding well-thought-out and well-informed conservative points of view, are for the most part simply apathetic and uninterested. It might be said that they are conservatives by omission rather than commission. As

---

[23] As is always the case, regardless of race, the percentage reporting they voted in an election (and that they voted for the winning candidate) is somewhat higher than the percentage who actually voted. Slightly over 90 per cent of our respondents who did vote said they voted for Kennedy. A Gallup Poll taken at the time of this election revealed that 68 per cent of the Negro vote went for Kennedy. However, our sample excludes those living in rural areas and oversamples those from the largest cities where the Kennedy vote was much stronger.

a Cleveland housewife put it: "I don't keep up with these things. My eyes are bad, and I don't read much. I take care of my grandchildren so I just don't keep up with what's going on. Now I told you at the start that I didn't have opinions on what's happening in this country. I just don't know."

Finally, the external validation of the index is completed by questions on whether Negroes and whites should go to the same schools and whether or not demonstrations had helped. These are among the most moderate items in the questionnaire in the sense that almost nine out of ten respondents accepted them. Still, as militancy increases, so does the percentage favoring integrated schools and thinking that demonstrations had helped. Differences are pronounced only when the extremes are compared. While 52 per cent of those with scores of zero on the index felt that demonstrations had done some good, among those with scores of eight, 100 per cent felt this way. At the bottom of the index 70 per cent felt whites and Negroes should go to the same schools, but at the top of the index this figure was 100 per cent.

Thus, the index seems to satisfy three main criteria of validity. The items included seem to be cogent measures of the kind of militancy represented by civil rights organizations in 1964; they relate to each other in a consistent fashion; and they predict responses to related questions not included in the index. This was the case for each of the samples.

In succeeding chapters we turn to the question of how Negroes come to be militant, moderate, or conservative on civil rights.

2

The Social Context
of Militancy

Beat and cuff your slave, keep him hungry and spiritless, and he will
follow the chain of his master like a dog; but feed and clothe him well,
work him moderately, surround him with physical comfort, and dreams
of freedom intrude.

—*Frederick Douglass*

Many [slave owners] agreed that bondsmen should not visit neighboring
estates. . . . By keeping them at home "they do not know what is going on
beyond the limits of the plantation, and feel satisfied. . . ."

—*Kenneth Stampp*

We turn now to some social and psychological sources of militancy. In
this chapter we locate militancy within the sociocultural structure of modern
America. In the following chapter we examine psychological factors affecting Negro militancy. While militancy is undoubtedly influenced by both
social and psychological factors, we do not mean to treat these as entirely
separate classes of variables. Clearly, much that is treated as a psychological
characteristic of persons is in turn greatly shaped by social circumstances.
Thus, while both kinds of factors are investigated separately, ultimately
their joint influence upon militancy will be examined. In this way it will be
possible to assess the extent to which certain psychological factors seem
to be the mechanisms by which social circumstances produce militancy.
For example, I shall try to show that high social status produces militancy
to the extent that status produces hope which in turn makes militancy seem
realistic. But this anticipates what is to come. First we must see the extent to
which social factors have consequences for Negro militancy.

For the sake of understanding, it is necessary to violate the seamless web of life and make analytic distinctions. Some of these are hierarchical or vertical distinctions; others are nonhierarchical or horizontal. Education, income, and occupational prestige serve to differentiate persons vertically. Other variables, such as region or sex, may be thought of as horizontal categories. In addition we distinguish between *attributes* of persons, such as their age, sex, or education, and their *behavior,* for example, participation in voluntary organizations or reading newspapers. In searching for the social determinates of militancy, we examine horizontal distinctions first, then the hierarchical, and finally various aspects of behavior bearing on social involvement and participation.

To avoid errors in interpretation, it should be clearly noted that our concern is with understanding the social and psychological factors that affect attitudes toward the civil rights struggle rather than the factors that affect actual participation in the civil rights movement. However, there is a strong relation between participation, as measured by membership in a civil rights organization, and attitudes toward civil rights, as measured by the Index of Conventional Militancy. Those classified as militant on the index were much more likely to report membership in a civil rights organization and to indicate willingness to take part in a civil rights demonstration than were those who were scored as conservative or moderate. If the definition of participation is broadened to include financial and other contributions, boycotting of products and stores, keeping children out of schools on protest days, and voting for more outspoken procivil rights candidates, then no doubt almost all of those termed militant have at one time or another been mobilized to some degree of participation.

However, our interest is not simply in civil rights activism, but rather in how a militant orientation develops and where it is located in the social structure. What we have done is characterize three main styles of response to the civil rights struggle among members of a "mass." "Mass" refers to a number of separate individuals each responding independently to the same stimulus (here the civil rights struggle). It implies a common focus of attention, but it is less than a collectivity since it lacks interaction tying the group together, as would be found among members of a civil rights group.[1] Thus, what we are exploring are the moods of the Negro community, not its modes of organization. However, when activism is analyzed the results are the same. In addition, as with any social move-

[1] The term "mass" is a familiar one in sociological literature; for example, Ralph Turner and Lewis Killian, *Collective Behavior,* Englewood Cliffs, N.J., Prentice-Hall, 1957, p. 167. Members of this "mass" are responding to what Blumer and Smelser have called "general social movements" as opposed to the specific "norm-oriented movements." (See Herbert Blumer, "Collective Behavior," in A. M. Lee, ed., *New Outline of the Principles of Sociology,* New York, Barnes & Noble, 1951, pp. 199-201, and N. Smelser, *Theory of Collective Behavior,* New York, Free Press, 1963, p. 273.)

ment, the civil rights struggle does not exist in isolation. In a society such as the United States which, ideally at least, permits groups to openly pursue their goals, civil rights leaders direct much attention toward mobilizing mass opinion in the black community. It is from this community that activists are recruited and that various forms of support so crucial for success in a direct action movement are obtained. Thus there is important reason for analyzing the response of the Negro community as a whole to the civil rights struggle.

Exposure to Race Relations Values of the Traditional South

The desire for radical social change and the belief that things are not as they should be requires an informing vision or perspective. In the case of race relations, such a vision must compete with contradictory perspectives on the proper place of the Negro. The extent to which modern American Negroes hold a perspective legitimating a struggle for equality ought to be partly contingent upon their exposure to and acceptance of the opposing value system of the traditional South.

Until very recently, the normative system governing race relations in the South was massive, and covered the most minute details of daily life down to segregated pet cemeteries, telephone party lines, blood plasma, and courtroom Bibles. In South Carolina, Negroes and whites were forbidden to look out of the same windows. This system was buttressed by a large set of formal laws, informal mores, and (white) economic, police, and juridical power. There is an ongoing debate among scholars about the role of coercion versus voluntary compliance in maintaining the patterns of Southern race relations both during and after slavery. Until recently the cheerful-compliance side has no doubt been overemphasized. However, the fact remains that the system rested (and rests) on something more than the police power of the white community.

This something is, of course, acquiescence in (to a greater or lesser degree) the system on the part of many oppressed by it. In the absence of sustained contact with an alternative pattern of race relations, or a different normative system, acceptance of the dominant pattern is easily understood. However, as the Negro's life circumstances operate to reduce his exposure to the Southern value system (and conversely, as exposure to the equalitarian value system of the rest of the country increases), individuals should increasingly question the legitimacy of the Southern "way of life" and militancy should increase.

We do not have a direct measure of the extent to which an individual has been exposed to the race relations values of the traditional South. However, certain indirect measures are available. The least ambiguous is whether a person was raised in the South or not.

Region and Type of Community

It is not surprising that among those raised in the deep South (but not necessarily still living there) only 19 per cent scored as militant (Table 28). This proportion increases steadily for those born in the border states and outside the South, up to 40 per cent for those raised outside the United States.

Table 28.   MILITANCY BY REGION WHERE MOST OF CHILDHOOD WAS SPENT

	Deep South	Border States	Non-South	Outside of U.S.
Militant	19%	31%	35%	40%
Number	(523)	(260)	(293)	(20)

Africans and West Indians in the United States have occasionally been critical of what they regard as the docility of American Negroes. Marcus Garvey and Denmark Vesey, two prominent protest leaders of the past, were both born outside the United States, as were Stokely Carmichael and a number of other contemporary civil rights leaders. However, while those raised outside the United States had the highest percentage militant, they were only slightly higher than those raised in the North.

Table 29.   MILITANCY BY TYPE OF COMMUNITY RAISED IN

	Farm	Small and Medium Cities	Big City
Militant	15%	28%	37%
Number	(321)	(483)	(287)

Being raised in a rural rather than in an urban area would also seem to be a good indicator of the value system to which an individual has been exposed. Rural areas, in the South and elsewhere, have traditionally been bastions of cultural conservatism, in addition to being a source of occasional populist reform. Today it is in the cities of the South that the traditional social structure is crumbling most rapidly. The anonymity of the city, its greater heterogeneity and mobility, its more cosmopolitan and sophisticated atmosphere, and its greater integration into the national life all militate against traditional Southern patterns. The data show that militancy increases from 15 per cent among those raised on farms to 37 per cent for those raised in big cities (Table 29). This finding holds independent of region.

Age and Sex

The color line in America, despite periods of regression, has slowly been shifting since the turn of the century, and each successive generation is born into a social milieu where less and less consensus exists over the traditional inferior position of Negroes in American life. The shifts in the color line have been particularly pronounced since the beginning of World War II and have gained increasing momentum in recent years. In view of this changing climate of opinion, it can be inferred that most of the old were raised to accept segregation and to limit their aspirations.

Table 30. MILITANCY BY AGE

	18–29	30–44	45–59	60–75	75+
Militant	31%	34%	23%	16%	9%
Number	(243)	(368)	(271)	(179)	(32)

The old should therefore be less likely to be militant than the young, and Table 30 shows that this is so. About one out of three under 44 scored as militant; this figure decreases to about one in ten for those 75 and over. The greater militancy of the young is also indicated by their visible prominence in picket lines, sit-ins, and voter registration drives. The Congress of Racial Equality estimates that as of early 1961 more than 95 per cent of demonstrators who had been arrested were in their early twenties or late teens.[2]

Sex differences are also also relevant. Men, being generally less insulated from society than women, are less traditional. This is true even in the Negro community, which in some respects, and partly for economic reasons, tends to be matriarchal. Men are more likely to be involved in the secular world and hence more likely to be exposed in a sustained way to values which would lead to rejection of the *status quo*. Negro males have traditionally been treated worse than females. It can be seen that about one in three of the men in the sample were militant while only about one in five of the women were (Table 31).

[2] As referred to in Jacob R. Fishman and Fredric Solomon, "Youth and Social Action: Perspectives on the Student Sit-In-Movement" in Bernard E. Segal, ed., *Racial and Ethnic Relations,* New York, Thomas Y. Crowell, 1966, p. 433.

In discussing age differentials among activists, Cothran notes that "a major source of conflict centers around adult conservatism and youthful aggressiveness" (Tilman C. Cothran, "The Negro Protest Against Segregation in the South," *Annals of the American Academy of Political and Social Science,* January 1965, p. 71). However, in considering the Negro community at large among those under 44, the percentage militant seems about the same, although it does drop down considerably as age increases beyond 44. This distinction roughly corresponds to those who reached maturity before and during or after World War II.

Table 31.   MILITANCY BY SEX

	Men	Women
Militant	32%	22%
Number	(495)	(600)

It has been observed that region, size of the community that one was raised in, age, and sex are each related to militancy, confirming the expectation that those most likely to be exposed to the values of the traditional South are the least likely to be militant. The effect of any one of these factors is independent of the effect of the others and, indeed, is independent of additional factors yet to be discussed.

A stronger measure of exposure to Southern values may be obtained by combining the four variables into a single Index of Exposure to Values Legitimizing Protest. This index shows that among those whose life circumstances combine to insure maximum exposure to the race relations values of the traditional South, only 11 per cent scored as militant while, at the other end of the index, among those least exposed to Southern values, 44 per cent were militants.

Thus, older Southern women reared in insulated rural areas are the least militant,[3] and younger Northern men reared in big cities are the most militant. When scores on the index are collapsed into categories of low (0, 1, 2), medium (3, 4), and high (5, 6, 7), the percentages militant are 12, 26, and 40, respectively (Table 32).

Table 32.   MILITANCY BY INDEX OF EXPOSURE TO VALUES LEGITIMIZING PROTEST

Score on Index[a]

	High on Presumed Exposure to Values of Traditional South				High on Presumed Exposure to Equalitarian Values		
	0	1	2	3	4	5	6	7
Militant	11%	12%	13%	24%	29%	38%	40%	44%
Number	(44)	(111)	(151)	(234)	(212)	(141)	(129)	(66)

Collapsed Scores

	(0, 1, 2)	(3, 4)	(5, 6, 7)
Militant	12%	26%	40%
Number	(306)	(446)	(336)

[a] Includes age, sex, region and type of community raised in. No point was given for each of the following: being over 60, a woman, brought up on a farm, and in the deep South. One point was given for being 45 to 59, a man, brought up in a small town, and raised in the upper South. Two points were given for being under 45, raised in a big city, and outside the South.

[3] These older Southern women now live in urban areas and are probably more militant in their attitudes than those still living in rural areas.

Heretofore it has been argued that exposure to values legitimating protest (or conversely lack of exposure to values precluding protest) seems to be required if militancy is to develop.[4] Being removed from the influence of the normative system of the traditional South seems to make it possible to adopt a new value system from which an individual can question the existing system. However, much more than this is involved in the development of militancy. An additional factor which ought to influence militancy is a certain amount of social privilege and the things associated with it.

Social Privilege

Militancy has already been located along some horizontal dimensions of social organization. Consideration will now be given to the vertical or hierarchial dimensions implied in social privilege. The effects of education, occupation, and income are investigated separately and then combined into a measure of social privilege.

Social groups differ markedly in the relative amounts of scarce social rewards distributed among their members. In some societies the gap between the privileged and less privileged is very pronounced while in others differences are small. But regardless of how great the relative gap between the "haves" and the "have nots," in all societies individuals differ in their share of social rewards. Laymen, and not only sociologists, categorize individuals by social class according to the relative amounts of social status, skill, and economic and political power they possess.

Education

James Vardaman, a Negro-baiting politician of another era, in commenting on Northern aid to Negro education stated, "What the North is sending South is not money but dynamite: this education is ruining our Negroes. They're demanding equality."[5] As a humanitarian Vardaman may leave something to be desired, but as a social analyst he was perceptive. As Table 33 indicates, education is strongly related to militancy. Among those with a grammar school education or less, only 15 per cent scored as militant, compared with 31 per cent of those who had attended high

[4] The fact that one in ten of those who appear to be least exposed to equalitarian values were still scored as militant does not necessarily weaken this assertion. The index only imperfectly measures such exposure. No doubt some older women brought up on farms in the South have obtained a relatively good education and are high in social participation (all of the respondents live in cities where contact with ideas legitimizing protest is more likely) and hence may have overcome the effect of these other background variables.

[5] Lerone Bennet, *Confrontation: Black and White*, Chicago, Johnson Publishing Company, 1965, p. 108.

Table 33. MILITANCY BY EDUCATION

	Grammar School	At Least Some High School	At Least Some College
Militant	15%	31%	42%
Number	(404)	(545)	(146)

school and 42 per cent of those with a partial or complete college education. This relation holds in both the South and the North.

Occupation

Strongly associated with but still independent of education is the individual's occupation. In Tables 34–37 several measures of occupation are related to militancy.

In considering employment, among those currently employed, 32 per cent scored as militant while for the unemployed and housewives this figure drops to 22 per cent and to 14 per cent for the retired (Table 34).

Table 34. MILITANCY BY EMPLOYMENT STATUS

	Employed	Unemployed or Laid Off	Housewife	Retired
Militant	32%	22%	22%	14%
Number	(589)	(119)	(265)	(111)

These findings are consistent with figures noted earlier, where women and the aged were lower in militancy. The unemployed are somewhat lower in militancy than are the employed despite their greater actual deprivation.

Among those currently employed it can be seen that, in general, as the status of a given occupation increases, so does militancy. In the category of service occupations only 24 per cent were scored as militant, and this figure increases consistently to 48 per cent among professionals (Table 35).

When occupations are grouped by prestige (here considering those currently employed and the "usual occupation" of the unemployed and retired), militancy increases from 22 per cent among those in lower-status occupations to 47 per cent among those in higher-status jobs. When housewives are included and assigned the occupation of the head of the household, a similar pattern is found: The higher the status of the occupation, the higher the percentage militant.

Since education is strongly related to both militancy and occupation, it is possible that those in higher-status occupations are more militant simply

Table 35.   MILITANCY BY OCCUPATION

Respondent's Occupation[a]

	Prof.	Semi-prof.	Man-agers	Cleri-cal	Sales	Crafts	Opera-tives	Labor	Service
Militant	48%	41%	54%	42%	42%	35%	27%	27%	24%
Number	(23)	(17)	(26)	(60)	(12)	(71)	(138)	(41)	(198)

Prestige of Respondent's Occupation[b]

	High	Medium	Low
Militant	47%	36%	22%
Number	(77)	(189)	(549)

Prestige of Occupation of Household Head[c]

	High	Medium	Low
Militant	45%	31%	22%
Number	(78)	(283)	(694)

[a] Among employed only.
[b] Professionals, semiprofessionals, managers, and proprietors were classified as high in occupational prestige; clerical, sales, and craftsmen as medium; and laborers, operatives, and service workers as low. Table includes the usual occupation of the unemployed and retired.
[c] Includes all respondents.

because they are more educated. However, Table 36 offers evidence that, even with education held constant, the higher the occupational position the higher the percentage militant. Similarly, the employed remain more militant than the unemployed even when education is controlled for.

Table 36.   MILITANCY BY EDUCATION AND OCCUPATION

(per cent militant)

Prestige of Occupation	Grammar School	At Least Some High School	At Least Some College
High	[a]	38%	57%
Number		(16)	(51)
Medium	27%	37%	44%
Number	(44)	(106)	(39)
Low	12%	32%	26%
Number	(250)	(272)	(27)

[a] Too few cases to compute percentages.

Among those in lower-status occupations, the employed are still higher in militancy than the unemployed (Table 37).

One of the reasons students are more active in the civil rights struggle is their relatively greater freedom, including freedom from the economic reprisals that may restrain employed people. Likewise, it has been theorized that one element in the civil rights activism of some Negro ministers is their independence of white employers. Although the present study did not inquire as to the race of the individual's employer, it did ask whether respondents were self-employed or employed by someone else. If one assumes that the self-employed are apt to be less subject to economic reprisal than those responsible to an employer, one might be led to predict greater militancy on their part. However, this is not the case. On the contrary, militancy is somewhat less pronounced among the self-employed than among those employed by others (Table 37).

Table 37.   MILITANCY BY PRESTIGE OF OCCUPATION AND EMPLOYMENT STATUS

(per cent militant)

Employment Status	Prestige of Occupation		
	High	Medium	Low
Employed	55%	41%	26%
Number	(45)	(133)	(366)
Self-Employed	33%	0%	14%
Number	(21)	(10)	(15)
Unemployed or Laid Off	a	37%	18%
Number		(24)	(87)
Retired	a	19%	11%
Number		(21)	(81)
Housewife[b]	44%	21%	20%
Number	(9)	(58)	(178)

[a] Too few cases to compute percentages.
[b] For housewives, the prestige of husband's occupation is used.

This finding certainly does not invalidate the hypothesis that those subject to strong economic reprisals are apt to be less militant than those not, particularly in concrete situations where action is called for.[6] However, it does suggest that, by itself the threat of economic reprisal need not hinder the development of a militant orientation just as freedom from economic reprisal may fail to encourage it.

[6] The report of SNCC field workers with respect to difficulties in obtaining cooperation among some rural Negroes obviously supports such a hypothesis, as does the 1966 electoral loss of the Lowndes County Freedom Organization. See also *Voting in Mississippi*, Report of the United States Commission on Civil Rights, Government Printing Office, Washington, D.C., May 1965.

Status Discrepancy and Social Mobility

It has sometimes been suggested that discrepancies among the various dimensions of social status—for example, being highly educated but in a low-prestige occupation, or being high on both of these yet belonging to a lowly esteemed racial or ethnic group—may lead to the development of radicalism.[7] It is argued that individuals in a position of status discrepancy are subject to pressures by the social order not experienced to the same extent by individuals with congruent statuses. This has often been thought to predispose them for radical political movements. The eighteenth century revolutionary zeal of the French bourgeoisie, denied recognition by the old aristocracy, and the support given in the fifties to Senator Joseph McCarthy by some recently arrived and upwardly mobile ethnic groups are often cited as examples.

How does militancy appear among those who manifest a pattern of status discrepancy, such as having considerable education, but being in a working-class occupation? It would seem that feelings of resentment against the social order would be particularly pronounced among this group whose education qualifies them for higher-status occupations, yet who are presumably denied such occupations and rewards simply because of society's arbitrary racial arrangement. One of our educated militant respondents in describing his occupation of garbage collector said that it was "subhuman beast-of-burden type work even though I was a student." Comments such as this would lead to the expectation that status discrepancy of this type would be an important factor in the development of militancy. However, in Table 36 it can be seen that this is not the case. Those with this type of objective status discrepancy (high education–low occupation) do not show a greater predisposition for militancy. In fact, among those whose consistent status stems from having a college education and being in a high-status occupation, 57 per cent were scored as militant while among the status-discrepant group, this figure was only 26 per cent.[8] Among American Negroes, apparently,

[7] For example, G. Lenski, "Status Crystalization: A Non-Vertical Dimension of Social Status," *American Sociological Review*, 1954, pp. 405–413.

[8] This measure suffers from the weakness of being an objective measure. As one school of sociology is continually reminding us, objective measures of social structure affect behavior most clearly when they lead to certain mental images and self-indications. If we had inquired as to whether people were actively aware of this objective discrepancy and then contrasted percentage militant among the group who were aware of and bothered by their discrepancy with those not in discrepant status positions, the pattern might have been very different.

When the status discrepants are compared with another group of status consistents, those with only a grammar school education in workingclass occupations, the former appear as somewhat higher in militancy. However, this is no doubt due to their greater education rather than to tension in their status positions.

A recent study of status consistency and political attitudes similarly notes that social class is a much better predictor of attitudes than discrepancies in status (K. Dennis Kelly and William J. Chambliss, "Status Consistency and Political Attitudes," *American Sociological Review*, June 1966).

rather than marked status discrepancies leading to radicalism they seem more likely to lead to resignation and a low morale. The joint effect of education and occupation on militancy is additive—the greater one's social status the greater one's militancy.

The notion of status discrepancy is closely related to the question of social mobility and its effect on attitudes. It is possible to view those who have been socially mobile as being status discrepants in the sense that their past status is inconsistent with their current status (independent of whether they have moved up or down in status).

The problem of intergenerational social mobility, or change in social position relative to one's parents, is an important factor in social behavior. It is becoming particularly relevant in the case of Negroes as the opportunity structure becomes more open.

Past research on social mobility in the United States has generally revealed a tendency for those who move up in the social structure to become more conservative in their political orientations than both the group they enter and the group they left. In the same way, those who are moving downward are more likely to hold on to the conservative outlook of the class they left so that downward mobility, too, is associated with conservatism.[9]

However, in the case of the Negro American and civil rights militancy, one would not necessarily expect to find this pattern. Instead, it might be thought that rather than becoming more conservative the downwardly mobile Negro would become more radical since, to a much greater extent than the downwardly mobile white, he has a built-in explanation (whether right or wrong) for his failure, his skin color.

Similarly, those who move up out of the ghetto world, instead of becoming satisfied and less militant, may merely have had their appetites whetted. More to the point, perhaps, is that recently arrived Negroes rarely have the large stake in the economic system which Frazier and others have suggested makes some members of the Negro elite almost as resistant to positive racial change as the white elite. Thus it may be hypothesized that those who have been socially mobile, regardless of the direction of their mobility, should be both more militant than the class from whence they came or the class into which they have moved.

These conjectures receive support in Table 38. Here we see that mobility is indeed related to militancy. Among the three groups who have been downwardly mobile (those of high-status parents who moved either into medium- or lower-status occupations and those of medium-status parents who moved into lower-status occupations), in every case the percentage scoring as militant is higher than among those in the status position moved out of or the new one moved into. Among those who moved down from a high-status

[9] These studies are summarized in S. M. Lipset and R. Bendix, *Social Mobility in Industrial Society*, Berkeley, University of California Press, 1960, pp. 64–71.

background to medium-status occupations, 56 per cent were militant, while among those who remained in medium-status positions this figure is only 30 per cent, and for those who remained in high-status positions it is 37 per cent. The pattern is the same for each of the three upwardly mobile groups. Among those who moved from lower-status and medium-status into relatively high-status positions, 48 and 76 per cent, respectively, are militant,

Table 38. MILITANCY BY SOCIAL MOBILITY

(per cent militant)

Prestige of Respondent's Occupation	Prestige of Father's Occupation[a]		
	High	Medium	Low
High	37%	76%	48%
Number	(19)	(17)	(27)
	(stationary)	(upwardly mobile)	(upwardly mobile)
Medium	56%	30%	41%
Number	(16)	(44)	(64)
	(downwardly mobile)	(stationary)	(upwardly mobile)
Low	39%	36%	20%
Number	(31)	(56)	(188)
	(downwardly mobile)	(downwardly mobile)	(stationary)

[a] Because of difficulty of classification, farm proprietors are excluded, as are the approximately 10 per cent of the sample who did not know their father's occupation.

while for those who remained in high-status positions only 37 per cent are militant. This finding is of particular interest because it suggests that although militancy is strongly related to social privilege, among those high in social privilege the *arrivistes* are more militant than others.[10] The higher-prestige, older, more-established Negro families may indeed have a vested interest in the *status quo* and thus be less militant than those newly arrived to their positions of prestige. However, among persons who have not been mobile, the higher the prestige, the greater the militancy. Both higher prestige and mobility produce militancy.

[10] A discussion of the background of SNCC workers (most of whom are young students) suggests that they are generally upwardly mobile. Zinn states: "These young people are not middle class reformers who became somehow concerned about others. . . . For the most part their fathers are janitors and laborers, their mothers maids and factory workers" (H. Zinn, *SNCC: The New Abolitionists*, Boston, Beacon Press, 1964, p. 9).

Similar findings are reported in a study of members of CORE (Ingeborg B. Powell, "Ideology and Strategy of Direct Action: A Study of the Congress of Racial Equality," Ph.D. dissertation, University of California in Berkeley, 1965, p. 191).

This pattern of upward mobility noted for both SNCC and CORE members suggests that exclusion from the entrenched Negro middle class is a factor encouraging militancy just as exclusion by the dominant white society encourages it.

Income

Due to discrimination, education and occupation are less closely related to income among Negroes than among whites. Nevertheless, the three are related. Table 39 shows the relation between income and militancy. The pattern is similar to that observed for the two other status variables:

Table 39. MILITANCY BY INCOME

	Less than $2,000	$2,000–$3,999	$4,000–$5,999	$6,000 and over
Militant	13%	19%	38%	35%
Number	(205)	(258)	(268)	(298)

The more privileged are much more likely to be militant than are the less privileged. Thus, among those earning less than $2,000 a year, only 13 per cent are militant; this proportion increases to 38 per cent among those with incomes of $4,000 to $6,000. Beyond $4,000 there are no meaningful differences. A ceiling effect seems to obtain: Beyond a certain point increased income does not influence militancy. That the relation between

Table 40. MILITANCY BY INCOME AND EDUCATION

(per cent militant)

Education	Less than $2,000	$2,000–$3,999	$4,000–$5,999	$6,000 and over
Grammar school	10%	13%	27%	20%
Number	(126)	(105)	(73)	(67)
At least some high school	15%	22%	43%	35%
Number	(68)	(135)	(157)	(153)
At least some college	36%	33%	40%	47%
Number	(11)	(18)	(37)	(79)

income and militancy is independent of education can be seen in Table 40. Status discrepancy, in this case between high education and low income, again fails to influence militancy.

A Combined Measure of Social Privilege

Since all three separate measures of social privilege are positively and independently related to militancy, it is proper to combine them into an over-all Index of Social Class. As is clear in Table 41, the joint effect of these three variables on militancy is very great. Among those lowest on the Social Class Index only 8 per cent scored as militant. This figure increases to 31 per cent for those in the middle of the class hierarchy and to 55 per cent for those with the highest social positions. When this measure is combined into categories of lower class, middle class, and upper class,[11] the percentage militant is 14 per cent, 31 per cent, and 45 per cent, respectively.

Table 41. MILITANCY BY SOCIAL CLASS

Index of Social Class[a]

	Lower Social Class					Upper Social Class	
	0	1	2	3	4	5	6
Militant	8%	19%	31%	31%	39%	49%	55%
Number	(182)	(252)	(269)	(210)	(105)	(47)	(32)

	Collapsed Scores		
	(0, 1)	(2, 3)	(4, 5, 6)
Militant	14%	31%	45%
Number	(434)	(479)	(184)

[a] No point was given for a grammar school education or less; at least some high school and at least some college were given one and two points, respectively. Occupation was also scored 0, 1, or 2, according to low, medium, or high status. No point was given for incomes under $2,000; incomes from $2,000 to $3,999 were given one point; all higher incomes, two points.

These data do not mean that there are not many lower-class people concerned with and involved in the struggle for equal rights or that those who are involved may not often be more militant than the involved of higher status. The data merely suggest that a militant orientation (as defined in terms of this index) increases as social position does. According to a number of observers, one of the distinguishing characteristics of the civil rights struggle is the fact that it draws support from all segments of the Negro community. For example, Rustin has stated that "Birmingham remains the unmatched symbol of grass-roots protest involving all strata of the black

[11] It should be emphasized that these categories are relative. Negroes labeled upper class in this study would be mostly middle and lower middle class in the broader American class structure. Frazier notes: "If members of the Negro upper class were integrated into American society, their occupations and incomes would place them in the middle class" (E. Franklin Frazier, *The Negro in the United States,* New York, Macmillan, 1949, p. 291. A full discussion of Negro class structure in Chicago may be found in St. Clair Drake and Horace R. Cayton, *Black Metropolis,* New York, Harper Torchbook, 1962, pp. 521–715.) An important gap exists in knowledge about Negro class structure.

community."[12] However this is not to say that the civil rights struggle draws its support in equal proportions from the various class groups.

On the basis of knowing that an individual is very low in social position, it is possible to predict that he will not be militant and be correct nine times out of ten. With each increase in social class there is a concomitant increase in the percentage militant. However, for those in the highest social positions predictions of militancy would be wrong slightly more often than they would be right. There are factors associated with being more privileged that lead to greater likelihood of militancy. But the fact that slightly less than half of the most privileged group scored as militant shows that there are still other factors which determine militancy in this class (some of which may not affect those low in status).

One factor which may reduce militancy among the high-status group is the conservatism often associated with higher-status positions. As Frazier has noted, the existence of a segregated Negro community, which is an exploitable economic unit, results in some Negroes, as well as whites, having a vested interest in the continuance of segregation. Higher-status Negroes often have a captive market within the ghetto.[13]

---

[12] Bayard Rustin, "From Protest to Politics: The Future of the Civil Rights Movement," *Commentary,* February 1965. Meier notes that a recent development "has been the involvement of lower-lower class people, many of whom are unemployed or chronically so," and that "a large part of the increasing militancy of middle and upper class Negroes is derived from the new militancy of the involved lower class" August Meier, "Negro Protest Movements and Organizations," *Journal of Negro Education,* Summer 1963, pp. 445 and 446).

It might be argued that lower-class Negroes are not concerned with integration per se, but rather with jobs and housing. However, the measure of militancy seems broad enough to cover these aspects as well, since it included questions about "equal rights," discrimination in employment, and civil rights demonstrations. In addition, the term integration has a symbolic meaning and refers to much more than simply equal treatment in expensive restaurants and residential areas. These items measuring militancy are all related to each other, and knowing how a person responded to any one of them helps predict his response to the remaining items. Most important, when the items are observed separately in relation to social class (even the items which did not mention integration, or discrimination in restaurants, or the sale of property), those lowest in social position were in every case the least militant.

Still the middle-class tone of the movement up until 1966 may help explain the lack of involvement of some workingclass Negroes. Much more as a result of a shared heritage and structural position in American society than of a common African past, a distinctive Negro working class culture does to some extent exist (for example, in language, food and music preferences, and perhaps in attitudes toward work and women). The fact that the civil rights movement has generally not worked within the framework of this subculture is no doubt relevant for the lack of involvement of some workingclass Negroes. The black power movement is trying to address itself to this lack.

[13] E. Franklin Frazier discusses the conservatism of this group in "The Negro Middle Class and Desegregation," *Social Problems,* April 1957, pp. 291–301, and in *Black Bourgeoisie,* New York, Free Press, 1957. In addition, some higher-status individuals may enhance their own self-image by depreciating their own group and in no way identifying with the Negro masses.

Although our study does not have any direct measure of the kind of vested interest just mentioned, certain inferences can be made as to who among the more privileged are most apt to have a vested interest in the *status quo*.

While we have observed that in general militancy increases with social privilege, we also noted variations in militancy among the privileged with respect to occupation and social mobility. Among higher-status individuals those who have been socially privileged for a longer time are lower in militancy than those who have arrived at their positions more recently. Furthermore, those earning over $6,000 a year were slightly less likely to be militant than those earning $4,000 to $6,000. This suggests that those who have been upper status for a longer period of time are more likely to have developed a vested interest in the system than those who have recently arrived, and the former are therefore less militant. Furthermore, among those who are already privileged, the more wealthy and generally better off might be expected to profit more from the system and hence be more conservative than the relatively well off, but less wealthy, people.

Table 42. MILITANCY BY HOME OWNERSHIP[a]

	Own Home	Rent
Militant	35%	54%
Number	(93)	(87)

[a] Among those classified as upper social class only.

An additional indication of economic well-being is the ownership of a home. In Table 42 home ownership is related to militancy for those of higher social status. Here it can be seen that the relation between privilege and militancy noted for the rest of the sample is reversed. Among those who are already relatively well off, the less privileged rather than the more privileged are the most militant. *Over half of the nonhome owners are militant, while only about one-third of those who own their homes were scored as militant.*

This question of a vested interest in the *status quo* among some of those in the highest social positions certainly does not entirely explain why many members of the group are not militant. However, by inferring its effect an important qualification must be made to the generalization that militancy increases with social privilege. We have perhaps isolated one of the factors that keep militancy from reaching higher proportions within this group.[14]

[14] It should be noted that even when this additional differentiation is made, even for those owning their own homes with their "relatively lessened" degree of militancy, militancy is still higher than among those in any of the less privileged groups. It is also interesting to note that the question of home ownership has slight effect on militancy among those lower in social status.

However, rather than being concerned with what prevents some of those high in social privilege from also being high in militancy, let us address ourselves to the more important question posed by the over-all relation between privilege and militancy. Social privilege is strongly related to militancy. The more education an individual has, the higher the prestige of his occupation, and the greater his income, the more likely he is to be militant (even when the effect of education on each of these other variables is controlled). This fact is even more evident when these items are combined into a measure of social class.

Why should social privilege relate to militancy the way it does? One might imagine the more privileged to be more satisfied—since the system has treated them relatively well—and hence less likely to be militant. However, social theorists have questioned the seemingly obvious idea that concern for social change is likely to be greatest among those most disinherited, and social science research has tended to support their claims.

The relation of deprivation to social upheaval has long been of interest to scholars. One of the most perceptive statements made about this subject was offered by the French political scientist Alexis de Tocqueville, well over 100 years ago:

So it would appear that the French found their condition the more unsupportable in proportion to its improvement. . . . Revolutions are not always brought about by a gradual decline from bad to worse. Nations that have endured patiently and almost unconsciously the most overwhelming oppression often burst into rebellion against the yoke the moment it begins to grow lighter. . . . Evils which are patiently endured when they seem inevitable become intolerable when once the idea of escape from them is suggested.[15]

Although Tocqueville was talking about revolutionary rather than reform movements, his statement has much relevance for understanding the increased tempo of the civil rights struggle within the United States in recent years. Protest has grown as the standard of living has risen (not fallen) and as the legal basis of segregation has been undermined (not strengthened). Tocqueville's analysis, which has led to theories of the revolution of rising expectations, is congruent with the regional differences we have observed. There is more militancy in the North, where living standards are higher and social justice more in evidence, than in the South, where objectively things are much worse. Thus, among Negro Americans, those who have experienced the most improvement and are least subject to objective deprivation are much more likely to be militant than those worse off.

Tocqueville suggested that the taste of better things serves, not to quell dissatisfaction, but to create and increase it. The many reforms and un-

---

[15] As quoted in J. Davies, "Toward a Theory of Revolution," *American Sociological Review*, February 1962, p. 5.

precedented prosperity of France just prior to the French Revolution, and the abolition of most of the remnants of serfdom prior to the Russian Revolution, are good examples of this. The situation seems similar for the pattern of militancy we have observed in this chapter. The more privileged recognize that change is possible and want more. The most deprived Negroes tend not to have a basis in experience for what "more" means.

Karl Marx, somewhat later than Tocqueville, stressed a different factor in his interpretation of why discontent is not necessarily related to the severity of objective conditions. He wrote in the *Communist Manifesto:*

Thus, although the enjoyments of the workers have risen, the social satisfaction that they [increased wages] give has fallen in comparison with the increased enjoyments of the capitalist. . . . Our desires and pleasures spring from society; we measure them, therefore, by society and not by the objects which serve for their satisfaction. Because they are of a social nature, they are of a relative nature.

Following through on the implications of Marx's idea, the author's of *The American Soldier,* a classic of survey research, develop the notion of relative deprivation to help understand why discontent among servicemen was not necessarily related to objective conditions of deprivation. The fact that soldiers in units with high rates of promotion were more critical of their chances of promotion than were soldiers in units where the chances for promotion "were about the worst in any branch of the army" is explained as follows: "such opinions represent a relationship betwen their expectations and their achievements relative to others in the same boat with them."[16]

In understanding discontent, what counts is not so much the individual's objective situation as that of the "others" with whom he compares himself. The group with whom the individual compares himself is called by sociologists his "reference group." If a person's reference group is as deprived as he is, the individual is apt to be content with his lot. If, however, a person's reference group is more successful than he is, the individual may have a sense of deprivation no matter how objectively well off he is.

The notion of relative deprivation and the related concept of reference group[17] have relevance for understanding the pattern of militancy observed in this chapter. The fact that militancy is more pronounced among the privileged than among the unprivileged suggests that the privileged have a broader perspective, derived from their greater education and social participation. With this perspective, an individual can evaluate his own and his group's position in relation to the more privileged segments of white

[16] S. Stouffer *et. al., The American Soldier: Adjustment During Army Life,* Princeton, N. J., Princeton University Press, 1949, Vol. 1, p. 251.
[17] Robert Merton, *Social Theory and Social Structure,* New York, Free Press, 1962, p. 237.

society rather than the limited framework of the depressed ghetto world.[18] This shift in perspective comes from the abiility of the more privileged to look horizontally at whites in similar positions and from their greater knowledge about how these whites live and are treated.[19] In addition to employing white society as the frame of reference, this perspective is likely to include greater intellectual sophistication, more substantive knowledge about the world, and an image of man more conducive to militancy.

The more privileged may be much more conscious of lack of acceptance due to race because they come so close to being accepted in every other way. They have reaped many of the fruits of middle-class existence and their image of themselves is likely to be severely contradicted when they find themselves assigned to an inferior racial status. The more deprived individual in the ghetto—uneducated, unskilled, underpaid or unemployed—may be less aware of the racial aspect of his low status because he is so consistently submerged. Thus, a subtle kind of status discrepancy may be an important impetus to militancy for the relatively privileged Negro.

There are far more concrete reasons, however, why militancy should vary directly with social privilege. These involve the energy, resources, morale, and self-confidence needed to challenge an oppressive and powerful system. The mental and physical energy of severely deprived people is occupied in simply staying alive. A concern with somewhat abstract principles of racial justice is a luxury of the more privileged, who need not worry where their next meal is coming from. They are freer in both a mental and a physical sense to challenge the *status quo*. In addition, their relatively well-to-do financial situation and the possession of occupational skills make them less vulnerable to economic reprisals for civil rights activities. Further, they are more likely to have the intellectual and organizational skills and the *savoir faire* that activism requires. Because they are less awed and overwhelmed by the power of society's institutions, and freer from concern for economic survival, they can more easily question and act.[20]

Those in very deprived positions may be less apt to feel the sense of solidarity needed for organized political challenge. A study of the effect

[18] Studies of social mobility indicate that only as people rise in the class structure do they realize how far down they previously were.

[19] From the mass media and employment by higher-status whites, lower-status people also come into contact with "white" values. However, such contact and whatever hope it may engender is, as Clark has indicated, more likely to involve "a pseudohope unaccompanied by an actual struggle to win better jobs, to get their children into college, to buy homes. Real hope is based on expectations of success; theirs seems rather a forlorn dream" (Kenneth Clark, *Dark Ghetto,* New York, Harper & Row, 1965, p. 32).

[20] Hoffer notes: "Those who are awed by their surroundings do not think of change, no matter how miserable their condition" and ". . . The poor on the borderline of starvation live purposeful lives. . . . The goals are concrete and immediate. Every meal is a fulfillment" (Eric Hoffer, *The True Believer,* New York, New American Library, 1964, pp. 17 and 32).

of unemployment on "revolutionary attitudes" reports that experiences of unemployment "do not lead by themselves to a readiness for mass action. . . . They can easily lead to outbreaks of distress in the form of single acts, but they leave the mass inert, since they lead to ever-increasing mutual estrangement, isolation, dispersion, destruction of solidarity, even to hostility among the laborers. . . ."[21] Literary depictions of the junglelike character of life in the urban ghetto with its "war of all against all" seem further to support such claims.

Furthermore, militancy requires at least some degree of hope, a belief in the possibility of beautiful tomorrows. Morale is needed which, although linked with dissatisfaction, is the opposite of despair. One can be "down," but he must not believe that he is "out." A sense of futility would seem to work against the development of the morale and hope required for a militant vision. One of the reasons that militancy is more pronounced among those in higher social positions may be that this group is more likely to have the high morale needed to sustain it. No matter how dissatisfied and distraught an individual may be over his personal and group situation, unless his discontent is found together with a positive morale, it is likely to lead not to militancy but to apathy, despair, and estrangement.

This does not mean that the underprivileged are filled with love or respect for the system that oppresses them. But they are likely to lack the energy, incentive, and will to challenge it in the disciplined way of civil rights organizations. If their concern does lead to attack, it is more likely to take the form of violent outbursts such as those of Richard Wright's protagonist, Bigger Thomas.[22] An Oakland, California, CORE spokesman described the absence of organized civil rights protest among impoverished young males in the ghetto by remarking, "If you want to go blow up something or fight, they'll do it, but they're not interested in carrying picket signs."

Closely related to morale is the question of self-image. One of the frequent consequences of lower social status is an unfavorable self-image, or at least a disparaging image of one's group. In the case of protest among Negroes, the question of self-image or group disparagement may be an extremely important factor. To believe that most Negroes are lazy, if not inherently inferior to whites, or that they are loud, dirty, and prone to violence often leads whites to fight to preserve segregation. Among Negroes, the acceptance of such beliefs probably leads to resignation. An unstated

[21] B. Zawadski and P. F. Lazarsfeld, "The Psychological Consequences of Unemployment," *Journal of Social Psychology*, May 1935, p. 249. In summarizing the results of a number of studies dealing with deprivation and political attitudes Davies indicates: "Far from making people into revolutionaries, enduring poverty makes for concern with one's solitary self or solitary family at best and resignation or mute despair at worst" (*op. cit.*, p. 7).

[22] In *Native Son*, New York, New American Library, 1961.

assumption made by militants is that Negoes are every bit as capable as whites, if not superior, and that they have the same vices and virtues as their pale counterparts. To believe otherwise would seem to justify differential treatment of Negroes and to shift the blame away from changing the social structure to changing the behavior of individuals. More privileged Negroes are probably better able to resist derogatory stereotypes of the Negro, as are more privileged whites, and this, too, may be a factor in the greater militancy of those in higher social positions.

In this section it has been suggested that important factors in the positive impact of social class on militancy are the greater intellectual sophistication, the higher morale and expectations, and the more positive self-image of those in more privileged social positions. In the next chapter these hypotheses are tested empirically.

Social Participation: Actual and Symbolic

A great deal of social participation takes in interpersonal settings in which there is face-to-face contact and communication occurs by word of mouth. But social participation also occurs when the individual reads newspapers, magazines, or books, watches television, or goes to a movie. For want of better terms, we call the first "actual" social participation, the second "symbolic" participation. Both, however, are forms of communication, and both are the opposite of social isolation and estrangement. The spread of militancy in the Negro community presupposes lines of communication which bring the message of protest and its legitimating values. By the same token, it also presupposes social participation on the part of its members, whether actual or symbolic. In this section both modes of social participation are examined to see the extent to which they are related to militancy. We consider actual participation first and then symbolic participation.

We have already learned that one aspect of social participation, employment, is positively related to militancy. Work is a major means by which persons participate in the larger society, gain a sense of responsibility for it, and acquire an interest in public affairs. The fact that men and employed women are more informed on news events than are housewives is well-known. The finding that employed Negroes are more militant than the unemployed (among both men and women) can be partly understood as a result of this process.

A similar pattern appears in Table 43 where three measures of social participation are examined. Membership in voluntary organizations[23] is

[23] Civil rights and church organizations are excluded here. The literature has suggested that membership in voluntary organizations offers Negroes an opportunity for participation and recognition denied them in the general society. Some investigators have found Negroes to be higher in membership in such organizations than whites (Gunnar Myrdal *et al.*, *An American Dilemma*, New York, Harper and Row, 1944,

positively related to militancy. Of those who belong to no voluntary organizations 23 per cent are militant compared with 30 and 38 per cent of those who belong to one or more than one such organization.

Furthermore, the more frequently an individual visits with friends, the more likely he is to be militant. Militancy ranges from 19 per cent among those who "almost never" visit to 34 per cent among those who do so every day.

An additional measure of social participation is voting. Those who failed to vote in 1960 were less likely to be militant (17 per cent) than were those who voted (31 per cent).

Table 43. MILITANCY BY INDEX OF ACTUAL SOCIAL PARTICIPATION

Number of Organizational Memberships[a]

	0	1	2+
Militant	23%	30%	38%
Number	(677)	(298)	(118)

Socialize with Friends

	Almost Never	Often	Every Day
Militant	19%	23%	34%
Number	(216)	(737)	(134)

Voted in 1960

	No	Yes
Militant	17%	31%
Number	(346)	(625)

Index of Actual Social Participation[b]

	Low 0	1	2	3	High 4, 5
Militant	11%	18%	27%	33%	43%
Number	(76)	(273)	(397)	(238)	(112)

[a] Excludes church groups and civil rights organizations.
[b] Composed of number of organizations belonged to, frequency of visits with friends, and voting in 1960.

p. 952, and more recently, N. Babchuk and R. Thompson, "Voluntary Associations Among Negroes," *American Sociological Review*, October 1962). However, when the data presented here are contrasted with data on whites obtained from the nation-wide study of anti-Semitism, differences in organizational membership by race are slight when social position is controlled for. A similar lack of difference in another nationwide sample is reported in C. Wright and H. Hyman, "Voluntary Association Memberships of American Adults: Evidence from National Sample Surveys," *American Sociological Review*, June 1958.

When these three aspects of social participation are combined into a single Index of Actual Participation, they show a powerful joint effect on militancy. Only 11 per cent of those scored zero on the index were militant as compared with 43 per cent of those high on the index (Table 43).

Symbolic Participation

Since the Civil War, Negro newspapers and magazines have been organs of racial protest (in spite of their advertisements for "straighteners" and "lighteners," which discredit black appearance). In fact, the existence of the Negro press can be traced to the desire to protest the treatment generally accorded Negroes by white newspapers. One observer has suggested that their singular dedication to the cause of Negroes "has been the prime reason for the effective organization of the Negro protest."[24] It is to be expected that those exposed to such publications should be more militant. Table 44 shows this to be the case. Of those who read no Negro newspapers, 19 per cent scored as militant, whereas this figure increases to 34 per cent for those who read two or more. Among those who read no Negro magazines only 13 per cent were militant, while among those reading two or more magazines this figure increases to 36 per cent. This phenomenon is not entirely due to the unique protest nature of the Negro media, since those who read general circulation newspapers or magazines are also more likely to be militant. Among those reading more than two general circulation magazines, 35 per cent were militant; among those who did not read such magazines this figure drops to 17 per cent. The questionnaire did not inquire how many general newspapers a respondent read, but it did ask how frequently he read a newspaper. It can be seen that the proportion of militants increases from 15 per cent among those who read newspapers less than once a week to 30 per cent for those reading a general newspaper every day. Thus, regardless of the medium, being plugged into channels of communication is associated with increased militancy. When these measures are combined into an Index of Symbolic Participation, the percentage militant increases from only 5 per cent among those who read no periodicals to 38 per cent for those who read a great many (Table 44).

The measures of actual participation and symbolic participation are strongly related to each other and for purposes of later analysis have been combined into an Index of Social Participation. On this combined index, the proportion militant increases from zero among those lowest on the index to 46 per cent among those scoring in the highest categories. Among collapsed categories of low, medium, and high, the proportions militant are

[24] D. Thompson, "The Rise of Negro Protest," *Annals of the American Academy of Political and Social Science,* January 1965, p. 27.

Table 44. MILITANCY BY INDEX OF SYMBOLIC SOCIAL PARTICIPATION

Number of Negro Newspapers Read

	0	1	2+
Militant	19%	26%	34%
Number	(245)	(521)	(329)

Number of Negro Magazines Read

	0	1	2+
Militant	13%	32%	36%
Number	(403)	(317)	(375)

Number of General Magazines Read

	0	1	2+
Militant	17%	32%	35%
Number	(472)	(189)	(433)

Read Other Newspapers

	Less Than Once a Week	Once a Week to Several Times a Week	Every Day
Militant	15%	24%	30%
Number	(165)	(283)	(708)

Score on Index of Symbolic Social Participation[a]

	0	1	2	3	4
Militant	5%	14%	20%	30%	38%
Number	(62)	(158)	(225)	(252)	(382)

[a] The total number of magazines was combined, and those reading no magazines were scored 0; those reading one or two, 1; and those reading three or more, 2. A combined measure of newspaper reading was then built up. Reading no Negro newspapers was scored 0; one, 1; and two or more, 2. Reading a general newspaper less than once a week was scored 0; several times a week, 1; and every day, 2. This measure was then trichotomized (scores of 0, 1–2, 3–4) and combined with the score on the measure of number of magazines read.

12, 25, and 39, respectively (Table 45). The advantage of combining these two measures is not that the percentage militant markedly increases at the extremes, but rather that cases become more evenly distributed over the index and subsequent analysis is facilitated.

The social participation–militancy pattern just considered is similar to that which historians have noted in analyzing Negro protest during slavery. Elkins has pointed to differences in the social participation of slaves in the United States, as compared with that in Brazil, to help account for the wider scope and greater success of the Brazilian protest against slavery.

Table 45.   MILITANCY BY INDEX OF SOCIAL PARTICIPATION

Score on Index of Social Participation[a]

	Low 0	1	2	3	4	5	6	7	High 8, 9
Militant	0%	5%	17%	12%	20%	28%	36%	41%	46%
Number	(14)	(43)	(96)	(143)	(176)	(205)	(210)	(130)	(72)

Collapsed Scores

	(0–3)	(4, 5)	(6+)
Militant	12%	25%	39%
Number	(296)	(381)	(412)

[a] Composed of indexes of Actual and of Symbolic Social Participation.

In Brazil the slave was more involved in society and had greater opportunity to play a number of roles beyond that of mere slave. The Brazilian slave could be a father and husband (while the American slave often could not), a communicant in the church, and a member of a religious fraternity. The law guaranteed him the time to engage in activities such as being an artisan, peddler, and petty merchant, and even a share of the profits. Elkins notes that such roles were all legitimized and protected outside the plantation and offered a diversity of channels for the development of personality. He adds:

Not only did the individual have multiple roles open to him as a slave, but the very nature of these roles made possible a certain range of aspirations should he someday become free. He could have a fantasy-life not limited to catfish and watermelons; it was within his conception to become a priest, an independent farmer, a successful merchant, a military officer. The slave could actually—to an extent quite unthinkable in the United States—conceive of himself *as a rebel*.[25]

It is of more than passing interest that the three most noteworthy slave revolts in the United States were led by individuals with social involvements and perspectives that extended beyond the institution that bound them. Thus Gabriel Prosser, Denmark Vesey, and Nat Turner all had the chance to play a variety of social roles denied to the average slave of the time, and are presumed to have been literate.[26] The majority of plots for slave revolts which have been recorded developed in urban areas.

[25] Stanley M. Elkins, *Slavery,* New York, Grosset and Dunlap, 1963, p. 136.
[26] H. Aptheker, *American Negro Slave Revolts,* New York, Columbia University Press, 1943, pp. 220, 268–269, 295–296.

While present conditions are fundamentally different from those under slavery, the effect of social involvement seems to be the same. Broader perspective extending beyond the insulated ghetto world seems especially relevant.

Those higher in participation live in a less constricted social environment and have mentally escaped the ghetto without necessarily leaving it physically. They also stand a greater chance of coming into sustained contact with others who have similar problems. Through their greater involvement, both actual and symbolic, distant civil rights activities become meaningful. Lack of involvement, on the other hand, isolates the individual from channels of communication which might transmit protest values and a more extensive view of the world. Living in the narrow, fairly homogeneous ghetto environment, often untouched even by newspapers or magazines, belonging to no formal organizations, and interacting only occasionally with friends are likely to lead to resignation or despair, a narrow and immediate view of the world, and a concern largely with the problems of daily existence. With restricted spheres of experience, the morale of such persons may be lower and their mental imagery less apt to encompass the larger community and the vision of broad social change necessary to militancy.

The Combined Effect

We have found militancy to be related to three clusters of variables. The first has to do with the nature of the value system an individual is presumed to have been exposed to, the second with social privilege, and the third with social involvement. What effect can be achieved by taking these variables together?

It is well known that older people, those raised in the South, and people from rural areas have less education and lower incomes than younger people, those raised in the North, and people from urban areas. Therefore, it is possible that the pattern of the Value Exposure Index (which combines age, region, sex, and community size) is due to the fact that those low on this index are also low in social position. However, the impact of the Value Exposure Index remains strong when social class is controlled (Table 46). Among those lowest on social class 9 per cent of those low on the Exposure Index are militant, while 30 per cent of those high on the index are militant. The effect of exposure remains strong within each class group. Reading across the table, the effect of social class also remains strong within all degrees of value exposure. Thus each has an independent effect on militancy. Together they strongly predict militancy, from 9 per cent militant among those low on both class and exposure to 52 per cent among those high on both.

A similar independence and joint effect can be seen when social participation and value exposure are simultaneously related to militancy (Table 47).

Table 46.   MILITANCY BY SOCIAL CLASS AND EXPOSURE TO VALUES
LEGITIMIZING PROTEST

(Per cent militant)

| | Social Class | | |
Value Exposure	Lower	Middle	Upper
Low	9%	18%	20%
Number	(203)	(88)	(15)
Medium	14%	30%	41%
Number	(155)	(212)	(79)
High	30%	39%	52%
Number	(73)	(174)	(89)

Within categories of social participation, the greater the value exposure the greater the proportion militant. Within categories of value exposure, the greater the extent of social participation the greater the likelihood of militancy.

Table 47.   MILITANCY BY SOCIAL PARTICIPATION AND EXPOSURE TO
VALUES LEGITIMIZING PROTEST

(Per cent militant)

| | Social Participation | | |
Value Exposure	Lower	Medium	High
Low	6%	13%	24%
Number	(142)	(98)	(64)
Medium	18%	23%	39%
Number	(107)	(166)	(161)
High	18%	36%	49%
Number	(46)	(114)	(175)

Nor is the effect of social participation merely a function of uncontrolled social class differences. Looking at Table 48, we see that both indexes have an independent effect upon militancy. Among all social classes, militancy increases with social participation, while in all categories of social participation, militancy increases with social class.

Militancy is not an idiosyncratic state of mind. Rather it most often occurs among persons whose location in society is conducive to developing aspirations for a better life. Thus, lack of exposure to Southern values (or, conversely, exposure to non-Southern values), social privilege, and access to the message of protest through actual and symbolic social participation all independently and powerfully affect militancy.

We have seen that a sizable percentage of the black community consistently holds militant attitudes and have examined some correlates of these attitudes. However, only a very small minority of these people become deeply involved as activists. For militant attitudes to lead to consistent action in an organization such as CORE an individual must first be "available" and in a position to undertake the often considerable risks involved.

Table 48. MILITANCY BY SOCIAL CLASS AND SOCIAL PARTICIPATION

(Per cent militant)

Social Class

Social Participation	Lower	Middle	Upper
Low	9%	17%	19%
Number	(190)	(92)	(16)
Medium	16%	28%	37%
Number	(151)	(184)	(46)
High	24%	40%	50%
Number	(90)	(202)	(120)

It would seem that the young, those with few if any familial responsibilities, and those not in occupations subject to the punitive control of whites would be most likely to be involved in direct action. A study of CORE reveals that activists do disproportionately possess these characteristics.[27] Furthermore, in the South, individuals who hold militant attitudes and are "available" for direct action are more likely to actually engage in protest activity when they are in communities with certain characteristics. For example, other factors being equal protest seems more likely in relatively urbanized communities, those with a higher socioeconomic level, those where organiza-

[27] Powell, *op. cit.,* pp. 215–216. Limitations of time and the importance of documenting the social and psychological factors associated with Negro response to the civil rights struggle have resulted in most of the analysis being directed toward factors which can be easily measured in an interview situation. A full understanding requires consideration of historical factors and variables related to the structure of a given community. Just because in most communities militants will share youth and higher social position or be alike in having a positive self-image and a high morale, this should not cause us to overlook the implications of variation in community structure for expressions of militancy. Nor should it be assumed that people with these common characteristics do not exhibit a wide variety of motives in becoming actively involved.

In contrasting regions, Breed explains the greater resistance of the Deep South to desegregation in terms of its being the least pluralistic area of the country. The one party system, the relative absence of labor unions, ethnic and religious homogeneity, and fewer associations all make it more difficult for competing definitions of the situation to emerge. Traditional elites committed to segregation have greater power and a monopoly on propaganda. (Warren Breed, "Group Structure and Resistance to Desegregation in the Deep South," *Social Problems,* Summer, 1962.) A consideration of these community structure variables also helps explain the greater ease with which protest has occurred in the North, the greater militancy of Negroes there, and the greater sympathy for the movement on the part of Northern whites.

tions such as the NAACP were viable before the beginning of the current struggle and where a Negro college is located, and those where Negroes are a relatively smaller percentage of the population.

Before turning from social to psychological factors, we shall examine the extent to which the findings in this chapter are consistent with empirical findings from other studies.

Numerous studies have found that lower-status people and those socially isolated are more likely to be apathetic about issues of public policy. However, in times of crisis it is precisely these alienated and isolated individuals who are most likely to be attracted to movements that seek change outside the framework of traditional values.[28] In a later chapter it will be observed that although a very large majority of all Negroes reject the Muslim variety of black nationalism, lower-status, isolated people were relatively more receptive to it than were those higher in social position and participation.

When such people do express opinions, they are likely to be conservative on noneconomic issues. Past research has shown that those lower in social position and involvement are least supportive of the civil liberties of dissenters and the civil rights of minorities.[29] If the Militancy Index is viewed as a measure of noneconomic liberalism,[30] the pattern that has emerged is clearly to be anticipated.

Past research dealing with Negro militancy is generally consistent with the results reported here. Studies of the two most militant civil rights organizations, CORE and SNCC, indicate that in spite of their antibourgeoisie emphasis, members are disproportionately middle class and younger.[31]

[28] Lipset notes: "In 'normal' periods, apathy is most frequent among such individuals (those in lower-status positions and isolated) but they can be activated by a crisis . . ." (S. M. Lipset, *Political Man*, New York, Doubleday, 1963, p. 116). Kornhauser states: "a greater proportion of people with few proximate concerns as compared to people with many such attachments, tend to be apathetic and uninformed on public matters; but . . . in times of crisis a greater proportion of people with few proximate concerns discard apathy and engage in mass movements outside of and against the institutional order." (W. Kornhauser, *The Politics of Mass Society*, New York, Free Press, 1961, p. 64.)

[29] S. Stouffer, *Communism, Conformity, and Civil Liberties*, New York, Doubleday, 1955; Lipset, *op. cit.*, pp. 87–126. P. Sheatsley, reports recent data on the attitudes of whites toward Negro rights ("White Attitudes Toward the Negro," *Daedalus*, Winter 1966, p. 229).

[30] The index is certainly a measure of liberalism on civil rights issues, asking as it did about discrimination and demonstrations. Furthermore, it was strongly related to a measure of tolerance for religious dissent. Almost half of those scored as militant said "yes" to the following question: "Suppose a man admitted in public that he did not believe in God. Do you think he should be allowed to teach in a public high school?" Among those scored as conservative on the Militancy Index less than one in five said "yes."

[31] On SNCC, see Zinn, *op. cit.*; on CORE, see Powell, *op. cit.*, p. 21. About CORE, Powell states: ". . . the outstanding characteristic of the activists is their exceptionally high occupational and educational status." However, she adds that Negro activists

One study of Negro college students found expressions of militancy to be greatest among those of higher-status backgrounds and those who participate more fully in extracurricular activities.[32] Another study of students found civil rights activism to be greater among relatively more privileged students from the better Negro colleges, and among those raised in urban areas and those best informed and most in touch with the mass media.[33] Other researchers have found that, in one community, enrollment of children in the first integrated school was positively related to higher social status and an urban background.[34] A study done on use of the open occupancy law in New York City found most complainants to be middle class.[35] Another found that in one small New York State community the least militant tended to be older, less educated, Southern-born, lower in participation, and female.[36] Studying this community, and two others, still another found that "militant group pride" existed significantly more often among upper-status individuals.[37] Brink and Harris report that, of non-Southern middle- and upper-income Negroes, 44 per cent reported marching in a demonstration and 63 per cent reported boycotting various stores, while for those with low incomes these figures drop to only 13 and 6 per cent.[38] Over twenty years ago, research on the American soldier, referred to earlier, discovered that opposition to segregated army PX's was greatest among the more educated and the Northern-born Negroes.[39]

---

are not "typical" of the entrenched and solidly established Negro middle class. Rather they are either recently upwardly mobile or have passed out of the established middle class ". . . into the same narrow layer of intellectual, left wing culture from which most [activist] whites are recruited" (pp. 21 and 22).

In addition, within CORE, those in the North, those brought up in larger urban areas, and those with more education have the most militant attitudes (*ibid.*, pp. 271–272).

[32] R. Searles and J. A. Williams, Jr., "Negro College Students' Participation in Sit-ins," *Social Forces*, 1962, pp. 215–220.

[33] D. Matthews and J. Prothro, *Negroes and the New Southern Politics*, New York, Harcourt, Brace & World, 1966, pp. 418, 423, 427. This study also notes that activism was most pronounced in private colleges and in communities where Negroes made up less than 20 per cent of the population. Also on the importance of urbanization and the percentage of Negroes in a county see Martin Oppenheimer, "Institutions of Higher Learning and the 1960 Sit-Ins: Some Clues for Social Action," *Journal of Negro Education*, Summer 1963.

[34] E. A. Weinstein and P. N. Geisel, "Family Decision Making Over Desegregation," *Sociometry*, 1961, pp. 21–29.

[35] H. Goldblatt and Florence Cromien, "The Effective Reach of the Fair Housing Law of the City of New York," *Social Problems*, Spring 1962.

[36] Robert B. Johnson, "Negro Reaction to Minority Group Status," in M. Barron, ed., *American Minorities*, New York, Alfred Knopf, 1957, p. 204.

[37] Donald Noel, *Correlates of Anti-White Prejudice: Attitudes of Negroes in Four American Cities*, Ph.D. dissertation, Cornell University, 1960, p. 225.

[38] William Brink and Louis Harris, *The Negro Revolution in America*, New York, Simon and Schuster, 1964, p. 203.

[39] Stouffer *et al., op. cit.*, pp. 568–580.

3

The Psychological Context
of Militancy

It matters not how strait the gate,
How charged with punishments the scroll,
I am the master of my fate;
I am the captain of my soul.
                    —*W. E. Henley*

Revolutionary movements seem to originate in the discontents of not
unprosperous people. . . . [They] are not worms turning, not children
of despair. These revolutions are born of hope.
                    —*Crane Brinton*

An even more basic force at work [producing passivity among the un-
educated] was their corroding sense of inferiority, which often expressed
itself in a lack of self-respect. Many unconsciously wondered whether
they actually deserved any better conditions.
                    —*Martin Luther King*

In the last chapter it was suggested that social class and social participation influence militancy because they result in intellectual sophistication,
high morale, and a positive self-image. In this chapter we see that these
factors are positively related to militancy and do in fact partly explain why
social privilege and social participation lead to militancy.

Intellectual Sophistication

The intellectually sophisticated, as a result of their greater cognitive
powers, their greater knowledge about the world, and to some extent the
possession of a unique set of values, are likely to view the world differently from the unsophisticated. In this section four separate indicators of
intellectual sophistication will be related to militancy.

The F Scale or Breadth of Perspective

An excellent indication of general sophistication are the well-known F-scale items.[1] Although the scale was originally designed to measure a personality characteristic—authoritarianism—ever since the publication of *The Authoritarian Personality* a lively controversy has existed among social scientists over the meaning of the items included in the F scale.[2] Much persuasive evidence argues for the view that the items in the F scale measure intellectual sophistication or the breadth of a person's perspective,[3] rather than deep-seated personality traits. Following this view, items from the F scale were combined into a measure of breadth of perspective.[4]

Table 49. MILITANCY BY SCORE ON F SCALE

Score on F Scale

	Narrow Perspective ⟶			Broad Perspective		
	5	4	3	2	1	0
Militant	12%	21%	21%	33%	41%	72%
Number	(101)	(267)	(315)	(261)	(117)	(25)

Table 49 shows that this index has a powerful inverse relation to militancy. Among those with a narrow view of the world and the most restricted perspective (agreeing to all five F-scale items), only 12 per cent were militant. This percentage increases to 41 and 72 per cent for those with the broadest perspective (accepting one or more of the F-scale items). Intellectual sophistication, as measured by these items, seems a crucial factor in determining militancy.

The broader and more liberated his outlook, the more likely a Negro is to be militant.

[1] T. E. Adorno *et al., The Authoritarian Personality,* New York, Harper & Row, 1950.

[2] For example, Richard Christie and Marie Jahoda, eds., *Studies in the Scope and Method of the Authoritarian Personality,* New York, Free Press, 1954.

[3] H. Kelman and J. Barclay, "The F Scale as a Measure of Breadth of Perspective," *Journal of Abnormal and Social Psychology,* 1963, pp. 608–615.

[4] The following items were used:

"Sex crimes, such as rape and attacks on children, deserve more than mere imprisonment; such criminals ought to be publicly whipped, or worse."

"No weakness or difficulty can hold us back if we have enough will power."

"Reading the stars can tell us a great deal about the future."

"People can be divided into two distinct classes—the weak and the strong."

"Much of our lives are controlled by plots hatched in secret places."

For each item an individual agreed to, or indicated he had no opinion on, a score of one was given.

Awareness of the Role of Social Factors

The *F*-scale items indicate a general kind of sophistication. But a more specific kind of sophistication is sensitivity to the way social factors shape human behavior: To what extent do persons recognize the degree to which their behavior is conditioned by their sociocultural environment? This requires an ability to detect the complexity of the world.

The questionnaire included several items designed to measure whether individuals were aware of the importance of environment in affecting social outcomes.[5] Militancy would seem almost to require recognition of the role of social forces in determining the present low status of Negroes. To think otherwise shifts the blame away from an unjust social order onto the failure of individual Negroes. The following questions were asked and combined into an index of awareness of how social factors shape behavior:

"Poor people have no one to blame but themselves."

"Most people on welfare could take care of themselves if they really wanted to."

"If you try hard enough you can usually get what you want."[6]

A score of one was given for each instance of disagreement.

This measure is strongly related to militancy. Among those least aware of the effect of the social environment, only about one in ten was militant. This percentage increases steadily up to five out of ten among those who indicated maximum awareness of the effect of the social environment

[5] In a recent paper Glock has suggested that people's attitudes on a wide variety of public issues are influenced by their conception of man's nature, especially the weight they give to the role of the social environment (Charles Y. Glock, "Images of Man and Public Opinion," *Public Opinion Quarterly,* Winter 1964).

[6] Kenneth Clark has recently noted that an important white rationalization for maintaining the *status quo* is the belief "that the poor are to blame for the squalor and despair of the slums; that the victims of social injustice are somehow subhuman persons who cause and perpetuate their own difficulties."

Clark further suggests that "in response to white society's criticisms of Negro family instability and the patterns of poverty, many *middle-class* [italics added] Negroes have tended to accept the judgment of many whites that they [Negroes in general] are responsible for their own troubles, that economic dependency is related directly to immorality" (Kenneth Clark, *Dark Ghetto,* New York, Harper & Row, 1965, pp. 75 and 55). It would be appropriate to add that such beliefs are held to an even greater extent by many workingclass Negroes. In response to the statement "Poor people have no one to blame but themselves," 30 per cent of those low in social class and 15 per cent of those high in social class indicated agreement.

In a somewhat similar vein Le Roi Jones has written of the "smell of the dry rot of the middle-class Negro mind: the idea that, somehow, Negroes must *deserve* equality." (Le Roi Jones, *Blues People,* New York, William Morrow and Co., 1963, p. 134.) In this regard it is interesting to note that in response to the statement, "Before Negroes are given equal rights, they have to show that they deserve them," 55 per cent of those low in social class indicated agreement, while for those high in social class this figure dropped to 27 per cent.

(Table 50). Thus, almost a necessary condition for militancy seems to be at least a mild awareness of how social factors affect behavior and, related to this, the perception that problems of Negroes are common to them as a group rather than as random individuals. Danzig has recently stressed the latter in noting that the concept of collective struggle rather than individual achievement is now dominant in the civil rights movement. He

Table 50. MILITANCY BY AWARENESS OF HOW SOCIAL FACTORS SHAPE BEHAVIOR

| | Score on Index of Awareness of Social Factors | | | |
| | Low | | | High |
	0	1	2	3
Militant	11%	22%	36%	50%
Number	(219)	(457)	(312)	(92)

notes: "What is now perceived as the 'revolt of the Negro' amounts to this: the solitary Negro seeking admission into the white world through unusual achievement has been replaced by the organized Negro insisting upon a legitimate share for his group of the goods of American society."[7] Recognition that the problems of Negroes are group problems, and that the rights and privileges of an individual depend in large measure upon the status of the group to which he belongs, is an important defining characteristic of the current civil rights movement, and those who have this perspective are much more likely to be miiltant than those who do not.

Knowledge of Negro Culture Figures

Factual knowledge about the world is a general indicator of sophistication and breadth of perspective, regardless of race. For Negroes, having greater knowledge of Negro history and of important Negro cultural and political leaders is a type of sophistication that should be strongly related to civil rights interest, a more positive self-image, and militancy. While the questionnaire did not ask about knowledge of Negro history, it did ask respondents to identify a number of prominent Negro figures. Inferences can be made from knowledge of these figures to general level of information. It can be seen in Table 51 that having knowledge of Negro civil rights leaders and writers is strongly related to militancy. Among those unable to identify any of the civil rights leaders (Martin Luther King, James Farmer, Medgar Evers, and Roy Wilkins) only 3 per cent were militant, and this figure consistently increases up to a high of 42 per cent

[7] D. Danzig, "The Meaning of the Negro Strategy," Commentary, February 1964, p. 43.

Table 51.   MILITANCY BY KNOWLEDGE OF NEGRO CULTURE FIGURES

| | Number of Civil Rights Leaders Correctly Identified | | | | |
	0	1	2	3	4
Militant	3%	9%	19%	20%	42%
Number	(32)	(193)	(151)	(268)	(448)

| | Number of Negro Writers Correctly Identified | | | |
	0	1	2	3
Militant	16%	29%	41%	57%
Number	(555)	(242)	(220)	(61)

for those able to identify all four. Similarly, in identifying three writers concerned with protest themes (Richard Wright, Ralph Ellison, and Langston Hughes) 16 per cent among those unable to identify any were militant, whereas for those correctly identifying all three, 57 per cent scored as militant. When these two measures are combined into an index

Table 52.   MILITANCY BY INDEX OF KNOWLEDGE OF NEGRO CULTURE FIGURES

| | Score on Index | | | | | | | |
| | Low | | | | | | | High |
	0	1	2	3	4	5	6	7
Militant	3%	9%	15%	19%	22%	35%	46%	60%
Number	(29)	(159)	(131)	(178)	(204)	(162)	(157)	(55)

of knowledge of Negro culture figures, the percentage militant goes from 3 for those with least knowledge to 60 for those with the most (Table 52). It is the informed Negro who is militant; the uninformed are more likely to be sunk in apathy.

Intellectual Values

The possession of intellectual values is also an important indication of a sophisticated world view. Respondents were asked to agree or disagree with the following three statements:

"I don't like to hear a lot of arguments I disagree with."
"A little practical experience is worth all the books put together."
"I like to hear all sides of an argument before I make up my mind."

These items were combined into an index of acceptance of intellectual values (a score of one was given for disagreeing with the first two items and agreeing with the third). This index shows a powerful relationship to militancy: Only 2 per cent of the "nonintellectually oriented" were militant, and this figure increases steadily to 50 per cent for those considered the most "intellectually oriented" (Table 53).

Table 53. MILITANCY BY ACCEPTANCE OF INTELLECTUAL VALUES

	Nonintellectually Oriented		Intellectually Oriented	
	0	1	2	3
Militant	2%	17%	31%	50%
Number	(41)	(511)	(373)	(165)

A Combined Measure

The indexes of Acceptance of Intellectual Values, Knowledge of Negro Culture Figures, and Awareness of Social Factors, as well as the F scale, are each powerfully related to militancy. They are also strongly interrelated and may be viewed as components of a general intellectual sophistication. When they are combined into a single index, the impact of general sophistication on militancy is shown to be great. The proportion militant steadily increases as intellectual sophistication increases, from a low of only *5 per cent* among those least sophisticated to *85 per cent* among the most sophisticated (Table 54). When this index is collapsed into categories of very unsophisticated, low on sophistication, and sophisticated the percentage militant are 9, 25, and 52, respectively.

Morale

As Crane Brinton recognized (see the quotation at the beginning of this chapter), movements for radical social change are unlikely to originate with "children of despair." They require a certain hope that a better future, if not just around the corner, is at least a possibility, and the will or desire to do something to help bring about change. Demoralized people are unlikely to believe that an improved future is possible, and their sense of futility is likely to lead to apathy, not action, and to despair rather than demonstrations.

Our questionnaire included the following three questions, which have been combined into an index of morale:

"You sometimes can't help wondering whether anything is worthwhile anymore."

Table 54. MILITANCY BY INDEX OF INTELLECTUAL SOPHISTICATION

Score on Index of Intellectual Sophistication[a]

	Very Unsophisticated											Very Sophisticated
	0	1	2	3	4	5	6	7	8	9	10	11, 12
Militant	5%	6%	7%	13%	22%	23%	31%	40%	56%	49%	67%	85%
Number	(20)	(88)	(102)	(143)	(175)	(141)	(118)	(107)	(72)	(41)	(27)	(20)

Collapsed Scores

	Very Unsophisticated (0–3)	Low on Sophistication (4–6)	Sophisticated (7–12)
Militant	9%	25%	52%
Number	(353	(434)	(264)

[a] Composed of F-scale score (5 scored 0; 3, 4 scored 1; 2 scored 2; 0, 1 scored 3); Awareness of How Social Factors Shape Behavior (0, 1 scored 0; 2 scored 1; 3 scored 2); Acceptance of Intellectual Values (0, 1 scored 0; 2 scored 1; 3 scored 2); and Knowledge of Negro Culture figures (0, 1 scored 0; 2 scored 1; 3 scored 2; 4 scored 3; 5 scored 4; 6 scored 5).

"Nowadays a person has to live pretty much for today and let tomorrow take care of itself."

"I often feel quite lonely."[8]

For each item disagreed with a score of one was given. This index is strongly related to militancy (Table 55). Of those with low morale (agreeing to all three questions) only 15 per cent were militant. This figure increases steadily up to 42 per cent for those with high morale (rejecting all three of the items).

Table 55.   MILITANCY BY MORALE

Score on Index of Morale

	Low Morale 0	1	2	High Morale 3
Militant	15%	22%	31%	42%
Number	(270)	(356)	(259)	(203)

That low morale is related to lack of militancy may also be seen by using a different indicator: subjective evaluation of one's health. Other factors being equal, people who consider themselves in poor health should be more likely to be demoralized and concerned with their own bodies than with the body politic. Respondents were asked to evaluate their own health with respect to the categories excellent, good, fair, or poor. It can be seen that having a low evaluation of one's health serves to reduce militancy. Only 7 per cent of those who described themselves as in poor health evidenced concern over the civil rights struggle. The figures are 24, 29, and 31 per cent, respectively, among those who said they were in fair, good, or excellent health (Table 56). This pattern was maintained even when the effect of age was controlled for.

[8] These items were all strongly interrelated. They are similar to those used in the past by Srole to indicate anomie (Leo Srole, "Social Integration and Certain Corollaries: An Exploratory Study," *American Sociological Review*, December 1956, pp. 709–716). The concept of anomie emphasizes weakening of an individual's attachment to society and his sense of isolation from others. However, they are used here simply as indicators of the somewhat less abstract concept of morale.

The criticism might be made that the middle question, rather than measuring morale, is simply a measure of acceptance of certain lower-class values involving the rejection of deferred gratification. But even the value itself no doubt arose from certain functional exigencies involving lack of opportunity, and hence can be seen as related to demoralization.

Two studies using somewhat similar items report findings comparable to those in Table 55. John M. Orbell, "Protest Participation Among Southern Negro College Students," *The American Political Science Review*, June 1967, and Pearl M. Gore and Julian B. Rotter, "A Personality Correlate of Social Action," *Journal of Personality*, March 1963.

A sense of life's utter futility and concern only with day-to-day existence have been found by novelists and social scientists to characterize a large proportion of Negroes in ghetto areas. Rainwater, in studying Negro life in the slums, notes: "In the white and particularly in the Negro slum worlds little in the experience that individuals have as they grow up sustains a belief in a rewarding world." He contrasts the "strategies of living" of the middle class to the "strategies for survival" of the slum Negro. One of the most prominent of the latter is the "depressive strategy."

Table 56. MILITANCY BY STATE OF HEALTH

	Excellent	Good	Fair	Poor
Militant	31%	29%	24%	7%
Number	(302)	(432)	(261)	(98)

"As members of the Negro slum culture grow older, there is the depressive strategy in which goals are increasingly constricted to the bare necessities for survival (not as a social being but simply as an organism). This is the strategy of I don't bother anybody and I hope nobody's gonna bother me: I'm simply going through the motions to keep body (but not soul) together."[9] Although our data imperfectly measure this strategy for survival, they do suggest that the "deadness of the depressed style" is a factor retarding the development of a militant orientation.

Nothing But a Man

Although slum children are still bitten by rats and their unemployed or underemployed parents face various types of subtle and blatant discrimination, for many the most biting and poignant aspect of the race situation in America lies at the symbolic rather than the material level.[10] It involves the denial of dignity to blacks and the acceptance among the subjugated of many negative attitudes about their own group.

A low self-image among Negroes was consciously created by many slave owners. According to those who wrote discourses on how best to manage slaves, a crucial factor was developing in them a sense of personal

[9] Lee Rainwater, "Crucible of Identity: The Negro Lower-Class Family," *Daedalus,* Winter 1966, pp. 206, 207. He notes that the "strategies for living" of the middle class "are predicated on the assumption that the world is inherently rewarding if one behaves properly and does his part. The rewards of the world may come easily or only at the cost of great effort, but at least they are there."

[10] King clearly notes this when he states: "Their minds and souls were so conditioned to the system of segregation that they submissively adjusted themselves to things as they were. This is the ultimate tragedy of segregation. It not only harms one physically but injures one spiritually. It sears the soul and degrades the personality" (Martin Luther King, *Stride Toward Freedom,* New York, Ballantine Books, 1958, p. 29).

inferiority. "They had 'to know and keep their places,' to 'feel the difference between master and slave,' to understand that bondage was their natural status. They had to feel that African ancestry tainted them, that their color was a badge of degradation."[11]

What was at one time consciously created became a natural product of the organization of race relations in America. No better example of the self-fulfilling prophecy can be found. The literature on race relations abounds with studies of "self-hate," "group disparagement," and "negative group identification" among Negroes and minority groups in general. Past research has clearly documented that the negative stereotypes held by whites about Negroes are often held by Negroes too.

One factor often thought to be associated with the upsurge of racial protest in America is a change in self-image on the part of American black men. The head of an important civil rights organization in the South states: "For years whites have decreed that Negroes must think of themselves as whites thought of them. Negroes are now insisting that the white majority revise its opinion of them in accord with their own newly fashioned self-conception."[12]

Since the present study collected data at just one point in time, it cannot document this presumed change in self-image. It also can tell us little about the deep-seated processes of identity through which this change is occurring. However, on the basis of two very general questions, respondents can be separated into those who seem to have a positive image of their group and those with a negative image.

Only 17 per cent of the sample agreed to the traditional stereotype "Generally speaking, Negroes are lazy and don't like to work hard." But 54 per cent agreed that "Negroes blame too many of their problems on whites."[13] These two questions have been combined into an index of self-image.[14] For each item disagreed with a score of one was given.

To protest the *status quo* would seem to entail the belief that the

[11] Kenneth Stampp, *The Peculiar Institution,* New York, Alfred Knopf, 1956, p. 145.

[12] Leslie W. Dunbar, "The Changing Mind of the South: The Exposed Nerve," in Avery Leiserson, ed., *The American South in the 1960's,* New York, Praeger, 1964, p. 11.

[13] Another question included in the study which might have been relevant in the past was: "In general, do you think that Negroes are as intelligent as white people —that is, can they learn things just as well if they are given the same education and training?" Ninety-nine per cent now say "yes." That Negroes have a higher estimation of their group's potentialities than whites is brought out by a recent nationwide survey of whites which found that among Southerners 57 per cent said "yes"; among Northerners, 80 per cent. The figures of 57 and 80 per cent represent a steady increase over a twenty-year period (P. Sheatsley, "White Attitudes Toward the Negro." *Daedalus,* Winter 1966, p. 223).

[14] It should be noted that in the strictest sense this measures group image rather than personal image.

disadvantages of Negroes as a group are traceable to the systems of status degradation imposed on Negroes by the white majority. It would also seem to entail rejection of the belief that Negroes are lazy and do not like to work hard, since to believe otherwise would shift concern away from changing the social world to changing the individual. The data show that, among those considered to have an unfavorable self-image, only 10 per cent score as militant, while militancy increases to 39 per cent for those having a favorable self-image (Table 57). People who have more doubts about their group's behavior will no doubt find it more difficult to argue convincingly with others on its behalf.

Table 57. MILITANCY BY SELF-IMAGE

Score on Self-Image Index

	Unfavorable Self-Image (0)	Neutral (1)	Favorable Self-Image (2)
Militant	10%	23%	39%
Number	(156)	(563)	(370)

It is difficult to say that having a positive self-image is a direct cause of militancy, since it is hard to establish which comes first. Most probably, the two go hand in hand and are themselves the result of other factors. However, Table 57 suggests an important fact about militancy. While it is obvious that militant attitudes are a precondition of efforts to change the external world, they are also apt to produce changes in individual self-conception as well. Thus the development of a positive concern over civil rights can be seen as combating the unfortunate consequences of America's racial system at two levels.[15]

Psychological Factors as Links Between the Social Structure and Militancy

In the last chapter, it was found that higher social position and greater social participation result in militancy. The suggestion was made that people with these characteristics are more likely to be intellectually

[15] This is brought out more clearly when we observe self-image among our three styles of response to the civil rights struggle. It may be recalled that those receiving scores of zero, one, and two on the Index of conventional Militancy were called conservative; those with scores of three, four, and five, moderates; and those with scores of six, seven, and eight, militants (the group which the analysis has been concerned with thus far). Among conservatives about one in four had an unfavorable self-image. For militants this figure was only one in twenty.

In considering the development of protest in historical perspective, Rose sees protest and the development of a positive self-image as intricately linked (A. Rose, *The Negro's Morale: Group Identification and Protest,* Minneapolis, University of Minnesota Press, 1948).

sophisticated, to have a more positive self-image, and to have a higher morale. It was hypothesized that these were important subjective mechanism through which sociocultural factors produce increased militancy.[16] We can now proceed to test the above hypotheses.

Table 58. MILITANCY BY INDEX OF SUBJECTIVE PREDISPOSITION

Score on Index of Subjective Predisposition to Militancy[a]

	Low (0, 1)	Medium (2, 3)	Medium High (4)	High (5, 6)
Militant	6%	22%	43%	56%
Number	(247)	(478)	(176)	(138)

[a] Composed of indexes of Intellectual Sophistication (0–3 scored 0; 4–6 scored 1; 7–12 scored 2); Morale (0, 1 scored 0; 2 scored 1; 3 scored 2); and Self-Image (0 scored 0; 1 scored 1; 2 scored 2).

We have seen in this chapter that these subjective factors are powerfully related to militancy. Furthermore, though each was positively related to the other, each had an independent effect on militancy. They are now combined into an index of subjective predisposition to militancy. On this measure, among those scored as low on subjective predisposition, only 6 per cent support militant attitudes. This figure increases to 56 per cent for those high in subjective predisposition to militancy (Table 58).

Since it is hypothesized that both social participation and social class relate to militancy for similar reasons, and since these measures are strongly related to each other, they have been combined into an index of social involvement. As Table 59 indicates, the percentage militant runs from 8 per cent among those low in social involvement to 50 per cent for those high.[17]

Table 59. MILITANCY BY INDEX OF SOCIAL INVOLVEMENT

Score on Index of Social Involvement[a]

	Low				High
	0	1	2	3	4
Militant	8%	16%	27%	39%	50%
Number	(188)	(243)	(290)	(247)	(118)

[a] Based on Social Class and Social Participation indexes. Scores of 0, 1, and 2 were given for those in lower, middle, and upper social position and for those low, medum, and high in social participation.

[16] These hypotheses were developed on the basis of participation in CORE and from the literature before the analysis of the data began.

[17] It should be clearly noted that the figures in this index and the one just above are based on categories collapsed in such a way as to provide adequate cases for more refined analysis. When these two measures are observed uncollapsed, for the

We are now ready to consider the joint effect of social and psychological factors on militancy. We have suggested that the sociological variables summarized in the Index of Social Involvement are related to militancy primarily through the intervening mechanism of the psychological variables summarized in the Index of Subjective Predisposition. That is, the social variables result in the psychological, which in turn result in militancy. If this is the case, then when the Index of Subjective Predisposition is controlled, the relation between social involvement and militancy ought to disappear. To the extent that this relation disappears we can say that we have located the psychological consequences of social involvement that in turn are translated into militancy.

Table 60.   RELATION BETWEEN SOCIAL INVOLVEMENT AND MILITANCY
WITH SUBJECTIVE PREDISPOSITION HELD CONSTANT

(Per cent militant; number of respondents shown in parentheses)

Subjective Predisposition to Militancy

Social Involvement		High		Medium High		Medium		Low	
Very isolated	0	a		31%	(21)	7%	(81)	4%	(78)
	1	40%	(15)	34	(32)	13	(102)	8	(78)
	2	62	(37)	40	(35)	21	(138)	5	(62)
	3	49	(41)	50	(64)	33	(106)	12	(25)
Very involved	4	60	(40)	48	(27)	54	(48)	b	

a Of the two respondents, one scored as militant.
b Of the four respondents, none scored as militant.

Table 60 considers the joint effects of social and psychological variables on militancy. The outcome confirms our expectations. While the range of the original relation between social involvement and militancy was 42 percentage points, it tends to disappear into meaningless fluctuations within two of the four categories of the Index of Subjective Predisposition and is greatly reduced in a third category. Only among those classified as medium on the subjective index do the original effects of social involvement remain strong. Within the other three categories (reading down the table), relatively no important relation remains between social involvement

social involvement measure militancy goes from a low of 0 per cent to a high of 75 per cent and for the subjective orientation index from 0 to 70 per cent. However, the concern in this section is not with showing the separate predictive power of these measures (which has already been established in this and the previous chapter) but rather with seeing how much of the effect of social involvement can be understood in terms of subjective orientations when they are brought together.

The two measures are strongly related to each other. Among those lowest in social involvement, 44 per cent are low in subjective predisposition. This figure is only 3 per cent among those highest in involvement.

and militancy. With the exception of this one category, then, we see evidence that the social factors help produce militancy through the mechanisms of high morale, intellectual sophistication, and positive self-image.

Because this is an important but somewhat complex point, it should be elaborated. What we find is that, with the exception noted, social participation does not have much *direct* affect on militancy. Rather, social participation produces certain psychic states, such as high morale, and it is these which facilitate the development of a militant outlook. This is not to reject social factors as "causes" of militancy. Rather, it is to specify the way in which social factors seem to operate in producing militancy.

The failure of the relation to be reduced in the medium category of the Subjective Index may result from the fact that these persons are strongly predisposed neither toward nor away from militancy. They are likely to be neither very sophisticated nor very ignorant, to have neither a very high morale nor a defeatist morale, neither a positive self-image nor one that is consistently negative. Lacking a subjective view of the world that would prompt them either to militancy or to apathy, such people are more directly influenced by their social involvements. Among persons who lack a consistent subjective orientation (those scored medium) to inform their response to the civil rights struggle, external social considerations remain relevant. They may be primarily conforming to what those around them are doing (being militant if they are high in social involvement or apathetic if low), and their reactions are more likely to be fairly unstable and ambivalent. Where a consistent subjective orientation has developed, which either predisposes persons toward militancy or toward apathy, then the effects of social involvement are wiped out.

To an important extent, we have seen that the psychological factors examined in this chapter provide the mechanism by which social factors act upon militancy. The main reason why the most privileged and least socially isolated Negroes are the most militant is because they have the necessary psychological outlook to support and encourage militancy: morale, sophistication, and pride in self.[18] However, where such an outlook is found among the less privileged and more isolated, militancy is also found. When the privileged fail to hold such views, they also fail to be militant.

[18] While it is argued here that these factors tend to result from a high degree of social participation and higher social position, two qualifications should be noted. First, there is a margin of indeterminancy between the variables of social structure and subjective orientations, shown by the fact that some (but not many) of those low in social involvement were nevertheless high in subjective predisposition to militancy and some (but again not many) of those high in social involvement were low in subjective predisposition to militancy. Secondly, being subjectively predisposed to militancy may sometimes lead to social involvement. High morale and positive self-image are often no doubt relevant factors in determining an individual's eventual social position.

Religion: Opiate or Inspiration of Civil Rights Militancy?

> Let justice roll down like waters, and righteousness like a mighty stream.
> —*Amos 5:24*

> The white folks like for us to be religious, then they can do what they want to with us.
> —*Bigger Thomas*

> Did we not straitly command that ye should not teach in this name? And behold, ye have filled Jerusalem with your doctrine. . . . Then Peter and the other apostles answered and said, We ought to obey God rather than men.
> —*Acts 5:28*

> But God . . . is white. And if his love was so great, and if he loved all his children, why were we the blacks, cast down so far?
> —*James Baldwin*

The last two chapters analyzed the role of social and psychological factors in militancy. Religion might have been considered under either of these rubrics. Being religious may be regarded as one kind of institutional affiliation or it may be seen as a psychological phenomenon. Because it relates to both these areas, and because of the crucial bearing of the Negro church on the civil rights struggle, religion is considered separately.

The relation between religion and political radicalism is a confusing one. On the one hand, established religious institutions have generally had a stake in the *status quo* and hence have fostered conservatism. The other-worldly orientation of the masses, particularly as expressed in the more fundamentalist branches of Christianity, has been seen as an alternative to the development of political radicalism. On the other hand, as the source of both universal humanistic values and the strength that can come

94

from believing one is carrying out God's will in political matters, religion has occasionally played a positive role in movements for radical social change.

This dual role of religion is clearly indicated in the case of the Negro American and race protest. Slaves are said to have been first brought to this country on the ship *Jesus Christ*.[1] Despite occasional controversy over religion's effect, most slave owners eventually came to view supervised religion as an effective means of social control. Stampp, in commenting on the effect of religion, notes:

Through religious instruction the bondsmen learned that slavery had divine sanction, that insolence was as much an offense against God as against the temporal master. They received the Biblical command that servants should obey their masters, and they heard of the punishments awaiting the disobedient slave in the hereafter. They heard, too, that eternal salvation would be their reward for faithful service. . . .[2]

In discussing the period after the Civil War, Myrdal states: "Under the pressure of political reaction, the Negro church in the South came to have much the same role as it did before the Civil War. Negro frustration was sublimated into emotionalism, and Negro hopes were fixed on the afterworld."[3] A large number of other analysts, in considering the consequences of Negro religion after slavery until the early 1950s reached similar conclusions about its conservative effect.[4]

[1] Louis Lomax, *When the Word is Given,* New York, New American Library, 1964, p. 34. And in another context it has often been noted that when the missionaries came to the lands to be colonized, they had the Bible and the indigenous people had the land. When they left, they had the land and the native people still have the Bible.

[2] Kenneth Stampp, *The Peculiar Institution,* New York, Alfred Knopf, 1956, p. 158.

[3] Gunnar Myrdal *et al., An American Dilemma* (New York: Harper & Row, 1944), pp. 861–863. About the North he notes that the church remained far more independent "but on the whole even the Northern Negro church has remained a conservative institution with its interests directly upon other-worldly matters and has largely ignored the practical problems of the Negroes' fate in this world."

[4] For example, Dollard notes that "religion can be seen as a mechanism for the social control of Negroes" and that planters have always welcomed the building of a Negro church on the plantation while looking with less favor on the building of a school (John Dollard, *Caste and Class in a Southern Town,* Garden City, N. Y., Doubleday Anchor, 1957, p. 248). A few of the many others reaching similar conclusions are Benjamin E. Mays and J. W. Nicholson, *The Negro's Church,* New York, Institute of Social and Religious Research, 1933; Hortense Powdermaker, *After Freedom,* New York, Viking Press, 1939, p. 285; Charles Johnson, *Growing up in the Black Belt,* Washington, D. C., American Council on Education, 1941, pp. 135–136; St. Clair Drake and Horace Cayton, *Black Metropolis,* New York, Harper and Row, 1962, pp. 424–429; George Simpson and Milton Yinger, *Racial and Cultural Minorities,* New York, Harper & Row, rev. ed., 1958, pp. 582–587. In a more general context, the social control consequences of religion have been noted throughout history from Plato to Montesquieu to Marx to Nietzsche to Freud to contemporary social theorists.

However, the effect of religion on race protest throughout American history has by no means been exclusively in one direction. While many Negroes were no doubt seriously singing about chariots in the sky, Negro preachers such as Denmark Vesey and Nat Turner and the religiously inspired abolitionists were actively fighting slavery in their own way. All-Negro churches first came into being as protest organizations, and later some served as meeting places where protest strategy was planned or as stations on the underground railroad. The richness of protest symbolism in Negro spirituals and sermons has often been noted. Beyond this symbolic role, the all-Negro church brought together in privacy people with a shared problem. It was in the church that many leaders were exposed to a broad range of ideas legitimizing protest and obtained the *savior faire,* self-confidence, and organizational experience needed to challenge an oppressive system. A recent commentator states that the slave churches were "the nucleus of the Negro protest."[5] And another, that "in religion, Negro leaders had begun to find sanction and support for their movements of protest more than 150 years ago."[6]

Differing perceptions of the varied consequences religion may have on protest have continued to the present time. While there has been very little in the way of empirical research on the effect of the Negro church on protest,[7] the literature on race relations is rich with impressionistic statements which generally contradict each other about how the church

[5] Daniel Thompson, "The Rise of Negro Protest," *Annals of the American Academy of Political and Social Science,* January 1965, p. 26.

[6] Liston Pope, "The Negro and Religion in America," *Review of Religious Research,* Spring 1964, p. 145.

[7] The empirical evidence is quite limited. The few studies that have been done have focused on the Negro minister. Thompson notes that in New Orleans Negro ministers constitute the largest segment of the Negro leadership class (a grouping not necessarily the same as "protest leaders") but that "the vast majority of ministers are primarily interested in their pastoral role. . . . Their sermons are essentially biblical, dealing only tangentially with social issues" (Daniel Thompson, *The Negro Leadership Class,* Englewood Cliffs, N. J., Prentice-Hall, 1963, pp. 34–35). Studies of the Negro ministry in Detroit and in Richmond, California, also stress that only a small fraction of Negro clergymen show any active concern with the civil rights struggle (R. L. Johnstone, "Militant and Conservative Community Leadership Among Negro Clergymen," Ph.D. dissertation, University of Michigan, 1963, and J. Bloom, *The Negro Church and the Movement for Equality,* M.A. thesis, University of California in Berkeley, Department of Sociology, 1966).

It is worthy of mention that, although the number of cases was small, the Negro ministers in our sample had the lowest percentage militant of any occupational group. With respect to the sons of clergymen, the situation seems somewhat different. While the myth of the preacher's son gone bad is almost a part of American folklore, one would think that a comparable myth might develop within the Negro community —that of the preacher's son gone radical. Malcolm X, James Baldwin, A. Philip Randolph, Martin Luther King, James Farmer, Adam Clayton Powell, Elijah Muhammad, and a number of others had clergymen as fathers. To be taken into consideration is that clergymen make up a relatively larger segment of the Negro middle than of the white middle class.

either encourages and is the source of race protest or inhibits and retards its development. For example, two observers note: "As primitive evangelism gave way to a more sophisticated social consciousness, the church became the spearhead of Negro protest in the Deep South,"[8] while another indicates that "the Negro church is a sleeping giant. In civil rights participation its feet are hardly wet."[9] A civil rights activist, himself a clergyman, states: "The church today is central to the movement. . . . If there had been no Negro church, there would have been no civil rights movement today."[10] On the other hand, a sociologist, commenting on the more involved higher-status ministers, notes: "Middle class Negro clergymen in the cities of the South generally advocated cautious gradualism in race activities until the mid-1950's when there was an upsurge of protest sentiment among urban Negroes . . . but most of them [ministers] did not embrace the most vigorous techniques of protest until other leaders took the initiative and gained widespread support."[11] Another sociologist states: "Whatever their previous conservative stance has been, the churches have now become 'spearheads of reform.' "[12] Still another suggests that "the Negro church is particularly culpable for its general lack of concern for the moral and social problems of the community . . . it has been accommodatory. Fostering indulgence in religious sentimentality, and riveting the attention of the masses on the bounties of a hereafter, the Negro church remains a refuge, an escape from the cruel realities of the here and now."[13]

Thus one faces opposing views, or at best, ambiguity in contemplating the current effect of religion. The quietistic consequences of religion are all too well known, as is the fact that only a relatively small segment of the Negro church is actively involved. On the other hand, the prominent role of the Negro church in supplying much of the ideology of the movement, many of its foremost leaders, and a place where protest can be

[8] Jane Record and Wilson Record, "Ideological Forces and the Negro Protest," *Annals of the American Academy of Political and Social Science,* January 1965, p. 92.

[9] G. Booker, *Black Man's America,* Englewood Cliffs, N. J., Prentice-Hall, 1964, p. 111.

[10] Rev. W. T. Walker, as quoted in William Brink and Louis Harris, *The Negro Revolution in America,* New York, Simon and Schuster, 1964, p. 103.

[11] N. Glenn, "Negro Religion in the United States," in L. Schneider, ed., *Religion, Culture and Society,* New York, J. Wiley, 1964.

[12] J. Fichter, "American Religion and the Negro," *Daedalus,* Fall 1965, p. 1087.

[13] E. U. Essien-Udom, *Black Nationalism,* New York, Dell, 1962, pp. 357–358. Many other examples of contradictory statements could be offered, sometimes even in the same volume. For example, Lee stresses the importance of religion for protest while Logan sees the Negro pastor as an instrument of the white power structure in a book published to commemorate 100 years of emancipation (Carleton Lee, "Religious Roots of Negro Protest," and Rayford Logan, "Educational Changes Affecting American Negroes," both in Arnold Rose, ed., *Assuring Freedom to the Free,* Detroit, Wayne University Press, 1964).

organized, can hardly be denied. It would appear from the bombings of churches and the writing of Martin Luther King and other religiously inspired activists that, for many, religion and protest are linked.

Denomination

It has been long known that the more fundamental sects, such as the Holiness groups and the Jehovah's Witnesses, are relatively uninterested in movements for concrete, secular, political or social change.[14] Such transvaluational movements, with their otherworldly orientations and their promise that the last shall be first in the great beyond, are said to solace the individual for his lowly status in this world and to direct attention away from efforts at collective social change. While only a minority of Negroes actually belong to such groups, the relative percentage belonging is higher than among whites. Negro literature is rich in descriptions of these churches and their position on race protest.

Table 61 shows data on civil rights militancy which are consistent with past research on political radicalism among sects. The percentage of respondents scored as militant is about twice as high among members of the more conventional religious groups than among those who belong to sects. The percentage militant increases from only 15 per cent for the sects to 43 per cent for Episcopalians. It is perhaps ironic that those individuals in largely white denominations (Episcopalian, Presbyterian, and Catholic) appear somewhat higher in militancy than those in Negro denominations, in spite of the greater civil rights activism of the latter. This was true even when social class was held constant.

In their comments, some of which were noted earlier, members of the less conventional religious groups clearly expressed the classical attitudes of sects toward participation in the politics of the secular world. An automobile serviceman in Philadelphia stated, "I, as a Jehovah's Witness, cannot express things involving the race issue." A housewife in the Far West ventured, "In my religion we do not approve of anything except living like it says in the Bible. Demonstrations mean calling attention to you, and it's sinful."

The finding that persons who belong to sects are among the least likely to be militant was to be expected. Clearly, for most people, this type of religious involvement rules out the development of radicalism. But what of religious Negroes in the more conventional churches, which may put relatively less stress on the after-life and encourage various forms of secular participation? Are the more religiously inclined within these groups also less likely to be militant?

[14] Liston Pope, *Millhands and Preachers*, New Haven, Yale University Press, 1942, p. 137; J. Milton Yinger, *Religion, Society, and the Individual*, New York, Macmillan, 1957, pp. 170–173.

Table 61. MILITANCY BY RELIGIOUS DENOMINATION

Religious Denomination[a]

	Episcopalian	United Church of Christ	Presbyterian	Catholic	Methodist	Baptist	Sects and Cults
Militant	43%	42%	36%	36%	28%	25%	15%
Number	(23)	(12)	(25)	(107)	(141)	(657)	(106)

[a] Twenty-five respondents are not shown in this table because they did not specify a denomination or belonged to non-Christian religious groups or other smaller Christian groups.

Religiosity

The study measured several dimensions of religious involvement: the importance of religion to the respondent, the orthodoxy of his religious belief, and the frequency of his attendance at worship service.[15] Even with the sects excluded, irrespective of the dimension of religiosity considered, the greater the religiosity, the lower the percentage militant (Table 62).[16] Militancy increases consistently from a low of 22 per cent

Table 62. MILITANCY BY SUBJECTIVE IMPORTANCE OF RELIGION TO RESPONDENT[a]

	Per Cent Militant	Number
Religion is:		
Extremely important	22	(664)
Quite important	34	(194)
Fairly important	44	(96)
Not too important	56	(18)
Not at all important	62	(13)

[a] Members of sects are excluded here and in all subsequent tables in this chapter.

among those who said religion was "extremely important" to a high of 62 per cent for those who indicated that religion was "not at all important" to them. For those high in orthodoxy (having no doubt about the existence of God, the devil, or an after-life), only 20 per cent were militant, while for those totally rejecting these ideas 57 per cent indicated concern

Table 63. MILITANCY BY RELIGIOUS ORTHODOXY

Score on Index of Religious Orthodoxy[a]

	High						Low
	6	5	4	3	2	1	0
Militant	20%	26%	25%	24%	42%	41%	57%
Number	(284)	(158)	(210)	(129)	(110)	(51)	(42)

[a] Having no doubt about the existence of God, the devil, and the after-life were each scored two, being fairly certain in acceptance of these beliefs was scored one, while having some doubts was scored zero.

[15] These dimensions and several others are suggested by Charles Y. Glock, "On the Study of Religious Commitment," *Religious Education—Research Supplement*, July–August 1962, pp. 98–100.

[16] One of the items in the Militancy Index (the question of praying as against demonstrating) might be seen to lead to a certain amount of circularity in Tables 62–66. However, it is noteworthy that even when this item is deleted from the Militancy Index the results are the same (Gary T. Marx, "Religion: Opiate or Inspiration of Civil Rights Militancy Among Negroes?" *American Sociological Review*, February 1967).

over civil rights (Table 63). Militancy is also inversely related to frequency of attendance at worship service.[17] As seen in Table 64, while 18 per cent of those who attend church more than once a week are high on militancy, 32 per cent who attend less than once a year are high in militancy.[18]

Table 64. MILITANCY BY FREQUENCY OF ATTENDANCE AT WORSHIP SERVICE

	Per Cent Militant	Number
Attend church:		
More than once a week	18	(79)
Once a week	26	(309)
Once to several times a month	28	(354)
Less than once a month to once a year	34	(178)
Less than once a year	32	(61)

These items were strongly interrelated and have been combined into an over-all measure of religiosity. Those scored as very religious in terms of this index attended church at least once a week, felt that religion was extremely important to them, and had no doubts about the existence of God and the devil. As one moves down the index, frequency of church attendance, the importance of religion, and acceptance of the belief items decline consistently until for those scored not at all religious church is rarely if ever attended, religion is not considered personally important, and the belief items are rejected.

[17] There is a popular stereotype that Negroes are a "religious people," and social science research has shown that they are "overchurched" relative to whites, that is, the ratio of Negro churches to the size of the Negro population is greater than this ratio for whites. Using data from the nationwide survey of anti-Semitism, a brief comparison of the religiosity of Negroes and whites was possible. When the various dimensions of religiosity are examined, holding the effect of education and region constant, Negroes appear as significantly more religious *only* with respect to the subjective importance assigned to religion. In the North whites were more likely to attend church at least once a week than were Negroes, while in the South rates of attendance were the same. About the same percentage of both groups had no doubts about the existence of God, and while Negroes were more likely to be sure about the existence of a devil, whites, were more likely to be sure about a life beyond death. Clearly then, any assertions about the greater religiosity of Negroes relative to whites are unwarranted unless one specifies the dimension of religiosity being measured.

[18] The study also made use of an additional measure of religious involvement, membership in church organizations. It may be recalled from Chapter 2 that, as membership in organizations increased, so did militancy. Church organizations were purposely excluded because the relation between degree of involvement in a church organization was the opposite of that noted for most other types of organizations. Thus, among those belonging to none, one, two, or three or more church organizations, the percentage militant decreases from 28 per cent to 23 per cent to 15 per cent to 8 per cent, respectively. Thus, organizational involvement in churches serves to decrease militancy, unlike the pattern noted for other types of involvement.

Observing the effect of this measure on civil rights concern, it can be seen that militancy increases from a low of 19 per cent for those labeled very religious to a high of 49 per cent for those considered not at all religious (Table 65).

Table 65.   AS RELIGIOSITY INCREASES MILITANCY DECREASES

Score on Index of Religiosity[a]

	Very Religious (11, 12)	Quite Religious (7–10)	Not Very Religious (3–6)	Not at all Religious (0–2)
Militant	19%	24%	33%	49%
Number	(209)	(485)	(166)	(124)

[a] Those for whom religion was extremely, quite, fairly, not too, and not at all important were scored 4, 3, 2, 1, and 0, respectively. Those with scores of 6, 5 and 4, 3, 2 and 1, and 0 on the Orthodoxy Index were scored 4, 3, 2, 1, and 0, respectively. Those attending worship services more than once a week, once a week, once to several times a month, less than once a month to once a year, and less than once a year were scored 4, 3, 2, 1, and 0, respectively.

Religiosity and militancy are both related to age, sex, region of the country raised in, and denomination. Older people, women, those raised in the South, and those in Negro denominations were more likely to be scored as religious and to have lower percentages scoring as militant. Thus it is possible that the relation of religiosity to militancy is simply a consequence of the relation of both religiosity and militancy to some third factor. However, it can be seen that even controlling for these factors the finding remains the same (Table 66). Even among older people, women, those raised in the South, and those in Negro denominations, the greater the religiosity the less the militancy. This finding perists even when observed in light of the summary measures developed in the last chapters (the indexes of Exposure to Values Legitimating Protest, Social Class, Social Participation, and Subjective Predisposition to Militancy).

The incompatibility of piety and protest that these data show is evident in comments offered by respondents. Many religious people hold beliefs that clearly inhibit race protest. For a few, segregation and a lowly status for Negroes are somehow God's will and not for men to question. Thus a housewife in South Bend, Indiana, in saying that civil rights demonstrations had hurt Negroes, added, "God is the Creator of everything. We don't know why we all dark-skinned. We should try to put forth the effort to do what God wants and not question."[19] A Negro spiritual contains the lines,

[19] Albert Cardinal Meyer notes that the Catholic bishops of the United States said in their statement of 1958: "The heart of the race question is . . . religious." ("Interracial Justice and Love," in M. Ahmann, ed., Race: Challenge to Religion, Chicago, Henry Regnery Company, 1964, p. 126). Viewed from the perspective of the activist seeking to motivate Negroes on behalf of the civil rights struggle, this statement has a meaning which their excellencies no doubt did not intend.

"I'm gonna wait upon the Lord till my change comes." Rather than seeing segregation as God's will, our respondents more frequently stressed that God, as absolute controller of the universe, would bring about change in his own way and at his own time. In indicating her unwillingness to take part in a civil rights demonstration, a Detroit housewife said, "I don't go for demonstrations. I believe that God created all men equal and at his appointed time he will give every man his portion; no one can hinder it."

Table 66. MILITANCY RELATED TO RELIGIOSITY BY AGE, SEX,
PLACE OF UPBRINGING, AND DENOMINATION
(per cent militant; number of respondents shown in parentheses)

	Index of Religiosity						
	Very Religious		Quite Religious		Not Very Religious		Not at All Religious
Age:							
18–29	20%	(25)	28%	(110)	35%	(55)	43% (37)
30–44	22	(54)	31	(161)	37	(59)	53 (58)
45–59	21	(63)	21	(117)	24	(33)	52 (21)
60+	13	(67)	11	(96)	26	(19)	—ᵃ
Sex:							
Women	18	(133)	21	(286)	32	(76)	42 (38)
Men	20	(76)	28	(199)	33	(90)	52 (86)
Where raised:							
Deep South	16	(122)	19	(255)	25	(61)	38 (29)
Border states	29	(49)	28	(104)	31	(42)	54 (35)
Non-South	16	(38)	32	(126)	41	(63)	60 (52)
Denomination:							
Episcopalian, Presbyterian, or Congregationalist	17	(12)	39	(23)	46	(13)	58 (12)
Catholic	10	(10)	31	(49)	40	(20)	54 (28)
Methodist	35	(23)	20	(76)	36	(28)	50 (12)
Baptist	17	(161)	23	(325)	30	(101)	46 (68)

ᵃ Three out of six respondents scored as militant.

And in response to the question about whether or not the government in Washington was pushing integration too slowly, a clerk in Atlanta said, "You can't hurry God. He has a certain time for this to take place. I don't know about Washington."

Others who desired integration and immediate social change felt that, since God was on their side, man need not do anything to help bring it about. Thus a worker in Cleveland gave as his reason for desiring fewer civil rights demonstrations: "With God helping to fight our battle, I believe we can do with less demonstrations." And in saying that Negroes should spend more time praying and less time demonstrating, an Atlanta clergyman added, "Praying is demonstrating."[20]

Although the net effect of religion is clearly to inhibit attitudes of protest, many religious people are nevertheless militant. A religious orientation and a concern with racial protest are certainly not mutually exclusive. Given the active involvement of some churches, the singing of protest spirituals, and the ideology of the movement as it relates to Christian principles of love, equality, passive suffering,[21] and the appeal to a higher moral law, it would be surprising if there were only a few religious people among the militants. A study of Southern Negro CORE activists indicates that less than one person in ten never attends church while almost six out of ten attended church weekly.[22] A religious orientation and a concern with racial protest are certainly not mutually exclusive, and some of those in our study would no doubt agree with Thomas Jefferson that "resistance to tyranny is obedience to God."

However, what determines whether religion leads to an active concern with racial matters or results in quietism?

The classical indictment of religion from the Marxist perspective is that, by focusing concern on an after-life, the evils of this life are ignored. However, there are important differences among religious institutions and among individuals in the importance they give to otherworldly concerns. Like most ideologies, both religious and secular, Christianity contains many themes, which, if not in contradiction, are certainly in tension with one another. Here, no doubt, lies part of the explanation of religion's varied consequences for protest. One important strand of Christianity stresses acceptance of one's lot and glorifies the after-life. However, another is more concerned with the realization of Judaeo-Christian values in the current life. Martin Luther King clearly represents this "social gospel"

[20] The study of ministers in Richmond, California, referred to earlier, offered similar findings. While almost all of the ministers in the study were opposed to discrimination, very few had taken concrete action, in part no doubt because of their belief that God would take care of them. One minister noted, "I believe that if we all was as pure . . . as we ought to be, there would be no struggle. God will answer my prayer. If we just stay with God and have faith. *When Peter was up, did the people march to free him? No. He prayed, and God did something about it* [italics added]" (Bloom, *op. cit.*).

[21] A discussion of nonviolent resistance as it relates to Christianity's emphasis on suffering, sacrifice, and privation may be found in James W. Vander Zanden, "The Nonviolent Resistance Movement Against Segregation," *American Journal of Sociology* (March 1963).

[22] In the North the same figure, four out of ten, report never attending as indicate that they go to church weekly. (Ingeborg B. Powell, "Ideology and Strategy of Direct Action: A Study of the Congress of Racial Equality," Ph.D. dissertation, University of California in Berkeley, 1965, p. 207.)

tradition.[23] When one's religious involvement includes temporal concerns and acceptance of the belief that men as well as God have a role in the structuring of human affairs, then, rather than serving to inhibit protest, religion can serve to inspire and sustain it. This religious inspiration is clearly present in the writings of King and others.

However, among sect members and the religious with an otherworldly orientation, religion and race protest, if not mutually exclusive, are certainly what one observer has referred to as "mutually corrosive kinds of commitments."[24] Until such time as religion loosens its hold over these people, or comes to embody to a greater extent the belief that man as well as God can bring about secular change, and focuses more on the here and now, religion would seem to be an important factor working against the widespread radicalization of the Negro public.

[23] "Any religion that professes to be concerned with the souls of men and is not concerned with the slums that damn them, the economic conditions that strangle them, and the social conditions that cripple them is a dry-as-dust religion." He further adds that "such a religion is the kind the Marxists like to see—an opiate of the people" (Martin Luther King, *Stride Toward Freedom,* New York, Ballantine Books, 1958, pp. 28–29).

John Lewis, a former SNCC leader and once a Baptist divinity student, is said to have peered through the bars of a Southern jail and quoted the New Testament: "Think not that I am come to send peace on earth. I came not to send peace, but a sword" (Matthew 10:34).

[24] Rodney Stark, "Class, Radicalism, and Religious Involvement," *American Sociological Review,* October 1964.

CHAPTER

5

Black Nationalism

The white man is by nature a devil and must be destroyed. The black man will inherit the earth; he will resume control, taking back the position he held centuries ago when the white devil was crawling around the caves of Europe on all fours.

—Malcolm X

The Big Niggers as a class don't think. . . . Once a Negro reaches college level he is no good for anybody.

—Black nationalist leader

The Muslims purport to be separationists, but time and again they will lament the failing of integration. Theoretically, as separationists they should be pleased when integration doesn't work.

—W. Haywood Burns

In the late 1950s the mass media began to detect the presence of a new militant force in the Negro community. Almost overnight much concern was expressed over what was heralded as a rising tide of black nationalism. The most prominent nationalist group was the Muslims. Soon millions of Americans knew of Elijah Muhammad, and heard the Muslim program outlined in potent rhetoric by Malcolm X. The significance of the Muslims was thought to be the mood they exemplified rather than their membership, which has remained quite small. Still, signs of rising black nationalism aroused apprehension on the part of many. It seemed a clear portent of a developing impatience and anger.

Any general assessment of the mood of the Negro community and of the current status of racial protest requires an analysis of black nationalism. While much has been written on this subject, very few trustworthy facts are known. Is there considerable support for nationalistic programs and sentiments among Negroes generally, or is support pretty much limited to actual members of nationalist organizations such as the Muslims?

First of all, what does the term black nationalism mean? Broadly speak-

106

ing, it implies pride in being black—a positive regard for Afro-American origins, history, and culture. One finds much of this spirit in the recent writings of Negro intellectuals. As Lerone Bennet has written: "The mood is, in essence, an affirmation of Negro experience and Negro values. It is not necessarily a rejection of white-ness, but it is quite definitely an acceptance of blackness. . . ."[1] This aspect of black nationalism, coupled with an emphasis on the development of Negro institutions and programs of self-help, seems to be one meaning of the concept of black power.

But beyond this general sort of nationalism, or racial pride, lies a more extreme variety built of notions of racial superiority which, in the case of the Muslims, are grafted onto a radical eschatology. Indeed, the Muslims exemplify the link between present-day black nationalism and the earlier tradition of messianic cult movements among Negroes. The Muslims were one such movement for some decades before the emergence of the civil rights movement gave them new relevance and direction. It is this more radical and racist variety of black nationalism that we shall investigate in this chapter. Primary attention will be given to support for the Black Muslims since at the time of our study they were the dominant nationalist group.

Index of Support for Black Nationalism[2]

In building a measure of support for the Muslims, two issues from their platform (also supported by many other nationalist groups) were used: refusal to fight for the United States in the event of a war, and giving black Americans their own country. The index also included two questions which gave respondents the chance to single out the Muslims as the group doing the most to help Negroes, and Malcolm X, a leading black nationalist spokesman in 1964, as the individual doing the most to help. Responses to these questions were reported in Chapter 1. For each black nationalist response a score of one was given; scores thus ranged from zero to four.

The index is a quite permissive criterion of black nationalist support when contrasted with the Black Muslims' program and occasional statements by their spokesman. Thus it provides an absolutely maximum estimate of Muslim support, registering even the "softest" or mildest pro-Muslim sentiment. For example, to be counted in this study as sympathetic to black nationalism, one need not believe that the white man is a devil in the theological sense or that Negroes are genetically superior to whites or are God's chosen race.

---

[1] *Confrontation: Black and White,* Chicago, Johnson Publishing Company, 1965, p. 239.

[2] In the remaining parts of this chapter, when the term black nationalism is used, it refers to the separatist variety manifested by the Muslims and similar groups.

The data in Table 67 show that reports of a "rising tide" of black nationalism, at least in late 1964, were widely misleading; strong and consistent support for the Muslims was at best an infinitesimal ripple in the Negro community. In the summer of 1964, only three persons out of nearly 1,100 interviewed gave a pronationalist response on all four questions. Indeed, less than 1 per cent would accept three of these statements.

Table 67.   SUPPORT FOR BLACK NATIONALISM BY REGION

Score on Index of Support for Black Nationalism	Metro	N.Y.	Chic.	Atl.	Birm.	Total
0	75%	71%	65%	69%	73%	72%
1	21	21	28	28	26	24
2	3	4	6	3	1	3
3	0.0062	3	0	0	0	0.55
4	0	1	1	0	0	0.27
Total	100%	100%	100%	100%	100%	100%
Number	(481)	(174)	(130)	(194)	(199)	(1,093)[a]

[a] As noted in Table 1 those interviews from the metropolitan area sample which occurred in New York (44 cases) and in Chicago (54 cases) have been reported in both the metropolitan sample and the New York and Chicago samples. Hence the total number reported in this column is less than the total number of respondents for the samples shown separately.

In fact, less than 4 per cent of the combined sample gave a pronationalist answer to two of the four. Thus, 96 per cent of the Negroes sampled rejected at least three out of four moderately pronationalist statements, and 72 per cent rejected all four. Thus, even by this relatively loose definition of black nationalism, only one-third of 1 per cent of our respondents offered strong and consistent support for the Muslims, and only 4 per cent indicated moderate support. Furthermore, the 1966 *Newsweek* survey, although carried out almost two years later, reports that just 4 per cent favor the Muslims.[3]

Muslim national headquarters is in Chicago, and, according to Malcolm X, New York City is where they have the most members. Table 67 shows that sympathy for black nationalism is a bit higher in Chicago and New York than elsewhere. However, even in these two cities, more than nine out of ten Negroes showed little or no sympathy.

At this point in American history then, there seems to be relatively little support for the kind of black nationalism manifested by the Muslims. Only a minute fraction of American black people hold to such a point of

[3] *Newsweek*, August 22, 1966.

view with any consistency.[4] However, this fact tells us little about how much power the Muslims may be able to wield in various local situations or how indirectly useful they have been to the more conventional civil rights groups who could hold out the threat of driving the masses to black nationalism if concessions were not met. Malcolm X stated of the "so-called Negro leaders"; "They charge us [with] being extremists but if it was not for the extremists the white man would ignore the moderates." Nor does this pattern of support tell us anything about the importance of the Muslims' ideas in shaping some of the ideology of the black power movement. The lack of strong support for black nationalism also does not tell us much about attitudes toward whites and about nonviolence. No inference should be made from this finding as to the likelihood of collective disturbances such as riots. We have examined only the extent of consistent support for two positions advocated by the Muslims, and for an individual who had been their outstanding spokesman. Lack of support is not necessarily the same as active opposition.[5]

This relative lack of support is consistent with the very small number

[4] This lack of support made it necessary to reconceptualize the study. I had originally hoped to carry the analysis out around two dimensions of civil rights concern— conventional militancy and black nationalism. It was anticipated that the basic framework for analysis would be a typology such as the following, which emerges when hypothetical measures of conventional militancy and black nationalism are combined:

		Conventional Militancy	
		Low	High
Black Nationalism	Low	"Apathetic Conservatives"	"Conventional Militants"
	High	"Black Nationalist Separatists"	"Black Nationalist Militants"

Because of the virtual absence of black nationalist support, it was not possible to proceed in this fashion and, with the exception of this chapter, militancy is treated as if it were a unidimensional phenomenon (i.e., as if there were nothing other than conventional militancy).

One could no doubt develop a highly sophisticated typology of civil rights concern sensitive to the many nuances found among different civil rights groups. However, attempting to use such a typology to analyze a representative national sample of the black population is another matter altogether. The survey analyst faces a major problem in trying to reconcile logical types with the frequency with which these types are empirically manifested.

[5] A statement by Lomax is relevant: "In the end . . . the Negro masses neither join nor denounce the Black Muslims. They just sit at home in the ghetto amid the heat, the roaches, the rats, the vice, the disgrace, and rue the fact that come daylight they must meet the man . . ." (Louis Lomax, *When the Word Is Given,* New York, New American Library, 1964, p. 67). Our data did indicate that, when an individual or organization was disapproved of, it was almost certain to be Malcolm X and the Black Muslims. Still, consistent with the above statement, about one-half of those questioned did not offer disapproval of either. Our findings also say nothing about the intensity of support that some may feel for black nationalism.

of black people who have become active members of the Nation of Islam. For example, Essien-Udom states that "the appeal of black nationalism is very special and is not actively supported by the Negro masses," and, in referring to the Muslims as a vocal but insignificant minority, he suggests that active membership is between 5,000 and 15,000.[6] Most observers of the Muslims have seen fit to label them as "secessionist," seeing the more conventional civil rights groups as "pluralistic" or "assimilationist." It is true that much of the Muslim rhetoric is based on vague talk of some "land of our own" and "three, four, or more states." However, relative to the action taken earlier by other secessionist groups such as Garvey's UNIA (Universal Negro Improvement Association) or the Peace Movement of Ethiopia, the Muslims seem to have actually concentrated little effort in this direction. The building of a $20 million center in Chicago, and their investments in the rest of the country, seem to contradict the expectation that they soon hope to have a land of their own. The secessionist emphasis is also somewhat contrary to Muslim leader Elijah Muhammad's statement of "What the Muslims Want."[7] "We want equality of opportunity. We want equal membership in society."

Given these facts, and the Muslim's high degree of racial concern, it is not surprising that, in spite of the separatist theme, the black nationalist sympathizers in our sample are at least as high and even higher than others in their concern over integration and in their opposition to discrimination. For example, 56 per cent of this group (those with scores of two, three, or four on the index)[8] felt that the government was pushing integration too slowly, while only 32 and 36 per cent of those with scores of zero or one felt this way (Table 68). Almost nine out of ten of those

[6] E. U. Essien-Udom, *Black Nationalism*, New York, Dell, 1962, pp. 349 and 84. This modest statement stands in marked contrast to the undocumented wild assertions made by journalists and often by social scientists, too) as to the widespread support the Muslims have in the black community.

[7] The ten statements of "What the Muslims Want" and twelve statements of "What the Muslims Believe" appear in each issue of the Muslim newspaper *Muhammad Speaks*.

[8] There are several reasons for considering those with scores of two or more as sympathetic to black nationalism. It offers at least a minimum number of cases to work with and permits some confidence in the statistical inferences to be made. It permits inclusion of those who may support the policies of the Black Muslims and Malcolm X but who did not necessarily single them out as doing the most to help Negroes. It permits inclusion of those few cases who may have responded to the explosive break of Malcolm X from the Muslims in late 1963 by supporting one but not the other. It also permits inclusion of those who may be generally sympathetic toward the Muslims but who disagree with their idea of a separate country for Negroes.

Internal analysis of the index shows that almost all of those with scores of two, three, and four felt that the United States would not be worth fighting for in the event of a war, but only about two in three felt that it would be a good idea to give Negroes their own country. One out of three chose the Muslims as the group doing the most to help Negroes, while one out of five chose Malcolm X as the individual doing the most to help.

sympathetic to black nationalism felt that Negroes and whites should go to the same schools; almost eight out of ten, that a restaurant owner should not be allowed to discriminate; and six out of ten, that discrimination in the sale of property should not be permitted. For each of these three discrimination items, the percentage giving the antidiscrimination response was higher or about the same as the percentage giving such a response among those with scores of zero or one.

Table 68. CONCERN OVER INTEGRATION BY INDEX OF SUPPORT FOR BLACK NATIONALISM

| | Index of Support for Black Nationalism | | |
| | Unsympathetic | | Sympathetic |
	0	1	(2, 3, 4)
Per cent thinking that government is pushing intergration too slowly	32	36	56
Per cent thinking white and Negro children should go to the same schools	92	87	86
Per cent disagreeing that a restaurant owner should not have to serve Negroes if doesn't want to	79	74	77
Per cent disagreeing that an owner of property should not have to sell to Negroes if he doesn't want to	48	47	63
Per cent scored as militant on Index of Conventional Militancy	27	23	44
Number	(788)	(262)	(43)

As a result of this pattern it is not surprising that black nationalist supporters score relatively high on the Index of Conventional Militancy; 44 per cent of this group scored as militant, as against only 23 and 27 per cent of those with scores of one and zero respectively (Table 68).[9]

[9] Chapter 1 notes that for a few respondents conservative responses seemed to be based not on apathy, indifference, or "Uncle Tomism" but on separatist black nationalism. The comments of some respondents clearly showed that, while quite concerned about civil rights issues, they based their "conservatism" on secessionist black nationalist ideology. However, when the percentages in Table 68 were taken in the opposite direction, only 1 per cent of the conservatives were sympathetic to black nationalism and hence conservative in this special and unique way. Thus almost all of those labeled conservative in this study manifest this position because of apathy or Uncle Tomism and not because of a black nationalist perspective. In any current discussion on civil rights conservatism, it is important to differentiate between these two types.

In spite of the separatist rhetoric of the Muslims, black Nationalist sympathizers in our sample are fairly strong in their opposition to discrimination and concern over integration. This finding does not invalidate our measure.[10] Rather, it suggests that a concern over integration (at least in principle) and support for black nationalism can easily exist together. In fact, for many of our black nationalist sympathizers, their continued frustration, resulting from a deep concern over integration and the lack of radical changes in the Negro's position within American society, may well be the factor that led them to accept black nationalist ideology. Malcolm X himself is reported to have said that what the Muslims really want is equality now, but that they are driven to separatism because their aims are frustrated.[11] Similar frustration is relevant for whatever of separatist themes exist within the black power movement.

A Descriptive Portrait

In previous chapters we observed how groups with different demographic, social, and psychological characteristics differed from each other with respect to the proportion who are militant, and we attempted to explain militancy. Seeing that people born outside the deep South are higher in militancy than people born there suggested that there is something about where one is born that is casually related to militancy. However, in the case of support for the Muslims, the small number of sympathizers makes such explanatory analysis much more difficult. Extensive explanatory analysis of Muslim support must be left to a sample drawn from a special universe. The same thing is true when attempting to analyze support for groups such as the Birch Society or the Ku Klux Klan. In a nationally representative sample of ordinary size, too few such supporters would be found. However, the number of black nationalist sympathizers was adequate for a simple descriptive analysis. Descriptive analysis simply means presenting a picture

---

[10] Evidence of the external validity of the index may be seen in the fact that as scores increase from zero to four the percentage indicating disapproval of the Muslims decreases from 58 per cent to 0 per cent. The situation is similar for disapproval of Malcolm X. The percentage reading the Muslim newspaper, *Muhammad Speaks,* also increases with score on the index.

[11] W. H. Burns, *Voices of Negro Protest in America,* New York, Oxford University Press, 1963, p. 80.

To the extent that the Muslims are driven to their "radical" proposals by the frustrations of "respectable goals," they are clearly "extremists" of a very different nature from the KKK and the American Nazi party with whom they are often wrongly compared. In a complete reversal, it is the partial realization of "respectable goals" (nondiscriminatory treatment and the integration of the Negro into the mainstream of American life) that drive these white extremists to their separatist positions. The Muslims also do not wish to deprive whites of their rights while the white extremists clearly wish to deprive Negroes of theirs.

of the black nationalists by showing how they differ from other respondents in a variety of respects. In an explanatory analysis one asks, for example, whether the old and young differ in the extent to which they support black nationalism. In a descriptive analysis, one reverses the question and asks whether black nationalist sympathizers are generally older or younger than nonsympathizers.

The remaining part of this chapter will be concerned with how black nationalist sympathizers differ from nonsympathizers. By nonsympathizers is meant that 96 per cent of the sample who rejected three or all four of the index items. Involving as it does almost the entire sample, this is quite a varied group, and one can obtain a much clearer picture by further classifying those not in sympathy according to their position on the Index of Conventional Militancy. Thus, we shall compare black nationalist supporters with persons who take a militant or a conservative stance on civil rights. Simply to clarify the discussion, persons scored as moderates on civil rights are excluded from the data. Such persons invariably fell between the militants and the conservatives in the comparisons that follow.

Proceeding in this fashion, we shall compare black nationalist sympathizers with militants and conservatives. Two general comparisons are of central interest. First of all, how do militants and black nationalists differ from conservatives? The first two groups are similar in the sense that they are concerned about contemporary protest, while the third has remained apathetic. Secondly, how do militants differ from nationalists, since the former have retained their commitment to the structure and values of American society, while in many cases the latter have not?

Our descriptive portrait will begin with some questions on civil rights, and then turn to demographic, social, and psychological characteristics.

Some Differences and Similarities Regarding Civil Rights Issues

The Muslims have been critical of the civil rights movement. They have accused it of being a trick, and have called demonstrations ineffective and directed at what they perceive to be rather trivial ends (sitting next to the white man at a lunch counter when they should be more concerned with owning the establishment instead). They state that only token changes have occurred and that in fact no others can occur until Negroes and whites are completely separated. Consequently, it is not surprising that the black nationalist sympathizers in the sample rate the effectiveness of civil rights demonstrations lower than do militants. For example, as seen in Table 69, only 40 per cent, as compared with 67 per cent of the militants, felt that civil rights demonstrations had "helped a great deal." The conservatives, a disproportionate number of whom are older and low in social status and, hence, have had less direct benefit from demonstrations, were only slightly more likely to say that demonstrations had "helped a great deal" than were the black nationalist supporters.

For the black nationalists, this evaluation of the worth of demonstrations may be seen as just one strand of a more general pessimism about the situation of black people in American society. This is not true of the conservatives. For example, a full 40 per cent of the black nationalist supporters felt that things in this country were getting worse for Negroes, while only 6 per cent of the militants and 13 per cent of the conservatives felt this way. And in response to a question about whether Negroes were better

Table 69.   OUTLOOK FOR CIVIL RIGHTS: BLACK NATIONALIST SYMPATHIZERS COMPARED WITH MILITANTS AND CONSERVATIVES

Per Cent Agreeing	Black Nationalist Sympathizers	Militants	Conservatives
Civil rights demonstrations helped a great deal	40%	67%	42%
Things getting worse for Negroes in this country	40	6	13
Situation of Negroes is the same in North and South	53	27	32
The day will come when whites will accept Negroes	63	75	75
Negroes some day are going to rise to the leadership of the world	80	67	66
Negroes are God's chosen people today	24	5	5
Number	(43)[a]	(266)[a]	(220)[a]

[a] All subsequent tables have approximately the same number of respondents unless the contrary is indicated.

off in the North or the South, more than half of the black nationalist supporters responded "the same" while about one-third of the conservatives and one-fourth of the militants gave this essentially negative response. Nationalists tend to refuse to distinguish matters of degree in the Negro's condition—it's all bad. They were also slightly less likely to agree that "the day will come when Negroes will be fully accepted by whites" than were militants and conservatives.

However, they were more likely to agree with the statement "Negroes are someday going to rise to the leadership of the world." Eight out of ten nationalists agreed with this statement. This kind of optimism is consistent with Muslim ideology in which Allah has determined that the black man is "by nature divine" and is destined to rule, now that the ruling time allotted to whites is almost up.[12] It can also be seen that almost one in four of the black nationalist sympathizers felt that today Negroes were God's chosen people as against one in twenty of the other groups.

Police and Violence

A frequent complaint of the black nationalists is police brutality. The Black Muslims seem to have been subjected to particularly harsh treatment at the hands of the police, as an attack on the Los Angeles mosque indicated. Reflecting this is the finding that seven out of ten of the black nationalist sympathizers in our sample felt that police treated Negroes badly. The shared concern and racial awareness among both black nationalist supporters and militants can be seen in the fact that a majority of the latter also felt police treated Negroes badly, while for the conservatives less than three in ten gave this response (Table 70).

Table 70. ATTITUDES OF BLACK NATIONALIST SYMPATHIZERS, MILITANTS, AND CONSERVATIVES TOWARD POLICE, RIOTS, AND VIOLENCE[a]

	Black Nationalist Sympathizers	Militants	Conservatives
Per cent thinking police treat Negroes badly	72%	53%	28%
Number	(36)	(239)	(194)
Per cent thinking riots do some good	72	48	48
Number	(37)	(258)	(193)
Per cent disagreeing violence will never help Negroes	49	40	24
Number	(39)	(256)	(204)
Per cent high on acceptance of violence	39	24	16
Number	(36)	(248)	(184)

[a] Because for these questions a "don't know" response was more likely to represent a desire not to respond rather than a genuine lack of opinion, the data in these tables omit the "don't knows."

[12] This emphasis in Muslim ideology may help explain why a majority of the black nationalist sympathizers agreed that the day would come when whites would accept Negroes, in spite of their greater pessimism about the current situation of the black man within American society. One of the few Muslims in the sample, in agreeing that the day will come when Negroes will be accepted by whites, added, "If they [Negroes] have their own government." Malcolm X stated that "it is not the Negroes but the whites who are a race because they are racing with time."

While the Muslims talk in apocalyptic language about the coming Armageddon and the need for self-defense in their utterances to the white community, they do not go nearly as far as the leader of a New York-based black nationalist group who during the Harlem riots screamed for the "blood to flow" and was quoted as saying, "I'm preaching violence . . . the Negroes must be free and the state must be completely and totally smashed. We'll have to kill a lot of cops and judges. No revolution was ever won by peaceful means, so we must fight and then set up a state of our own choosing." Still, the Muslim attitude toward riots and violence at the time of the study was very different from that of the conventional civil rights groups. While the Muslims may have been unduly labeled as a violent group, an undercurrent of support for riots and lack of faith in nonviolence can easily be detected. More than seven out of ten of those receptive to the Muslim appeal felt that riots do some good, while less than one-half of the militants and conservatives felt this way. Similarly, about half the nationalists denied that "violence will never help Negroes get equal rights." This figure is 40 per cent for militants and only 24 per cent for conservatives. Although the acceptance of violence is relatively high among black nationalist sympathizers, even among this group about half felt that violence would not help, and about three in ten agreed that no good can ever come from riots. When these two questions are combined into a measure of acceptance of violence, only about four out of ten nationalists scored as high on the acceptance of violence in contrast to 24 per cent of militants and 16 per cent of conservatives. That many black nationalist sympathizers do not seem to be high in the acceptance of violence is consistent with the official teachings of the Muslims.[13] In urging his followers to respect law and order the leader of the Muslims states: "Obey those in authority" and "be yourself . . . a righteous Muslim. Follow the Golden Rule. . . . Be polite, courteous and respectful so that you may inspire respect from the police officers."[14]

Black nationalists are often extremely critical of white merchants in Negro ghettoes. They claim these merchants treat Negroes with disrespect, sell inferior goods at quality prices, and, in addition, often employ Negroes only in menial positions at substandard wages. In later chapters the relationships between Negroes and ghetto merchants will be considered in some detail. However, here it can be noted that the black nationalist supporters were much more critical of the way white store owners treated Negroes than were nonsupporters of nationalism. Among the former, 44 per cent said that almost all white store owners take advantage of Negroes. This figure drops to only 15 per cent among militants and conservatives.

Criticism of white businessmen is usually matched by a plea for purchasing from black businessmen who don't "put shellac on spoiled meat to

[13] However, as noted in Chapter 1, these questions have some limitations.
[14] Essien-Udom, *op. cit.,* p. 292.

make it look fresh" and who "pay a living wage." The Muslims put great emphasis on the development of Negro-owned businesses and themselves own a number of enterprises. This agitation does not seem to have had an important effect on consumer behavior. The percentage of black nationalist sympathizers who report they shop at none or only a few white-owned stores (14) is about the same as the percentage of militants (10) and conservatives (17) who report this. Regardless of what Negroes would like to do, there are relatively few Negro-owned stores in many areas, and those that do exist are not diverse enough to cover all consumer needs, making it almost impossible not to shop at some white-owned stores. This "entrapment" by the white merchant of those already hostile may operate to intensify black nationalist feelings.

Exposure to Protest Values

With regard to a number of variables presumably related to exposure to values legitimizing protest, black nationalist sympathizers and militants are quite similar and differ considerably from conservatives. About seven out of ten of the former two groups were under 44 years of age, as against less than half of the conservatives. A majority of both black nationalist supporters and militants were men, whereas two out of three conservatives were women. Conservatives were also much more likely than the others to have been raised in the deep South and in a rural area.

Table 71. DEMOGRAPHIC CHARACTERISTICS OF BLACK NATIONALIST SYMPATHIZERS, MILITANTS, AND CONSERVATIVES

Per Cent Affirmative	Black Nationalist Sympathizers	Militants	Conservatives
Men	72%	54%	31%
Under 44	70	67	45
Raised in a big city	33	40	19
Raised in deep South	27	36	57
High on Index of Exposure to Values Legitimizing Protest	45	46	15

When these factors are observed together in the Index of Exposure to Values Legitimizing Protest, used in Chapter 2, 45 per cent of the black nationalist sympathizers and 46 per cent of the militants scored as high, while only 15 per cent of the conservatives did (Table 71). Thus, regardless of the type of protest, those who show civil rights concern are more likely to be men, younger, and raised in big cities outside the deep South. These four factors may be seen as predisposing an individual to be in a milieu (either temporal, social, or geographical) in which exposure to values legitimizing protest is more likely to occur.

The literature suggests that new immigrants to the city, especially from Southern rural areas, are especially attracted to black nationalism because of their dislocation and the normal tensions of urban slum living.[15] However, black nationalist supporters in our sample were less likely to come from rural areas than were conservatives. They were also the least likely to have migrated from the South. Among those now living in the North, 46 per cent of the black nationalist sympathizers had moved from the South as against 65 per cent of the conservatives and 55 per cent of the militants. However, black nationalist sympathizers have been more geographically mobile than the rest of the sample. Thirty per cent of the nationalist sympathizers reported that they had lived in their present city less than six years, as against only 11 per cent of the conservatives and 15 per cent of the militants. Although black nationalist supporters were least likely to have come from the South or from rural areas, they were most likely to have come from some place else recently. For them the tension and strain associated with moving from the South to the North, from a rural area to an urban one, or between urban areas, may facilitate receptiveness to the nationalist appeal.

An additional type of strain, not unrelated to the problems of migration, is the disparity between ambitions and the opportunity for their actualization. Merton suggested that an imbalance between means and ends could lead to various types of deviant behavior, and numerous analysts have pointed out that the frustration of rising expectations is an important impetus for radical social change.[16] In the case of Negroes this strain may be particularly acute. Living in the world's most affluent society and socialized to have the same success values as whites, they are nevertheless largely denied the opportunity for actualizing these values because of discrimination and its bastard offspring, the lack of acquired skills. Our study included two questions which roughly measure the fit between ambition and opportunity. Respondents were asked first, "How important is it to you to get a promotion on your job?" and then, "Would you say your chances of promotion in the next few years are excellent, good, fair, or poor?" Compared to others, black nationalist sympathizers were more likely to evidence frustration. Of this group, 50 per cent reported that a promotion was important to them yet they had a poor or only a fair chance of getting one, while for conservatives this figure drops to 25 per cent and for militants, to 34 per cent (Table 72).

15 *Ibid.*, p. 23; Burns, *op. cit.*, p. 65.

16 Robert Merton, *Social Theory and Social Structure*, New York, Free Press, 1962, pp. 131–160.

This measure was computed only for those for whom the question of a promotion was relevant, those presently employed. Additional evidence of the greater strains experienced by black nationalists may be seen in the fact that one in four of this group was unemployed or had been laid off at the time of the interview, while this was the case for only one in ten of the militants and conservatives.

Table 72. JOB OPPORTUNITIES OF BLACK NATIONALIST SYMPATHIZERS, MILITANTS, AND CONSERVATIVES

	Black Nationalist Sympathizers	Militants	Conservatives
Per cent for whom a promotion is important yet who report having a poor or only a fair chance to obtain one (Only among those employed)	50%	34%	25%
Number	(18)	(141)	(72)
Per cent unemployed	26%	9%	10%

Social Position

It has been seen that Muslim sympathizers and militants are similar in characteristics which are presumably related to exposure to protest values and that both differ greatly from conservatives in these ways. However, black nationalist supporters are markedly different from militants in social position. Indeed, pronationalists are much more like conservatives than militants in this respect. Analysis showed that a majority of nationalists and conservatives earned less than $4,000 a year while fewer than three in ten of the militants earned this little. They were also somewhat more likely to be in blue-collar occupations than militants. In addition, while 52 per cent of the conservatives and 35 per cent of the black nationalist sympathizers had no more than a grammar school education, this was true for only 22 per cent of the militants. When these factors are combined into an Index of Social Class, 58 per cent of the conservatives and 40 per cent of the black nationalist sympathizers, as opposed to only 22 per cent of the militants, scored as lower class. At the other extreme, 29 per cent of the militants scored as upper class as contrasted with only 7 and 6 per cent of black nationalist supporters and conservatives (Table 73).

The relation of black nationalism to social class noted here is consistent with the reports of contemporary observers about the lower class base of

Table 73. SOCIAL POSITION OF BLACK NATIONALIST SYMPATHIZERS,
MILITANTS, AND CONSERVATIVES

Social Class	Black Nationalist Sympathizers	Militants	Conservatives
Lower	40%	22%	58%
Middle	53	49	36
Upper	7	29	6
Total	100%	100%	100%

such movements.[17] The failure of the Garvey movement and the Communist Party to gain appreciable support from middle-class Negroes also attests to this group's general rejection of the more radical solutions to the plight of the black man. However, the failure of black nationalism to attract more than a minute proportion even of the most disadvantaged indicates the general rejection of radical solutions in the Negro community at the time of the study.

Social Participation

Those who support black nationalism and apathetic conservatives are again similar and differ from militants in their "symbolic" and "actual" social participation. About half of both black nationalist sympathizers and conservatives report they do not read either Negro magazines or general circulation magazines. Among militants, more than four out of five report reading Negro magazines; and about three out of four, general magazines. The pattern for reading Negro and general newspapers is the same. However, in spite of their relative isolation from ordinary communications channels, more than one in four of the black nationalist sympathizers report reading the newspaper of the Nation of Islam, *Muhammad Speaks,* while almost none of the other two groups report reading this paper.

In considering actual participation, seven out of ten of both black nationalists and conservatives report belonging to no organizations, while this is true of only about half of the militants. Black nationalist supporters and conservatives were also similar in the proportion who did not vote in 1960 and the percentage socializing with friends infrequently; on each count, militants were much higher in participation.[18]

When the factors observed here are combined into the Index of Social

[17] C. Eric Lincoln, *The Black Muslims in America,* Boston, Beacon Press, 1961, p. 22; Essien-Udom, *op. cit.,* p. 32 and p. 201; Burns, *op. cit.,* p. 65.

[18] In spite of their civil rights concern and racial awareness one might predict that black nationalists would be relatively low in voting, in part because of their lower status and social isolation, in part because of a sense of futility in electing a white man or a middle-class Negro to office. In addition, until recently the Muslims have not shown much interest in politics and have generally refrained from voting (Lincoln, *op. cit.,* p. 18; Essien-Udom, *op. cit.,* p. 312).

Participation used in Chapter 2, more than four out of ten black nationalist sympathizers and conservatives score as very low in social participation compared to only 12 per cent of the militants (Table 74).

Table 74. SOCIAL PARTICIPATION OF BLACK NATIONALIST SYMPATHIZERS, MILITANTS, AND CONSERVATIVES

Index of Social Participation	Black Nationalist Sympathizers	Militants	Conservatives
Low	42%	12%	44%
Medium	28	31	34
High	30	57	22
Total	100%	100%	100%

Some Psychological Factors

Given the lower level of social participation and lower class position of both the black nationalist supporters and the conservatives, it is not surprising that on the measures of intellectual sophistication used in Chapter 3 these groups were found to be similar and scored much lower than militants (Table 75). For example, about one out of two scored as high on the F-scale items as against less than one in four of the militants.[19] With respect to knowledge about civil rights leaders, only 31 per cent and 23 per cent were able to identify four leaders, compared to 66 per cent of the militants. The pattern is comparable for the other items used in the Index of Intellectual Sophistication—the indexes of awareness of the role of social factors, knowledge of writers, and intellectual values. On this larger measure, almost four in ten of the black nationalists and five in ten of the conservatives but only one in ten of the militants were labeled unsophisticated (Table 75).

In considering the measure of morale, black nationalist supporters and conservatives are again similar and differ from the militants. About one in

[19] The F scale is considered here as a measure of breadth of perspective rather than of deep-lying authoritarian personality characteristics. However, one of the original intentions of the authoritarian personality studies was to document the existence of a fascist or authoritarian personality, which presumably was especially likely to be attracted to antidemocratic authoritarian social movements. The finding that a sizable percentage of black nationalist sympathizers are high on the F scale is consistent with this as with Essien-Udom's assertion that "many turn to the Nation of Islam because they feel a need for a strong leader and an important personality with whom to identify" (*op. cit.,* p. 110).

Unlike the participatory democracy found among other civil rights organizations (where virtual anarchy occasionally marks the relationship between local groups and the national office), the Muslims are very tightly organized and "authority in the Nation of Islam on all matters of ideology, theology, and policy rests solely in the Messenger of Allah" (*ibid.,* p. 160).

Table 75. SOME PSYCHOLOGICAL CHARACTERISTICS OF BLACK NATIONALIST
SYMPATHIZERS, MILITANTS, AND CONSERVATIVES

Per Cent Reporting	Black Nationalist Sympathizers	Militants	Conservatives
High score on F scale (4,5)	53%	23%	46%
Correctly identify all four civil rights leaders	31	66	23
Correctly identify two or all three authors	25	44	13
High score on Index of Awareness of How Social Factors Shape Behavior (2,3)	23	57	31
High score on Index of Acceptance of Intellectual Values (3)	14	29	7
Score as unsophisticated on Index of Intellectual Sophistication (0,1,2)	39	11	54
Very low morale (0)	36	12	36
Unfavorable self-image (0)	14	6	26

three of these groups were found to have a very low morale as against slightly more than one in nine of the militants.

With respect to self-image, only about one in twenty of the militants, as opposed to one in seven of the black nationalist supporters and one in four of the conservatives, had an unfavorable self-image.[20]

Religion

In the last chapter it was observed that religion seemed to inhibit conventional militancy. It seems reasonable to suppose that commitment to Christianity would particularly inhibit black nationalism, especially the Muslim variety. The Black Muslims constitute a competing religion, and it would make as little sense to speak of a Christian Muslim as to speak of a Baptist Catholic. Muslims are especially aware of their direct contradiction

[20] In exploring group image among black nationalists, one finds opposing tendencies. On the one hand, one of the most significant aspects of black nationalism is its attempt to create a sense of pride and dignity in being black. For the Muslims, black is beautiful and black men are God's chosen people. However, when one makes a distinction between the Negro potential and his current situation a much more negative self-image emerges. Negroes who are as yet "unredeemed" are referred to as "dead" and severely criticized for their complacency. Of them, the Muslim leader states, "You cannot find any other people in the world whose morals are so low" (ibid., p. 91).

of Christianity and refer to it as a "slave religion" and "white man's religion." The Bible they regard as a "poison book,"[21] meant to trick Negroes into accepting their suffering.[22] That support of Christianity and of the Muslims tend to be mutually incompatible is borne out by the data. One out of two black nationalist sympathizers were scored as not at all religious or not very religious within the context of Christian religiosity, while only one out of five of the conservatives and one in three of the militants were scored this way.

In summary, this chapter has noted that only a small fraction of black Americans in 1964 offered even minimal support for black nationalism of the Muslim variety and, among those who did, many still favored integration, at least in principle.

The rejection of separatist black nationalism is consistent with the whole of the Negro's American experience which, however snail-like in pace, has been a gradual move toward inclusion into the world's most abundant material civilization. Since the enemies of the Negro have traditionally stressed separation, until recently the militant Negro and his allies have felt it necessary to posit integration as the key objective. In much the same way, Jews have been driven to the political left because the anti-Semites are on the right. Any movement for separation must fly in the face of the American experience and of the changes that have and are taking place. As James Baldwin realized in his Parisian exile, whatever else the American Negro may be, he is fundamentally American.[23]

[21] Although the Muslims are critical of the Bible, they frequently quote from it to support the veracity of their prophecies.

[22] Elijah Muhammad states: "No one after death has ever gone any place but where they were carried. There is no heaven or hell other than on earth for you and me, and Jesus was no exception. His body is still . . . in Palestine and will remain there" (Lincoln, op. cit., p. 123).

It is interesting to note that although the black nationalists are strong in rejecting Christianity and its otherworldly emphasis, their heavy reliance on a deterministic Allah may nevertheless lead to political inactivity. Essien-Udom notes: "The attainment of black power is relegated to the intervention of Almighty Allah sometime in the future. . . . Not unlike other religionists the Muslims too may wait for all eternity for the coming of the Messiah, the predicted apocalypse in 1970 notwithstanding" (op. cit., pp. 313–314). Opposition to this policy of nonengagement was a factor in Malcolm's X's breaking with the Muslims.

It was noted in the last chapter that in order for religion to be socially relevant it must place heavy emphasis on the here and now and in addition involve the notion that men, as opposed or in addition to, a deterministic God, may play a crucial role in the structuring of human affairs.

[23] A recent remark of Baldwin's is also relevant in this context: "I remember coming home from school, you can guess how young I must have been, and my mother asked me if my teacher was colored or white, and I said she was a little bit colored and a little bit white. . . . And as a matter of fact I was right. That's part of the dilemma of being an American Negro; that one is a little bit colored and a little bit white, and not only in physical terms but in the head and in the heart" (James Baldwin in Kenneth Clark, ed., The Negro Protest, Boston: Beacon Press, 1963). Parenthetically, although few realize it, "white" Americans are also a little bit colored.

While black nationalist sympathizers were much more pessimistic about their prospects in American society than were other Negroes, one of the interesting things our data revealed was the optimism of the vast majority of those surveyed. The belief that progress is being made and that a brighter future can come without radical change no doubt hinders receptiveness to the Muslim appeal, as well as to other radical solutions.

Another factor which would seem to hinder the Muslims is the black man's traditional attachment to Christianity. Even in its activist social gospel form, which may provide impetus to race protest, it still preaches nonviolence, the brotherhood of man, and love for one's enemy, and hence does not seem likely to inspire support for the nationalists. So long as Christianity either of an otherworldly or a social gospel variety retains its hold over American black men, it will remain an obstacle to black nationalist support.

In Chapter 2 it was noted that a major theory of extremist behavior suggests that, in times of severe crisis, those isolated and in lower social positions, being unsophisticated and having little to lose but their degradation, are more likely than the privileged to support movements for radical social change that go outside the framework of established values. However, in normal times, the unsophisticated and alienated are disproportionately apathetic. Consistent with this theory, Chapter 2 found that a relatively large segment of the more depressed and alienated part of the black community did not score as militant. However, we have now seen that those few who are sympathetic to black nationalism are relatively low in both social position and social participation.

Unless or until a major economic crisis or a series of important and sustained civil rights setbacks shakes the optimism of middle-class Negroes or the apathy of the Negro masses, Negroes will probably continue to be relatively unresponsive to the appeals of the black nationalists. And even then, increased feelings of despair and futility may be the predominant consequence. Such events might well increase acts of racial violence and increase feelings of hostility without this energy becoming channeled into an organized movement for social change. In the event of such an occurrence, however, it seems reasonable to conclude that black nationalists will be disproportionately drawn from the more deprived and isolated segments of the black community and will be predominantly younger males, raised in big cities outside the South.

Barring such catastrophes, the data clearly indicate a number of major impediments to black nationalist, and especially Muslim, aspirations. For the Muslims to gain any appreciable support they probably would have to surrender the eschatological and apocalyptic components of their ideology. They would have to cease to be a religion in order to become a mass movement. Furthermore, they would have to modify their antipathy toward the civil rights struggle, for American Negroes want in, not out. They might also need to ease the puritanical moral demands they impose on members. In short, they would have to become much more like a conventional civil rights organization, perhaps attracting support by being the most militant civil rights group. The movement which Malcolm X tried to get started after his break with the Muslims did in fact embody many of these changes.

We have seen in this chapter that American Negroes have rejected the solutions to the race problem advocated by the Muslims. In the chapters that follow we shall see the extent to which they agree with Muslim indictments of the white man.

Negroes and Jews

The white man is the man they must meet every morning when they go to work in the garment district; the man . . . when the rent is due; the man . . . when they go to the pawnshop; the man who comes and sells things on credit; the man who gets work when they cannot . . . the man, the man, the white man, the goddamn white man!

—*Louis Lomax*

They [Jews] understand colored better because they have been through some of the same kind of discrimination. They have more heart. They are more in sympathy with our people's problems.

—*Laundry worker, Manhattan*

He is a benefactor for our people. I have always felt friendly toward a Jew. There is a distinct difference between a Jew and a white man and I hate a white man.

—*Foundry worker, Pittsburgh*

The widespread and enduring character of anti-Semitism in American life forces the conclusion that in a certain sense anti-Semitism is a "normal" aspect of our culture. The average American feels at least some ambivalence toward his Jewish countrymen. As Americans, Negroes are exposed to this common anti-Semitic component of our culture, and negative attitudes toward Jews may be as "normal," in the sense of being as typical, among Negroes as among whites. Indeed, according to James Baldwin, anti-Semitism is common in the Negro community: "I remember meeting no Negro in the years of my growing up, in my family or out of it, who would really ever trust a Jew, and few who did not indeed, exhibit for them the blackest contempt."[1]

Recently, however, many have come to believe that anti-Semitism among Negroes represents something more than a mere reflection of the anti-

[1] James Baldwin, *Notes of a Native Son*, Boston, Beacon Press, 1962, p. 68.

Jewish component of our common culture. Negroes, it is claimed, have special sources of anti-Semitism, and are more likely to be hostile toward Jews than are whites. It is often further claimed that Negroes feel greater hostility toward Jewish whites than they do toward non-Jewish whites. These interpretations cite the disproportionate role of Jewish merchants and landlords in the Negro ghettoes as a source of bitter experience which provides a special focus and impetus to Negro anti-Semitism. The destruction of Jewish-owned stores[2] during recent riots has been interpreted as a clear manifestation of the intensity of Negro anti-Semitism.

But it is also the case that Jews have been prominent in the Negro struggle for social justice, and that Jews share with Negroes many of the problems of an excluded and discriminated-against minority group. These facts suggest that there is a basis for special sympathy between Jews and Negroes, and that Negroes will be found to be less anti-Semitic than whites.

Thus, there are plausible reasons for several quite different expectations about Negro anti-Semitism.

1. That it is equally common among Negroes and whites because it stems from the same cultural sources;

2. That Negroes have a special set of grievances against Jews which makes them dislike Jews more than they dislike other whites;

3. That a special affinity between Jews and Negroes makes them less anti-Semitic than whites, and indeed to prefer Jews to other whites.

In this chapter we try to discover which of these expectations about Negro anti-Semitism is correct. How widespread is anti-Semitism among Negroes? How does it compare with anti-Semitism among whites? How do attitudes toward Jewish whites compare with attitudes toward non-Jewish whites? And how do certain factors unique to Negro-Jewish relationships influence anti-Semitism?

An Index of Anti-Semitism

Before we may ask about the current state of Negro anti-Semitism, it is necessary to select some empirical measure of anti-Semitism. The interviews contained questions designed to assess agreement with a number of the stereotypes about Jews which are typical elements in anti-Semitic ideology.[3] The extent of anti-Semitism revealed by these questions varied considerably; some were widely agreed to; others were accepted by only a minority of

[2] According to one observer, 80 per cent of the furniture stores, 60 per cent of the food markets, and 54 per cent of the liquor stores burned and looted in the Watts riot were owned by Jews (Paul Jacobs, "Negro-Jewish Relations in America," *Midstream*, December 1966, p. 53).

[3] An extensive analysis of the meaning and validity of these items will appear in the volume reporting the national study of anti-Semitism previously referred to.

respondents.[4] For example, only 12 per cent said "yes" to the question "Do you think the Jews have too much power in the United States?"; only 11 per cent said "false" to the statement "Jews are warm and friendly people," and only 14 per cent disagreed with the statement "The more contact a person has with Jewish people the more he gets to like them." On the other hand, 59 per cent said "true" to the statement "Jews are more willing than others to use shady practices to get what they want" and 44 per cent agreed that "Jewish businessmen are so shrewd and tricky that other people

Table 76. ATTITUDES TOWARD JEWS BY REGION[a]

	Metro.	N.Y.	Chic.	Atl.	Birm.	Total
"Jews have too much power in the United States."						
True	15%	18%	5%	9%	7%	12%
False	74	73	77	78	79	76
Don't know	11	9	8	13	14	12
Total	100%	100%	100%	100%	100%	100%
"Jews are warm and friendly people."						
True	79%	71%	85%	85%	84%	81%
False	12	16	11	8	7	11
Don't know	9	13	4	7	9	8
Total	100%	100%	100%	100%	100%	100%
"The more contact a person has with Jewish people, the more he gets to like them."						
True	75%	59%	74%	84%	80%	75%
False	15	29	16	8	8	14
Don't know	10	12	10	8	12	11
Total	100%	100%	100%	100%	100%	100%
"Jews are more willing than others to use shady practices to get what they want."						
True	62%	56%	62%	61%	54%	59%
False	28	36	29	25	28	29
Don't know	10	8	9	14	18	12
Total	100%	100%	100%	100%	100%	100%
"Jewish businessmen are so shrewd and tricky that other people don't have a fair chance in competition."						
True	48%	44%	50%	44%	39%	44%
False	38	44	37	29	41	38
Don't know	14	12	13	27	20	17
Total	100%	100%	100%	100%	100%	100%

[4] Because preliminary analysis, as well as common sense, suggested that using white interviewers to ask Negroes about attitudes toward whites biased responses, those subjects from the metropolitan area sample who were interviewed by whites (because no Negro interviewers were available) are excluded from all analysis of intergroup attitudes among Negroes.

Table 76.   (*Continued*)

	Metro.	N.Y.	Chic.	Atl.	Birm.	Total
"Jews stick together too much."						
True	45%	44%	51%	39%	40%	43%
False	49	50	44	51	51	50
Don't know	6	6	5	10	9	7
Total	100%	100%	100%	100%	100%	100%
"Jews don't care what happens to anyone but their own kind."						
True	39%	38%	44%	40%	32%	38%
False	51	52	49	46	49	50
Don't know	10	10	7	14	19	12
Total	100%	100%	100%	100%	100%	100%
"Jews are just as honest as other businessmen."						
True	59%	59%	57%	60%	69%	61%
False	31	33	33	30	19	29
Don't know	10	8	10	10	12	10
Total	100%	100%	100%	100%	100%	100%
Number	(330)	(190)	(133)	(198)	(200)	(957)[b]
"Jews have too much power in the business world."[c]						
True	29%	38%	34%	24%	13%	26%
False	60	56	58	63	74	63
Don't know	11	6	8	13	13	11
Total	100%	100%	100%	100%	100%	100%
Number	(297)	(164)	(121)	(163)	(198)	(870)

[a] In this and all subsequent tables, the 162 cases from the metropolitan area sample who were interviewed by whites are excluded. Furthermore, the number of respondents in each sample remains approximately the same, as shown in Table 76, eighth question, unless the contrary is indicated.

[b] As noted in Table 1, those interviews from the metropolitan area sample which occurred in New York (44 cases) and in Chicago (54 cases) have been reported in both the metropolitan sample and the New York and Chicago samples. Hence the total number of respondents reported in this column, and throughout this chapter, is less than the sum of the numbers for the samples shown separately.

[c] Due to a defective printing format, not all respondents were asked this question.

don't have a fair chance in competition." For two of the remaining statements in Table 76—"Jews stick together too much" and "Jews don't care what happens to anyone but their own kind"—roughly four out of ten gave the anti-Semitic response. For the last two items in the table—"Jews have too much power in the business world" and "Jews are just as honest as other businessmen"—just under three out of ten gave an invidious response.

It is interesting to note that here again the percentage of respondents who said "don't know" or had no opinion is relatively small, although it is slightly larger than the percentage having no opinion on the questions dealing with civil rights.

These statements about Jews vary considerably both in content and extent to which they are believed. By combining them into an index of anti-Semitism, an individual's orientation to Jews can be more adequately characterized than by simply considering single items. The items include beliefs about Jewish economic behavior, clannishness, and power, all components of traditional anti-Semitism. In addition, the Anti-Semitism Index includes two items on Jewish sociability (thinking that Jews are warm and friendly people and that contact with Jews increases friendly feelings). These questions, which were worded positively, help control for acquiescence.[5]

This index measures *beliefs* about Jews, not the emotional feeling accompanying such beliefs or an individual's willingness to engage in overt discriminatory behavior. The relation among beliefs, emotions, and overt action is a highly complex one, highly dependent on situational factors. Still, while the attitudes measured here do not necessarily determine overt behavior, they may have important implications for it.

In constructing the index, one point was given for every response of an anti-Semitic nature; those who said "don't know" to an item or who did not give an anti-Semitic response were scored zero.[6] Scores thus run from zero to nine. From Table 77 it can be seen that respondents are clustered at the lower end of the index. As scores increase from zero to nine, at each interval there is a decrease in the proportion of the sample who fall at that point. Thus, 19 per cent of the combined samples gave no anti-Semitic responses, and this percentage decreases consistently to 1 per cent who gave the anti-Semitic response to all nine questions. The average score on the index was 2.74; thus, out of the nine questions asked, the average respondent exhibited anti-Semitism on almost three.

For analysis, respondents were combined into three categories. Those with scores of zero or one on the index were considered non-anti-Semitic. Those with scores of two, three, or four were classified as low in anti-Semitism. Only those with scores of five or more were considered to be anti-Semitic. At times, this last group will be separated into those high on

[5] Studies have shown that some proportion of the public tends to agree with any statement made in a survey regardless of content. This tendency to agree indiscriminately is called acquiescence. By including these two postively worded items (as well as the positively worded item about Jews being just as honest as other businessmen), the chance that those who scored as anti-Semitic received their scores because of acquiescence is greatly reduced. Those scored as anti-Semitic (as well as those considered not at all anti-Semitic) had to demonstrate much greater discrimination in their response pattern than those scored in the middle of the index.

[6] The "don't knows" for most people seemed to represent a genuine lack of opinion rather than evasiveness. This is inferred from the fact that the "don't knows" had much less contact with Jews and had less knowledge about them.

anti-Semitism (scores of five or six) and those very high (scores of seven, eight, or nine). In order for an individual to be considered anti-Semitic, he had to have agreed to five or more items, well above the average number of items agreed to. These people are anti-Semites in the sense that they were more likely to acknowledge anti-Semitic beliefs than was the average respondent, and gave an anti-Semitic response a majority of the time. They also are anti-Semitic in the sense that they tended to accept negative statements about Jews in a wide variety of areas.

Table 77. DISTRIBUTION OF SCORES ON INDEX OF ANTI-SEMITISM

Score on Index of Anti-Semitism	Per Cent of Sample	Number[a]	Collapsed Scores
0	19%	(181)	36% non-anti-Semitic
1	17	(162)	
2	15	(138)	40% low on anti-Semitism
3	14	(136)	
4	11	(106)	
5	10	(89)	18% high on anti-Semitism
6	8	(72)	
7	3	(29)	6% very high on anti-Semitism
8	2	(24)	
9	1	(5)	
Total	100%		
Number	(942)		

Average score 2.74

[a] This table excludes 162 cases interviewed by a white person and 15 cases in which it was not possible to score the respondent either because one or more of the questions were not asked or the respondent refused to answer. In addition, due to a defective printing format, 87 respondents were not asked the question concerning power in the business world. Because they were so numerous these cases were not dropped from the index; rather, it was assumed that the response would not have been anti-Semitic, since all the individuals involved had indicated that they did not think Jews have too much power in the United States. The probability is that only 19 would have given an anti-Semitic response to the business question. Hence, the amount of error involved in assuming a non-anti-Semitic response is minimal.

Index Validity

An analysis of the intercorrelations among items included in the index revealed that the items are powerfully related to one another, and that scores on the index were obtained in a systematic fashion. The nature of response patterns provides important insights into the nature of contemporary Negro anti-Semitism.

Table 78. EXTERNAL VALIDATION OF INDEX OF ANTI-SEMITISM

	Score on Index of Anti-Semitism										
	0	1	2	3	4	5	6	7	8	9	Total
"Do you think that something should be done to take some power away from the Jews?" *(asked only of those who felt Jews had too much power in the business world)*											
"Yes"	0%	0%	17%	17%	31%	33%	42%	41%	58%	60%	35%
Number											(244)
"The Jews have suffered through no fault of their own."											
Per cent agreeing	47	41	45	35	33	27	28	35	13	0	37%
Number											(942)

Among those who accepted anti-Semitic beliefs, the vast majority accepted items suggesting that Jews are somehow unethical or unfair in their business practices; even a great many of those with scores of only two or three on the index held such beliefs. Those with scores of four or more were likely to go on and accept beliefs about Jewish clannishness. In contrast, the national study of anti-Semitism found that whites were most likely to accept statements about Jewish clannishness and less likely to accept statements impugning Jewish business ethics. Only among those with scores of six or more was the traditional conspiratorial item about Jewish power widely accepted, and only those with scores of seven or higher tended to go out of their way to reject the positively worded items about Jewish sociability.

That Negroes should be most prone to negative stereotypes about Jewish economic behavior and less prone to stereotypes about Jewish clannishness seems logical when examined in light of the impoverishment of the Negro and the involvement of Jews in the ghetto economic life. Negroes do, of course, see Jews as clannish though it is possible that they see all whites as sticking together too much and, indeed, as generally dishonest in their business dealings with Negroes. The items on sociability and Jewish power (with its possible implications for an international Jewish conspiracy) are much less salient for Negroes, and hence the fact that only a small minority of the sample accepted them is understandable. But it must be acknowledged that these beliefs are given little support by whites, and thus this does not indicate a peculiarly Negro variety of anti-Semitism.

External evidence of the validity of the index is provided by the data in Table 78 where it is shown that, as score on the index increases, so does the percentage giving the anti-Semitic response to related items. Those who felt that Jews had too much power in the United States or in the business world were asked if they thought something should be done to take some power away from the Jews. It can be seen that the percentage saying "yes" to this question steadily increases from 0 per cent for those with scores of one to 60 per cent for those with a score of nine. Though the relation is less systematic, the percentage thinking that "Jews have suffered through no fault of their own" decreases from 47 per cent among those with scores of zero to 13 per cent and 0 per cent for those with scores of eight and nine.

Thus the Anti-Semitism Index appears valid in the three ways discussed in Chapter 2. The items included certainly seem to measure negative attitudes toward Jews, they are positively related to each other, and taken together they are useful in predicting responses to related questions not included in the index.

The extent of anti-Semitism among Negroes differs considerably by region. High scores on the index were more common among those living outside the South. In each of our non-Southern samples (the nationwide metropolitan area and New York and Chicago) roughly three in ten appeared as anti-Semitic, that is, gave an anti-Semitic response to five or more of the nine items (Table 79).[7] Furthermore, 7 per cent of the metropoiltan area sample, 9 per cent in Chicago, and 11 per cent in New York City scored as very high on anti-Semitism. An additional four out of ten were low, accepting some anti-Semitic statements but not others, but still tending to reject more than they accept. Finally, among those outside the South, slightly more than three out of ten showed no signs of anti-Semitism in the sense that they gave no anti-Semitic responses or at most one. In the South,

Table 79. ANTI-SEMITISM BY REGION

Score on Anti-Semitism Index	Metro	N.Y.	Chic.	Atl.	Birm.
Non-anti-Semitic (0, 1)	34%	33%	30%	38%	42%
Low (2, 3, 4)	38	39	40	43	44
High (5, 6)	21	17	21	14	13
Very high (7, 8, 9)	7	11	9	5	1
High plus very high	28%	28%	30%	19%	14%
Total	100%	100%	100%	100%	100%

on the other hand, less than one in five scored as anti-Semitic. In Atlanta, 5 per cent scored as very high on anti-Semitism while in Birmingham this figure was only 1 per cent. About four out of ten Southerners showed no signs of anti-Jewish feeling.[8]

Independent of the current level of anti-Semitism among Negroes is the impressionistic assertion made by many that anti-Semitism among black

[7] Most relevant to any discussion of Negroes and Jews is of course the extent of anti-Negro attitudes among Jews. As part of the white majority and people with a strong communal spirit, the presence of what may be interpreted as anti-Negro attitudes on the part of many Jews is not surprising.

Data from the Survey Research Center's national study reveals that while Jews were much more tolerant than white Protestants and Catholics some anti-Negro sentiment was certainly present. For example, rougly three out of ten felt that "Negroes are lazy and don't like to work hard," that "Before Negroes are given equal rights, they have to show that they deserve them" and that "Negroes are demanding more than they have a right to." Furthermore, although only one Jew in five did not want his children to go to school with Negroes and felt that there should be a law against marriages between whites and Negroes more than seven out of ten felt that "an owner of property should not have to sell to Negroes if he doesn't want to."

As the civil rights struggle becomes more prominent in the North and as Jews and other whites come to be more directly affected by it, an increase in anti-Negro sentiment and the surfacing of latent hostility seem likely. A study of Jewish response to a program to desegregate several New York City grammar schools indicates that approximately seven out of ten Jews were against the desegregation proposal. The figure for white Catholics was about the same (Kurt and Gladys Lang, "Resistance to School Desegregation: A Case Study of Backlash Among Jews," in Bernard E. Segal, ed., Racial and Ethnic Relations, New York, Thomas Y. Crowell, 1966).

[8] It should be noted that this Southern pattern is based on the South's two largest urban areas and these cities may not be representative of other Southern metropolitan areas or of Southern rural areas.

Americans is on the increase.[9] One way of measuring this would be to inter-view the same people about their feelings toward Jews at different points in time. This the present study could not do. However, it did ask people to compare their present feelings toward Jews with their feelings in the past. Respondents were asked the question "Thinking of Jews as a group, would you say you feel more friendly toward them now than you used to, less friendly, or have you always felt as you do now?" Most of those interviewed said that they felt the same toward Jews now as in the past. However, among those who reported a change in their feelings, the overwhelming majority indicated that this change has been in a positive direction (Table 80). Of those who reported feeling differently toward Jews, almost 90 per cent said that they now felt more friendly than they used to. Differences by region were slight.[10]

Table 80.   FEELINGS OF FRIENDSHIP TOWARD JEWS

Reply to: "Thinking of Jews as a group, would you say you feel more friendly toward them now than you used to, less friendly, or have you always felt as you do now?"

More friendly	12%
Less friendly	1
Same	85
Don't know	2
Total	100%
Number	(956)
Per cent more friendly[a]	88%
Number	(127)

[a] Among those who report feeling either more or less friendly.

Respondents were asked why they now felt differently and, among those who felt more friendly, comments almost always dealt in some way with Jewish support of civil rights:

They seem more friendly toward Negroes. He has done more on our fight toward civil rights. They have integrated more of their places faster.
> —*Railroad club car attendant, St. Louis*

I feel more friendly now because Jews have spoken out for the Negro cause. Have helped demonstrate and have written articles in papers saying the Negro has been treated unfair.
> —*Crane operator, Birmingham*

[9] For example, Louis Lomax, *The Negro Revolt,* New York, Harper & Row, 1962, p. 184; and B. Berry, *Race and Ethnic Relations,* Boston, Houghton Mifflin, 1958, p. 448; and numerous articles in "Negro-Jewish Relations in America," *Midstream,* December 1966.

[10] Here and in many subsequent tables the marginal distribution by area of the country is not shown; this is because no important differences emerge when region is controlled for.

I see the way they try now to help Negroes. They will more readily speak to you.

—Forklift operator, Atlanta

They are a member of the CORE. Maybe the Jews haven't changed but the CORE has made me notice them. . . . During the bombing here in Birmingham, many of them gave food, money and clothing.

—Ice truck worker, Birmingham

They have helped colored people more by radio and television and through all the means of communication. Their philosophy has helped the Negro in recent years. They seem more willing to join other groups in fighting for the rights of all people.

—Shirt ironer, New York

This perception of increased Jewish support for civil rights was also revealed in comments offered to a question which asked, "Do you think that Jews have changed in some ways in recent years?" About one in four felt that Jews had changed. When asked how Jews had changed, the largest percentage again answered in terms of civil rights. However, many respondents also felt that Jews had changed in the sense of becoming more assimilated. For example:

Their religion, thoughts and ways of living. Even their appearance [has changed]. It's impossible to distinguish if they are Jewish.

—Post office clerk, Chicago

You used not to be able to open your door but what one wasn't there trying to sell you some kind of inferior junk for double the price it was really worth. You just don't see them now doing that.

—Housewife, Birmingham

The Jew is more Americanized. He is getting more and more like the American white man. He is more socially inclined.

—Fireman, Pittsburgh

They have changed, more Americanized in dress, speech, manners, even marrying outside their race.

—Retired clerk, Chicago

Assimilation was also mentioned by many white Americans in the national study of anti-Semitism. It would seem to suggest that anti-Semitism, to the degree that it was related to the perception of Jews as aliens, readily identifiable on the basis of their foreign speech and behavior, might be declining.

Jewish and Non-Jewish Whites

It has been seen that many Negro Americans indicate acceptance of anti-Semitic beliefs in an interview situation. But the question remains: Is this hostility directed against Jews per se, or is it simply part of a general hostility toward whites? Are Jews singled out from non-Jewish whites for special hostility by Negroes? Are Jews a scapegoat for Negro discontent, as has often been suggested?[11]

Any judgment of a special Negro affinity for anti-Semitism requires evidence that Negroes do single out Jews negatively. Attitudes toward Jews must be examined within the context of attitudes toward non-Jewish whites, or whites in general. The next chapter will take up this analysis in greater

Table 81. ATTITUDES TOWARD JEWISH AND NON-JEWISH WHITES BY REGION

	Metro.	N.Y.	Chic.	Atl.	Birm.	Total
Employer						
Better to work for a Jew	31%	36%	33%	36%	35%	34%
Better to work for a non-Jew	23	19	23	16	15	19
About the same	10	16	12	10	2	10
Don't know	36	29	32	38	48	37
Total	100%	100%	100%	100%	100%	100%
Merchant						
Jewish store owners better than other white store owners	16%	10%	15%	32%	28%	20%
Jewish store owners worse	9	7	8	4	5	7
About the same	70	79	71	60	61	68
Don't know	5	4	6	4	6	5
Total	100%	100%	100%	100%	100%	100%
Landlord						
Jewish landlords better than other white landlords	25%	19%	22%	31%	19%	24%
Jewish landlords worse	12	11	7	4	4	7
About the same	29	42	37	27	27	32
Don't know	34	38	34	38	50	37
Total	100%	100%	100%	100%	100%	100%

[11] For example, Srole notes, "the inevitable hostility, overt or covert, which Negroes bear toward whites and the white 'system' is specially directed toward Jews." ("Remarks by Discussant Leo Srole," *Jewish Social Studies,* January 1965, p. 31). Simpson and Yinger note: "Negro anti-Semitism, not uncommon among urban Negroes, is partly a displaced prejudice, using another minority group as a substitute target for the hostilities felt toward the more powerful white gentiles" (George Simpson and Milton Yinger, *Racial and Cultural Minorities,* New York, Harper & Row, rev. ed., 1958, p. 220). Many other references could be cited.

It is often further suggested that anti-Semitism offers a means of venting hostility toward the white man (as Jew) and yet identifying with the dominant white group who often express similar ideas.

detail. As a necessary preliminary, we first consider some specific questions which asked Negroes to contrast Jewish and non-Jewish whites.

In response to the question "Do you think it is better to work for a Jewish person or for a white person who is not Jewish?" about half the sample responded "the same" or "don't know."[12] But the remainder of the sample was much more likely to favor a Jewish employer over a non-Jewish one, particularly in New York City (36 to 19 per cent), Atlanta (36 to 16 per cent), and Birmingham (35 to 15 per cent). Similarly when asked: "Compared to other white store owners, do you think Jewish store owners are better, worse, or about the same?" roughly seven out of ten respondents made no distinction. However, in those cases where a distinction was made, there was a slight tendency in the North and a pronounced tendency in the South to see Jews as better (in Atlanta 32 per cent felt Jewish store owners were better as against only 4 per cent who said they were worse; in Birmingham these figures were 28 and 5 per cent). Even when asked to compare Jewish landlords with non-Jewish white landlords, the situation was the same. Most respondents did not make a distinction, but when they did, Jews again were seen in a more favorable light than non-Jews[13] (Table 81).

These various items were combined into an index of attitudes toward Jewish and non-Jewish whites. For the situations asked about, Jews are by and large not singled out as being worse than other whites, nor are they generally seen as better than other whites (Table 82). Just as most whites

Table 82.   INDEX OF ATTITUDES TOWARD JEWISH AND NON-JEWISH WHITES

	Score on Index	Per Cent of Sample	
Jews better	0	6%	20%
	1	14	
Jews neither better nor worse	2	24	75%
	3	39	
	4	12	
Jews worse	5	4	5%
	6	1	
Total		100%	
Number		(949)	

[12] Some of those who responded "don't know" said they really could not say because they had worked for, or rented, from Jews alone, and hence had no basis for comparison.

[13] This finding is interesting when considered in light of Kenneth Clark's statement that "antagonism toward the 'Jewish landlord' is so common as to have become almost an integral aspect of the folk culture of the northern urban Negro . . . and all his obvious housing ills are attributed to the greed and avarice of the Jewish landlord" ("Candor on Negro-Jewish Relations," *Commentary*, February 1946, p. 8).

fail to make a distinction between Negro Protestants and Negro Catholics, or between native-born Negroes and West Indians, for a majority of our Negro respondents "white folks is jes white folks" as one man put it.[14] Approximately three out of four respondents had scores in the middle of the index (two, three, or four) indicating that no distinction was made or that differentiation between Jewish and non-Jewish whites was not consistent. This is congruent with the pattern to be observed in the next chapter where, for most respondents, degree of hostility toward Jews is roughly comparable to degree of hostility toward whites generally. The major fact to be recognized is that among 25 per cent of Negroes who made a distinction between Jewish and non-Jewish whites, *Jews were seen in a more favorable light than other whites by a four-to-one ratio.*[15]

In considering this measure in relation to the Anti-Semitism Index, further assessment of the scapegoat interpretation is possible. The majority of anti-Semitic Negroes did not see Jews as different from other whites. However, when a distinction was made, even among anti-Semites there was a slight tendency to see Jews as better than other whites, not worse (Table 83). If the present study is any indication, the scapegoat interpretation does not have widespread applicability.[16] Furthermore, six of seven studies done in the past twenty years report that Jews are seen in a more favorable

[14] A report about the pattern of rioting in Philadelphia, where many Jewish-owned stores were attacked, is consistent with this. There "not one eyewitness to the riot recalls the mobs shouting anti-Semitic slogans, although anti-white epithets abounded. . . . It was as whites and as merchants and realtors rather than as Jews *per se* that they bore the brunt of the Negro's attack" (Lenora Benson, *Case Study of a Riot,* New York, American Jewish Committee, 1966, p. 46). Similarly a large number of Jewish-owned businesses were destroyed in Watts (see footnote 2, p. 127); yet when Watts residents were asked who the targets of attack were, only 5 per cent singled out the Jews, although eight out of ten mentioned whites or merchants. (D. O. Sears, "Riot Activity and Evaluation: An Overview of the Negro Survey," paper prepared for the American Psychological Association Conference in New York, September 1966.)

[15] Although their statements are sometimes contradictory, even the militantly anti-white Muslims have occasionally suggested that Jews are better than other whites. An article in *Muhammad Speaks* (April 15, 1966) says: "As often pointed out by the Honorable Elijah Muhammad, the Jewish people have a greater sense of justice and humanness than their white gentile brothers. . . . Jewish people have shown a greater sympathy toward the plight of black peoples . . . and have developed a higher sense of ethic, less tainted with the crimes of colonialism, white supremacy and prejudice characterizing the Christians."

Malcolm X reports that, before coming to agree that all white men were devils, he felt that "Jews were different . . . I had known good ones . . . I knew them, men and women, and liked them" (E. U. Essien-Udom, *Black Nationalism,* New York, Dell, 1964, p. 115). Of course, contrary statements made by Muslim spokesmen could also be cited.

[16] In like manner, the next chapter reports that only 4 per cent of those scored as anti-Semitic were free of general antiwhite feelings. One might be led to question Baldwin's assertion "But just as society must have a scapegoat, so hatred must have a symbol. Georgia has the Negro and Harlem has the Jew" (Baldwin, *Notes,* p. 72). Even in New York City, only one in eight who scored as anti-Semitic felt Jews to be worse than other whites in the situations asked about.

light than other whites or that less hostility is expressed toward them than toward other whites.[17]

The minority of the sample who did make a distinction between Jews and non-Jews were asked why they felt this way, and some comments are revealing:

Table 83.   ATTITUDES TOWARD JEWISH AND NON-JEWISH WHITES BY ANTI-SEMITISM

Score on Index of Attitudes Toward Jewish and non-Jewish whites	Anti-Semitic	Low on Anti-Semitism	Not Anti-Semitic
Jews better (0, 1)	21%	23%	16%
Jews same (2, 3, 4)	62	75	82
Jews worse (5, 6)	17	2	2
Total	100%	100%	100%
Number	(219)	(375)	(338)

[17] J. A. Bayton and E. F. Byoune, "Racio-national Stereotypes Held by Negroes," *Journal of Negro Education*, 1947, pp. 49–56; E. T. Prothro and J. A. Jensen, "Comparison of Some Ethnic and Religious Attitudes of Negro and White College Students in the Deep South," *Social Forces,* May 1952, pp. 426–428; R. L. Simpson, "Factors in the Attitudes of Two Minority Groups Toward Each Other," M.A. thesis, Cornell University, 1952.

Studies by Cothran and by McDaniel and Babchuk found Jews were seen as more sympathetic than other whites (Tilman C. Cothran, "Negro Conceptions of White People in a Northeastern City," *American Journal of Sociology,* March 1951; and P. McDaniel and N. Babchuk, "Negro Conceptions of White People," *Phylon,* Spring 1960, pp. 7–19).

The *Newsweek* survey reported on by Brink and Harris indicated that Jews were seen as more helpful with respect to the struggle for Negro rights than ten of fourteen groups (William Brink and Louis Harris, *The Negro Revolution in America,* New York, Simon and Schuster, 1964, p. 133).

The only contrary evidence is reported in G. Lenski, *The Religious Factor,* New York, Doubleday, 1963, pp. 60–71.

The picture with respect to social distance feelings is less clear. Two studies have found feelings of social distance to be less toward Jews than toward white southerners, and while one of these studies reports feelings of social distance to be the same toward Jews and Northern whites in general, the other suggests a preference for Northern whites over Jews. (J. B. Edlefsen, "Social Distance Attitudes of Negro College Students," *Phylon,* I, 1956, pp. 79–83, and A. Goins and M. Meenes, "Ethnic and Class Preferences Among Negro College Students," *Journal of Negro Education,* Spring 1960.

Another study reports social distance feelings to be about the same toward Jewish whites as whites in general, and still another found less social distance feelings toward the latter. (J. Stanley Grey and A. H. Thompson, "The Ethnic Prejudices of White and Negro College Students," *Journal of Abnormal and Social Psychology,* April 1953, and R. Derbyshire and E. Brody "Social Distance and Identity Conflict in Negro College Students," *Sociology and Social Research,* April 1964.

Better to Work for a Jewish Person

A Jew will give you an advance in your pay quicker than a cracker will. A Jew seems to feel that the people who work for him is part of his responsibility. If you need medical care, a Jew sees that you get that and holds your job for you. A cracker lets you go when you get sick. A Jew stick by you for the good you have been. I know several Jews who still pay rent, buy groceries, helping people who used to work for them, but now they are sick.

—Auto mechanic, Atlanta

They are not so quick to fire you as other people. They have more patience with you . . . they seem to find jobs for Negroes.

—Shirt ironer, New York

I felt he was a relative. I could go to him with my problems and he would help me. Moneywise, he goes out of his way to help.

—Automobile painter, Chicago

They treat you better. They don't stand over and watch you. They pay you better than others. If you can do jobs better, they let you know it. They explain to you that they would like for you to have certain jobs—but because of certain other white workers it makes it impossible.

—Student nurse, Birmingham

They treat you as a man, not someone beneath them. They give you due credit for your abilities.

—Butcher, Chicago

They hire the colored quicker, also good to the colored woman. A Jew will allow us a chance to a certain extent to work for him, he is just an all-round friend to the colored man.

—Truck driver, Philadelphia

Well I found a lot of white people who are not Jewish who think no matter how much education we get we still have a place. Jews mention nothing about color—not even to their children.

—Housewife, New York

Better to Work for a Non-Jewish White

'Cause the Jews have a tendency to be cheap, like keeping the money for themselves. I don't think they believe in giving a fair salary. They want to work you to death for just a little pay.

—Housewife, Chicago

I find that Jews have a standard line of sympathy which I dislike. We don't need sympathy. Our forefathers shared disaster may be true but what I want is to be hired on my capabilities. They seem to use this sympathy as an excuse to pay me less money.

—Unemployed secretary, New York

I worked for a Jewish family. They expect more out of you. You can't use soap powder or certain ones. You have to wash all those special dishes for special occasions. It's a lot of special fussin'. . . . They never let you rest even for a minute. They keep after you and always have another job ready for you as soon as you finish up one. They hound you and you are dead tired and plumb wore out by the end of the day.

—*Maid, McKeesport, Pennsylvania*

It is better to work for someone who is not Jewish because you get a better salary and a shorter working day. They will not expect you to work when you are sick.

—*Crane operator, Birmingham*

I consider gentiles as whites not Jews. Jews are just Jews not white. Someone not Jewish they treat you with respect in their house and on the job, make you feel like a human being. They pay you lots more money, working conditions much better. Jews don't trust you, they don't treat you right, they take advantage of you, put more work on you. No feeling for you, treat you like an animal.

—*Presser in a dress factory, New York*

In my opinion, I don't like Jewish food. You know when they have Yom Kippur and things like that, you get very little to eat. You have to eat what they eat. When you have a sleep-in job, you have to do about the same things for everybody, so I guess my main objection is to the food in Jewish homes.

—*Nurse's aide, Brooklyn*

Jewish Store Owners Better

They are more nicer to the colored people than the Southern whites to me. They treat you just like you were white or a Jew. I could buy groceries on credit at the Jewish store and some of these white store owners won't even cash my check.

—*Nurse's aide, Atlanta*

They will let you have things a little cheaper than other white people. They will cut the price on goods so that you won't leave the store without buying. They will give you a job quicker in their stores too.

—*Machine operator, New York*

The way I think they are better they sell something cheaper and gain more. If they have an item for 89¢ they sell it for 69¢ and count on volume to make more money. The other whites stick to selling the 89¢ item for its regular price and sell only one.

—*Salesman, Chicago*

He will give you a better chance to pay bills—just call him when you don't have the money and he will give you time to pay and talk very courteous to you. He will show you all qualities of goods for your selection. The other race will show you goods depending how you look and are dressed. The Jew will always put a handle on your name and not just call you Mary or Susie. They call you Mrs. or Miss and they also address you properly on their mail that is sent to you.

—Practical nurse, Birmingham

Well, they treat you a little better. They give you a little better break than these crackers. I think they talk to you better, take up more time with you.

—Factory worker, New York

They treat Negro customers better. They will serve you just as fast as they serve anybody else. They will donate money faster to the Negro causes.

—Truck driver, Atlanta

Jewish store owners are better because they will keep cutting the price of an item you want until you can afford to buy it. They do not want you to leave the store without buying. They will follow you to the door urging you to buy, at least you know they want your business.

—Housewife, Birmingham

Jewish Store Owners Worse

Because they want to deal in the colored neighborhood and get more . . . Negroes have to patronize their place of business. If there's a Jewish market and an Italian the Jewish would put his prices higher. When a Jew buys whole-sale he pays less and then he sells it at high prices especially in our neighborhood.

—Unemployed power machine operator, New York

I think the Jew depends upon using a lot of psychology on you. Well, he always tried to talk faster than you and to show you right where the particular article or garment is. He tries to get your money from you whether you are receiving fair trade for it or not. He forgets principles and just has his mind on your money.

—Housewife, Birmingham

They are, in my opinion, much worse than any other merchant, trying to pass off inferior merchandise on unsuspecting Negroes. They take great advantage of the less literate Negro in selling him low-quality items at high prices.

—Housewife, Los Angeles

Try to put a product over to you which they know is not good. No standard price. If you talk to him, he will drop the price.

—Practical nurse, Chicago

Jewish Landlords Better

Jewish landlords are one hundred per cent better. They are more lenient if you are behind in rent payments. They are better about fixing repairs. I would rather have a Jewish landlord than a white one.

—Machine operator, Chicago

He gives you a little more time when you are short and goes along with that ... he's better than our color on that subject. He gives you a job and makes sure you have somewhere to live even if he charges you more, sure he's better, some white people don't want you around them.

—Apartment maintenance man, Cleveland

They are more tolerant. They'll go along with anything as long as you give them a story. I have seen Jews bend over backwards, go out of their way to try and help, not a person to put you out on the street.

—Housewife, Chicago

The Jew automatically kind of gives you a chance to pay. Even if he has a white man collecting. The white man will want to put you out the minute you don't pay or get behind, but the Jew, you can call him, and he will make the white man extend you time. This is better when you're poor like I am and other Negroes.

—Unemployed worker, Birmingham

They will give you a chance to catch up, if you get behind in your rent or with other bills you owe. A cracker will set your things out-doors. A Jew will keep up his property a little better for his tenants.

—Domestic, Atlanta

They were very considerate. They would be giving us something every time when we paid the rent. They always gave us some clothes and goodies. If it weren't for the Jews I wouldn't be here today. It was hard to get along with no father.

—Housewife, New York

Jewish Landlords Worse

The white landlord who is not Jewish is better. He goes out of his way to help a Negro. He'd lend you money if you was short. Well, the Jew landlord he'll put you in this apartment and you'd pay an arm or a leg and it isn't worth it. The apartment is raggedy. There are rats in them. They are falling down, shabby. They won't fix anything. They won't repair. All they want is their money. He may have 10 or 12 houses and all he's doing is sitting down collecting his money and rubbing his bald head ... he don't care about fixing it up because he feels we're just trash.

—Housewife, New York

Jews are worse because they will put your furniture out-doors. Do not want to keep the house in good repair, will not paint up and put hot water in the house.

—Maid, Birmingham

They don't care too much about the buildings and whatever else they own. They don't rebuild. You have to fight to get him to paint. You practically have to take him to court in order to get important things for the home that the landlords should give. Like in here it's rather on the cool side because there's no heat. They allow the building to become run down ... you very seldom see the landlord. We have a few things inside this apartment that should be done. The kitchen stove leaks gas, the window is broken. When we called the landlord, he said he doesn't usually speak to tenants that you should go to the super.

—Merchant seaman, Brooklyn

The data observed in this section indicate something about attitudes toward Jewish whites relative to attitudes toward non-Jewish whites but nothing about the hostility felt toward Jews per se. The data do not suggest that friendly feelings toward Jews *necessarily* exist among those who feel them to be better than other whites, or among those who fail to make a distinction. For some, Jews are simply seen as a lesser evil, or equally as bad as other whites, and in these cases such beliefs did not preclude the expression of considerable hostility toward Jews.[18]

Thus far we have established several facts. About three in ten Northern Negroes hold relatively anti-Semitic views (as did 19 per cent in Atlanta and 14 per cent in Birmingham). In view of commonly held beliefs of rampant anti-Semitism among Negroes, one might have expected this proportion to be considerably higher. Indeed, to the extent that Negroes single out Jews from other whites, they overwhelmingly prefer Jews, while the majority of Negroes do not see Jews as in any way different from other whites.

If it was true in the 1930s, as Richard Wright indicated, that "all of us black people who lived in the neighborhood hated Jews" and "to hold an attitude of antagonism or distrust toward Jews was bred in us from childhood . . . it was part of our cultural heritage,"[19] today the majority of Negroes do not share the endemic anti-Semitism of Western culture.

[18] However, some respondents who felt Jews to be better than other whites did make a clear distinction in that they expressed considerable hostility toward non-Jewish whites yet had only friendly feelings for Jews. A parallel may be drawn to the attitudes of South African Bantus toward the Boers and the British (who are at least a statistical minority). A study of African attitudes notes that for many people a marked difference existed with respect to the hostility expressed toward the Dutch and toward the English, and stereotypes exist of the "bad" Dutch and the "good" English. This study notes that "the lesser of two evils may, under the circumstances, appear to be a positive good." Like the attitudes of Jews in America, English attitudes in South Africa have also traditionally been more liberal (I. D. MacCrone, "Reaction to Domination in a Colour-Caste Society: A Preliminary Study of the Race Attitudes of a Dominated Group," *Journal of Social Psychology,* 1947, p. 88). While only a very small fraction of the total population of South Africa is Jewish, the comments of several respondents in the South African study, with a change in a word or two, were identical to the comments of some of our respondents who felt Jews to be better than other whites. For example, "The Jews in this country are the better people of the Whites. They are liberal, good natured and sympathetic. They very rarely show signs of ill-feeling towards the Africans" (*ibid.,* p. 82). Any comparative study of Jews in multi-ethnic or multiracial societies would do well to start with the assumption that, as a result of their values and experiences as a minority group, Jews in general may differ from other whites in their treatment of subordinate peoples, although in a society where they are dominant, such as Israel, this may not be the case.

[19] Richard Wright, *Black Boy,* New York, New American Library, 1964, p. 70.

Negro Versus White Anti-Semitism

Although it has been observed that very large segments of the Negro American population do not hold strong anti-Semitic beliefs, and that Jews do not seem to be singled out for special hostility, it is still possible that Negroes are somewhat higher in anti-Semitism than are whites. Recently, the violently anti-Semitic remarks of an occasional rioter have led many observers to conclude that Negroes are more likely than whites to be anti-Semitic.

We shall now consider this question by comparing Negroes and whites on the Index of Anti-Semitism. In doing this it is necessary to control for the effects of education. It is well known that the acceptance of anti-Semitic beliefs decreases with education (this is further substantiated by all the

Table 84. ANTI-SEMITISM OF WHITES AND NEGROES BY REGION AND EDUCATION[a]

	North		South	
	Whites	Negroes	Whites	Negroes
Grammar school				
Non-anti-Semitic	36%	25%	32%	36%
Low on anti-Semitism	34	45	32	52
High on anti-Semitism	21	23	12	8
Very high on anti-Semitism	9	7	24	4
High plus very high	**30%**	**30%**	**36%**	**12%**
Total	100%	100%	100%	100%
Number	(195)	(43)	(25)	(25)
At least some high school				
Non-anti-Semitic	39%	42%	48%	21%
Low on anti-Semitism	51	41	28	51
High on anti-Semitism	12	11	12	21
Very high on anti-Semitism	8	6	12	7
High plus very high	**20%**	**17%**	**24%**	**28%**
Total	100%	100%	100%	100%
Number	(454)	(62)	(58)	(28)
At least some college[b]				
Non-anti-Semitic	64%	47%		
Low on anti-Semitism	28	47		
High on anti-Semitism	5	11		
Very high on anti-Semitism	3	5		
High plus very high	**8%**	**16%**		
Total	100%	100%		
Number	(215)	(19)		

[a] Based on data from national study only.
[b] For the South, there were too few cases to make comparisons.

studies in this series), and that Negroes are less educated than whites. Since we are concerned here with the effects of race, not of education, we must compare the anti-Semitism of Negroes and whites with roughly equivalent educations. This is done in Table 84. The respondents, both white and Negro, used to provide the comparison were interviewed as part of the national study of anti-Semitism referred to in earlier chapters.[20] In addition to education, region is also controlled in the table since region, too, is related to anti-Semitism.

The data shown in Table 84 indicate no consistent pattern of differences when education and region are controlled. Of the five comparisons possible, Negroes are a bit less likely to be anti-Semitic in two, slightly more likely to be anti-Semitic in two, and in one Negroes and whites are tied. When only the proportions scored as very high on anti-Semitism are considered, Negroes are less likely than whites to be extreme anti-Semites in four of the five comparisons. On the other had, in three of the five comparisons, Negroes are less likely to score as non-anti-Semitic. All in all, however, no case can be made for the prevalent notion that anti-Semitism is more widespread among Negroes than among whites, anymore than it could be shown that they single out Jews for special enmity.

This lack of an over-all pattern of differentiation obscures the differences between whites and Negroes that did emerge when comparisons were made with respect to separate items included in the index. Negroes were more likely to accept negative economic stereotypes about Jews than were whites. On other negative stereotypes, however, such as that Jews stick together too much, the percentage giving the anti-Semitic response was about the same regardless of race. On still others, such as thinking that Jews have too much power, Negroes were less likely to appear as anti-Semitic than whites.[21]

On measures not involving stereotypes, however, Negroes consistently emerge as less anti-Semitic. Compared with whites, they more frequently opposed passage of a law to stop further Jewish immigration, more frequently said they would vote against a congressional candidate who declared himself against the Jews, and more frequently said they would not mind if their party nominated a Jew for President. In addition, Negroes expressed greater opposition to occupational and social club discrimination against Jews than did whites. It seems that their position as a persecuted

[20] Comparisons are made here between whites and Negroes in the national study and not Negroes in the present study. This is done because the questionnaires were in many respects different. However, when Negroes in the metropolitan area sample are compared with non-Southern urban whites, the pattern remains essentially the same.

[21] In other words, whether Negroes apear as more or less anti-Semitic than whites depends upon how anti-Semitism is defined or measured. An index containing many power stereotypes will show Negroes to be less anti-Semitic, just as an index containing many economic stereotypes will show Negroes to be more anti-Semitic.

minority leads black Americans to reject discrimination against Jews, if not always negative stereotypes.

These contrasts between whites and Negroes are all the more interesting when one recalls that, in questioning Negroes about Jews, one is asking about a different racial group as well as a different religious-ethnic group. One might expect that there would be an important element of antiwhite feeling in Negro anti-Semitism not found in white anti-Semitism. Furthermore, given their oppression by the white society of which Jews are a part, and the involvement of Jews in ghetto economic life, widespread feelings of hostility toward Jews would be readily understandable. That the above factors have not resulted in appreciably greater anti-Semitism among Negroes may surprise common sense.[22] However, it is worthy of note that other studies in this series report comparable findings.[23]

Unique Aspects of the Negro-Jewish Relationship

While Negroes and whites in similar situations do not differ significantly from each other with respect to their scores on the Index of Anti-Semitism, it does not necessarily follow that their attitudes stem from the same sources. It could still be true that certain aspects of Negro-Jewish relations operate to generate hostility among Negroes, without which Negroes would be much less prone to anti-Semitism than are whites. Additionally, there could be factors in Jewish-Negro relationships which act to produce good will, and indeed such factors may cancel out those popularly believed to produce hostility. This section will investigate these questions.

Negro Identification with Jews: Biblical and Contemporary

An important factor differentiating Negro-Jewish relations from Jewish-gentile or Negro-white relations is that both Jews and Negroes have long suffered persecution and discrimination. Both can potentially sympathize

[22] That Negroes generally do not appear as higher in anti-Semitism than whites is of further significance when one remembers the inferior education Negroes receive within a segregated system. Given the crucial effect of education on attitudes, Negroes with the same number of years of schooling as whites might be expected to be more anti-Semitic than their counterparts because of their relatively inferior education.

[23] In fact in the two other studies where comparisons are possible, Negroes emerge as less likely to be anti-Semitic than whites when those in similar social positions are considered. Thus a study of the intergroup attitudes of adolescents being conducted by Brewster Smith and Jane Hardyck reports that in general Negro youths appear somewhat less anti-Semitic in both feelings and stereotypes than white non-Jewish youths. Negroes also emerged as slightly less anti-Semitic than whites in the study of public response to the Eichmann trial (Charles Y. Glock, Gertrude J. Selznick, and Joe L. Spaeth, *The Apathetic Majority*, New York, Harper and Row, 1966, pp. 180 and 197).

with one another's minority group experiences. For the Negro there is the further possibility of identifying with the Biblical Jew.

Although the actual contact between Negroes and Jews becomes amenable to analysis only in the latter part of the nineteenth century,[24] long before this, as slaves and Christians, Negroes may have come into contact with ideas about Jews which could have led them to see the latter as a particular kind of white group. As Christians, Negroes may have developed or absorbed hostile beliefs about Jews as religious outsiders. However, unique to the Negro, and a factor possibly working to produce positive feelings for Jews, was Negro enslavement and identification with the Israelites of the Old Testament. It is possible that for many there came to be an identification with the Jews as another people of bondage who struggled and obtained their freedom. The richness of Negro spirituals based on the exploits of Old Testament heroes such as David, Daniel, Joshua, and of course one of the first nationalists of them all, Moses, who led the children of Israel out of bondage, all attest to this identification. And indeed, even James Baldwin has written: "The Negro identifies himself almost wholly with the Jews. The more devout Negro considers that he is a Jew, in bondage to a hard taskmaster and waiting for a Moses to lead him out of Egypt."[25]

The comments of some of our respondents suggest this identification. A professional dancer in Springfield Gardens, New York, said, "I think as far as civil rights are concerned they are conscious and more outspoken. . . . They can compare the Negro with their ancestor's plight in Egypt." A plasterer in Los Angeles, also low on anti-Semitism, said, "They are Christ's chosen people, and they are blessed."

Although the questionnaire did not ask directly about this identification, it contained two items from which limited inferences can be made. These involved seeing the Jews as the chosen people of the Old Testament and still God's chosen people today. When these factors are combined in an index, it can be seen that people who perceive Jews as the chosen people are less likely to be anti-Semitic than are those who do not, regardless of their view of the present religious status of Jews (Table 85).

A more current source of Negro identification with Jews might stem from the fact that both are contemporary minority groups, who have suffered in the past and now receive differential treatment from the dominant group.[26]

[24] Before this time there were few Jews in the United States and Negroes were generally confined to Southern plantations. Jewish slave owners do not appear to have been different from others, and Jews were prominent in the leadership of the Confederacy. Southern Jews were largely in favor of slavery, and this caused Horace Greeley and other abolitionists to turn against them. However, there were also Jewish abolitionists, and two Jewish brothers rode and were executed with John Brown.

[25] Baldwin, Notes, p. 67.

[26] These factors no doubt help explain why Negroes showed greater opposition to discrimination against Jews and political anti-Semitism than did whites in the national study of anti-Semitism.

This shared minority group consciousness may be inferred from several questions which measured sympathy for Jews as a minority group. Those questioned were asked whether they thought that Jews are being discriminated against at the present time and whether they felt that Jews had suffered

Table 85. ANTI-SEMITISM BY BIBLICAL IDENTIFICATION OF THE JEWS

	Jews as Chosen People of Old Testament and as God's Chosen People Today	Jews as Chosen People of Old Testament But Not as God's Chosen People Today	Jews as Neither Chosen People of Old Testament nor God's Chosen People Today[a]
Anti-Semitic	16%	19%	28%
Number	(84)	(405)	(451)

[a] This category includes those who said "All are the chosen of God" as well as those who said "don't know."

in the past. A majority of the sample felt that Jews are currently discriminated against. With respect to Jewish suffering, 42 per cent felt that "Jews have suffered no more than anybody else"; 11 per cent felt that "Jews have suffered but they generally brought it on themselves"; and 37 per cent felt that "Jews have suffered through no fault of their own."[27]

In many comments offered about the situation of the Jews, an identification with the Jews as a fellow minority group could be noted.

The Jewish plight and the Negro plight is about the same—have the same things to go through.

—Worker, Birmingham

I think Jews are almost like Negroes.

—Machine operator, Chicago

As immigrants they were abused worse than Negroes.

—Waitress, Oakland, California

They are like us. We Negroes suffer but through no fault of our own.

—Housewife, Detroit

They know how it feels to be mistreated. Their hearts go out to the Negro.

—Cab driver, Birmingham

Jews seem to me like colored people.

—Housewife, Jamaica, New York

[27] This question unfortunately leaves something to be desired as a measure of sympathy for Jews as a minority group. In view of the Negro experience, many who chose the response "Jews have suffered no more than anybody else" might be aware of and sympathize with Jews as a minority group, yet not think that Jews have suffered more than Negroes. If considered in a relative sense, the question is still useful.

They are not as strong armed as other whites are. Deep down inside they are not as prejudiced as other whites are because they are discriminated against themselves. . . . They will socialize with you when Italians, Irish, and others will not. I think also it is because of their origins, it is closest to the Black Man.

—Musician, New York

I hear they treat Jews the same way they treat Negroes in the South.

—Housewife, Philadelphia

When the questions about discrimination against Jews and Jewish suffering are combined into an index of sympathy for contemporary Jews,[28] it is seen that anti-Semitism decreases with increased awareness of Jews as a minority group that has also suffered. Thirty-one per cent of those lowest in sympathy for Jews scored as anti-Semitic against 15 per cent of those highest in sympathy[29] (Table 86).

Table 86. ANTI-SEMITISM BY SYMPATHY FOR CONTEMPORARY JEWS

Score on Index of Sympathy for Contemporary Jews[a]

	Low 0	1	High 2
Anti-Semitic	31%	28%	15%
Number	(192)	(311)	(254)

[a] One point was given for feeling that Jews are discriminated against and one point for feeling they have suffered through no fault of their own. Those without opinions are excluded.

Jews as Civil Rights Supporters

Another factor in Negro-Jewish relationships is the disproportionate involvement of Jews in the Negro's struggle for equality and the fact that Jews may be less prejudiced and discriminatory.

[28] The opinionless were excluded from this as well as the next two indexes. When the "don't knows" are included, the import of Table 86 remains essentially the same, although the magnitude of the difference is reduced. This is because people who said "don't know" to items on the Index of Sympathy were also likely to say "don't know" to many of the anti-Semitism items. Hence the percentage scoring as prejudiced is artificially lowered, since a "don't know" response was scored as non-anti-Semitic. A purer test of the effect of sympathy for Jews was possible when only those with opinions are considered.

[29] Although sympathetic awareness of the minority status of Jews inhibits anti-Semitism the relation could be much stronger. One reason why it may not be stronger is that the realization that Jews have suffered may lead an individual to expect very much more from them than they are willing to give. Even though Jews may be relatively more sympathetic than other whites, many are still prejudiced in their attitudes and discriminatory in their behavior. James Baldwin has written that Jews of all people should "know better" and that "an understanding is expected of the Jew such as none but the most naive and visionary Negro has ever expected of the American gentile" (Baldwin, *Notes* p. 69). When this understanding is not forthcoming it may intensify feelings of hostility among some of those aware of Jewish minority status.

Since Julius Rosenwald played his important early role in providing educational and other opportunities for Negroes, Jews have often been in the forefront of the struggle to realize the values of the Constitution and the Bill of Rights. Jewish philanthropists and activists played a role in the founding and funding of the Urban League and the NAACP in the early 1900s and have been active participants in and donors to these organizations to the present day. The president of the NAACP has traditionally always been Jewish. Civil rights activists have a disproportionate number of Jews in their ranks, and it was not by chance that of the three martyrs of the 1964 summer civil rights crisis the two whites were Jewish. Jewish defense agencies have in recent decades cooperated with Negro organizations in securing legislation and political action beneficial to both groups. Predominantly Jewish unions, such as the International Ladies Garment Workers Union, played pioneering roles in involving Negroes in the labor movement. Even the masses of Jews have traditionally supported more liberal candidates and have tended to take the pro-civil rights stand on various issues to a much greater extent than other white ethnic groups. This is perhaps related to Talmudic values as well as Jewish minority group experience.

Responses to several questions gave evidence that Negroes do tend to perceive Jews as being more in favor of civil rights and as less discriminatory. Thus, in response to the question "On the whole, do you think that Jews are more in favor of civil rights for Negroes than other white people are, less in favor, or is there no difference?" 45 per cent of the sample said "more in favor," only 3 per cent said "less," and 35 per cent said "the same." When asked whether it was true or false that Jews were better than other whites about hiring Negroes, 69 per cent of the sample said "true" and only 15 per cent said "false."[30] This pattern emerged even in the South where Jews have not been so openly supportive of Negro rights.

To the extent that Jews are perceived as being more supportive of Negro rights, one would imagine that this would operate to curtail anti-Semitism.[31]

[30] This perception of Jewish support for Negro rights is consistent with past research on the subject. Cothran, in 1949, used an open-ended interview to determine Negro conceptions of white people. He found that one of the more frequently mentioned conceptions was: "Jews are more sympathetic toward the Negro than other whites." He then asked a random sample of Negroes to agree or disagree with various statements about whites. He discovered that approximately 53 per cent of his sample agreed with this statement about Jews, 30 per cent were not sure, and only 17 per cent disagreed (Cothran, *op. cit.*). Similar findings are reported by McDaniel and Babchuk, *op. cit.*

[31] Ironically, however, for some respondents these factors may produce anti-Semitism. That Jews may be more willing to hire, sell, and rent to Negroes is a factor in their disproportionate contact, and hence feelings of class resentment may inspire anti-Semitism. In addition, ambiguities in the role of the white liberal are relevant. Jews have occasionally been criticized for dominating civil rights organizations.

To test this notion, the previous questions were combined into an index of perception of Jewish support for civil rights. Among those high on this index, 20 per cent scored as anti-Semitic compared with 38 per cent of those who saw no difference in the support given to civil rights by Jewish and non-Jewish whites (Table 87).

Table 87. ANTI-SEMITISM BY PERCEPTION OF JEWS AS SUPPORTIVE OF CIVIL RIGHTS

| | Index of Perception of Jews as More Supportive of Civil Rights[a] | | |
	Low 0	1	High 2
Anti-Semitic	38%	30%	20%
Number	(38)	(265)	(343)

[a] One point was given for belief that Jews are more in favor of civil rights than other whites and one point for belief that Jews are better than other whites in hiring Negroes. Those without opinions are excluded.

In their comments, respondents again gave numerous examples of how and why they felt Jews to be more supportive of civil rights; these need not be repeated here. However, it is significant to note that, the claims of some leaders of the Jewish community notwithstanding, *a sizable percentage of the black population is aware of the support that Jews give to civil rights.* And this awareness seems to have an effect on inhibiting the anti-Semitism that might otherwise develop.

Three factors which tend to be unique to the Negro-Jewish situation have been observed as they affect anti-Semitism. These factors were empirically related to each other and, since they all pertain to Jewish minority group status, may be treated as a single dimension. When they are combined into a larger measure which summarizes the perception of Jews as a minority group supportive of Negro rights, their effect on inhibiting anti-Semitism becomes pronounced.[32] Among those highest on this summary index, only 8 per cent scored as anti-Semitic. This percentage increases steadily to 62 per cent for those with the lowest score on the index (Table 88). If one looks just at the extreme category, the increase in the proportion who scored as very high in anti-Semitism is from zero to 39. Clearly, the anti-Semitism of Negroes is strongly inhibited by their perception of Jews as a disadvantaged minority group sympathetic to the Negro struggle for civil rights.

[32] Scores of the indexes of Sympathy for Contemporary Jews and Perception of Jews as Supportive of Civil Rights were added; seeing Jews as the chosen people of neither the Old Testament nor the chosen people today was scored two; seeing Jews as the chosen people of the Old Testament but not today was scored one.

Economic Relations

The preceding section has considered factors unique to Negro-Jewish relationships which operate to produce friendly feelings toward Jews. Other factors also tend to make their relationship a special one, and these may be found in the economic realm. However, here conditions may well generate anti-Semitism rather than inhibit it.

Table 88.   ANTI-SEMITISM BY PERCEPTION OF JEWS AS A MINORITY GROUP SUPPORTIVE
OF CIVIL RIGHTS

Score on Index of Perception of Jews as a Minority Group
More Supportive of Civil Rights

	Low 0	1	2	3	4	5	High 6
Per cent anti-Semitic (including those very high)	62%	44%	35%	25%	17%	14%	8%
Per cent very high on anti-Semitism	39	19	10	6	2	1	0
Number	(13)	(57)	(110)	(168)	(147)	(88)	(12)

During the generations following the emancipation of the slaves, Negroes and Jews began to come together on a much wider scale than they had previously. Both were involved in the great process of migration that has been such a key factor in the development of American society. As Jews and other groups immigrated to the United States, native-born Americans were moving from farms to cities. As Negroes left the relatively isolated and ethnically more homogeneous rural Southern areas for the ethnically mixed cities, their confrontation with whites became one in which ethnic diversity was more relevant for the structuring of group relations. Whereas in the South it was just "Massa Charlie," in the North it became "the micks," "the dagoes" and "the kikes." Given their lack of resources as new immigrants, Negroes, Poles, Jews, and the Irish were drawn to the same poorer sections of urban areas.

However, unlike other immigrant groups, Jews came with a commercial tradition and often began life in America as peddlers or small tradesmen. Both as Jews and as immigrants, they were perhaps less inclined to accept traditional American beliefs about Negroes. In any event, their business tradition encouraged them to deal with outsiders no matter who they might be.[33] The relationship of Jews to Negroes thus tended to differ somewhat

[33] Wirth, in his classic study of the Jewish ghetto in the 1920s, quotes a Jewish clothing merchant on Maxwell Street as saying, "A dollar is just as good whether a white hand or a black hand hands it over." However, perhaps as a concession to American race attitudes, the merchant adds, "Anyway, their hands are white on the inside" (L. Wirth, *The Ghetto,* Chicago, University of Chicago Press, 1962, p. 231).

from the latter's contact with other recently arrived ethnic groups. For example, Negro-Irish contact, occurring somewhat earlier, tended to be one of competition in the unskilled labor market, though this decreased as the Irish moved more into the mainstream of middle-class American life. However, from the beginning, Negro-Jewish contact was more likely to involve a dominant-subordinate relationship, first as merchant to client, later, as Jews met with financial success, as landlord to tenant and employer to employee.

In addition, the pattern of ethnic ecological succession was often one in which Negroes, as the most recent of a long line of impoverished migrants, moved into urban areas being vacated by socially mobile Jews (who themselves had replaced earlier migrants).[34] However, although Negroes tended to replace Jews as residents of the slums, businesses tended to remain in Jewish hands. As a result, in many areas Jews are definitely overrepresented in Negro economic life, and since the 1920s the presence of Jewish-owned businesses in what have become largely Negro neighborhoods has often been in evidence.[35] The disproportionate economic contact of these groups seems to have important implications for Negro attitudes.

Just how frequent Negro-Jewish economic involvement is becomes evident when various types of impersonal contact are considered. Of the combined samples, seven out of ten report that some of the stores in the areas where they live or do their shopping are owned by Jews; and, in such areas where Jewish-owned stores exist, more than nine out of ten currently patronize these Jewish-owned stores. Among those not now shopping at Jewish-owned stores (including those in areas where no Jewish-owned stores exist), nine out of ten report having shopped at such stores in the past (Table 89).

Differences by region in shopping at Jewish stores are not pronounced.

[34] Writing about Chicago in the 1920s, Wirth noted: "The transition . . . of the ghetto community has been proceeding at such a speed that the complexion of the area changes from day to day. Dilapidated structures that a decade ago were Christian churches have since become synagogues and have now been turned into African Methodist Episcopal or colored Baptist churches. Under the latest coat of paint of a store-front colored mission there are vestiges of signs reading, "Kosher Butchershop" and "Deutsche Apotheke" (ibid., p. 231).

However, this pattern of residential displacement is due to something more than natural urban processes since, even outside ghetto areas, middle-class Negroes are likely to move into Jewish areas (N. Glazer, "Negroes and Jews: The New Challenge to Pluralism," Commentary, December 1964, p. 31).

[35] Even where there are relatively few Jewish-owned stores, they may receive a disproportionate share of Negro business. In writing about a small Southern town in the 1930s, Dollard noted that Jewish merchants received most of the Negro's business and that "over and over again one hears from Negroes that Southern [non-Jewish] merchants have been crowded out of the territory by their rough categorical treatment of Negroes" (John Dollard, Caste and Class in a Southern Town, Garden City, N. Y., Doubleday Anchor, 1957, p. 129). Scattered throughout the voluminous literature of American race relations similar statements may be found.

Table 89. ECONOMIC CONTACT WITH JEWS BY REGION

	Metro.	N.Y.	Chic.	Atl.	Birm.	Total
"Are there Jewish-owned stores in your area?"						
Yes	66%	78%	66%	78%	60%	70%
No	20	13	18	15	35	20
Don't know	14	9	16	7	5	10
Total	100%	100%	100%	100%	100%	100%
Number[a]	(328)	(190)	(132)	(198)	(199)	(954)
Per cent shopping at Jewish-owned stores (among those in areas with Jewish-owned stores)	92%	98%	94%	92%	90%	93%
Number	(217)	(148)	(87)	(154)	(121)	(664)
Per cent who have shopped at Jewish-owned stores in the past (among those not now shopping at Jewish-owned stores)[b]	86%	88%	92%	100%	90%	90%
Number	(104)	(34)	(35)	(45)	(87)	(280)
"Have you ever worked for someone who is Jewish?"						
Yes, now	11%	23%	17%	10%	4%	12%
Yes, in the past	63	58	57	43	41	53
No	23	18	24	45	53	33
Don't know	3	1	2	2	2	2
Total	100%	100%	100%	100%	100%	100%
"Has anyone else in your family ever worked for a Jewish person?"						
Yes, now	17%	24%	15%	8%	6%	14%
Yes, in the past	43	46	40	30	24	36
No	27	22	32	49	50	37
Don't know	13	8	13	13	20	13
Total	100%	100%	100%	100%	100%	100%
"Is your doctor or dentist Jewish?"						
Yes	34%	43%	29%	10%	10%	25%
No	61	54	65	86	87	71
Don't know	5	3	6	4	3	4
Total	100%	100%	100%	100%	100%	100%

[a] When the number of respondents is not reported, it is approximately the same as shown here.

[b] Due to interviewer error, 57 respondents were not asked this question.

They become more evident when considering the question of a Jewish employer. Twenty-three per cent in New York, 17 per cent in Chicago, and 11 per cent in the metropolitan area sample reported they currently have a Jewish employer. Indeed, more than half of these samples claim to have had a Jewish employer in the past. Thus, in all regions, at least half either presently work for a Jew or have done so.[36]

When asked if their doctor or dentist was Jewish, 34 per cent of those in the metropolitan area sample, 43 per cent in New York, 29 per cent in Chicago, but only 10 per cent in Atlanta and 10 per cent in Birmingham said yes (Table 89). When an index of impersonal contact is built, based on working for, shopping from, and having a Jew as one's doctor or dentist,

Table 90.   IMPERSONAL ECONOMIC CONTACT WITH JEWS BY REGION

	Metro.	N.Y.	Chic.	Atl.	Birm.	Total
Two or more impersonal economic contacts	29%	47%	29%	16%	8%	25%
Number	(324)	(188)	(132)	(197)	(199)	(942)

not surprisingly those in New York City report the most contact, followed by the other two Northern samples (Table 90). Respondents in Atlanta and Birmingham report much less contact.

While there is considerable impersonal contact between whites and Negroes in American society, those interviewed reported much less personal contact of an equal-status nature. When asked if they currently had contact with Jews in any clubs or organizations to which they belonged, only 13 to 15 per cent of those in the Chicago, New York, and metropolitan samples said "yes." The comparable figures for Atlanta and Birmingham were 7 and 2 per cent respectively. However, when asked if they had ever had a close friend who was Jewish, about four in ten outside the South, 28 per cent in Atlanta, and 19 per cent in Birmingham said "yes."

A frequently noted finding of social scientists concerned with race relations is that equal-status contact with members of disprivileged groups tends to reduce prejudice. In our data those who reported having had a Jewish friend were slightly less likely to score as anti-Semitic. However, the effect of dominant-subordinate contact, especially on those in subordinate roles, has been approached much less frequently. In considering the situation of the ghetto Negro and his contact with Jews, one might be led to hypothesize that, as this impersonal, dominant-subordinate contact increases, feelings of hostility might also tend to increase.

To begin with, regardless of race or ethnicity, or questions of dishonesty

[36] The import of these figures becomes clearer when it is realized that Jews make up 3 per cent of the United States population (although they are a much larger percentage of the middle class in larger urban areas).

and exploitation, the merchant-customer, employer-employee, or landlord-tenant relationship provides a basis for conflict and tension. When this potential for hostility is buttressed by a situation where the subordinates are often of very low income and of a different race, religion, or ethnic group, then the development of hostility is even more understandable. Wright, Baldwin, and Ellison, and many others have written of what it does to an individual always to see a white (and in major urban centers often a Jewish white) looking down at him in every impersonal relationship he enters into. For some, class resentment may easily merge with and perhaps inspire racial and religious hostility.

Table 91.   ANTI-SEMITISM BY IMPERSONAL ECONOMIC CONTACT WITH JEWS AND SOCIAL CLASS

(per cent anti-Semitic)

| Social Class | Extent of Impersonal Contact[a] | | |
	Low (0, 1, 2)	Medium (3, 4)	High (5, 6)
Lower or middle (0, 1, 2, 3)	20%	27%	38%
Number	(371)	(293)	(118)
Upper (4, 5, 6)	12%	11%	11%
Number	(73)	(54)	(27)

[a] For each current impersonal contact with Jews (as employer, merchant, or doctor), a score of two was given. Those not currently having a Jewish employer but who have had one in the past received a score of one.

Thus, it is not surprising that (excluding those highest in social position) as impersonal contact increases so does the percentage scoring as anti-Semitic. Among those who currently have a high degree of impersonal contact, 38 per cent score as anti-Semitic, while for those with the least contact this figure drops to 20 per cent (Table 91). The relationship of the college-educated, higher-status Negro to Jews differs markedly from that of the urban poor, and for this group only about one in ten scored as anti-Semitic, regardless of the extent of their impersonal contact.

However, increased economic contact is accompanied by a slight increase in the perception of Jews as a minority group which supports civil rights. This operates to limit the over-all effect of economic contact on anti-Semitism. When perception of Jews is held constant (Table 92), important changes occur in the original relation. Among persons with a high degree of impersonal contact with Jews, those who did *not* perceive the minority status and pro-civil rights stance of Jews were very likely to be anti-Semitic (73 per cent), while those who did recognize the Jews as a pro-civil rights minority group were very unlikely to be anti-Semitic (21 per cent). Looked at another way, among persons who recognized the minority status and civil rights activism of Jews, impersonal economic contact had almost no anti-Semitic consequences. Sixteen per cent of such persons with no impersonal economic contact with Jews scored as anti-Semitic, while only 21 per cent of those with considerable contact did so. Thus, the impact of ghetto economic relations between Negroes and Jews on anti-Semitism depends on whether or not such contact is accompanied by Negro recognition of the Jews as a fellow minority group committed to social justice. When this is the case, the potential for anti-Semitism in this relationship is almost totally suspended. But when Negroes do not see

Table 92. ANTI-SEMITISM BY IMPERSONAL ECONOMIC CONTACT WITH JEWS AND PERCEPTION OF JEWS AS A MINORITY GROUP SUPPORTIVE OF CIVIL RIGHTS[a]

(per cent anti-Semitic)

| | Extent of Impersonal Contact | | |
Perception of Jews as a Minority Group More Supportive of Civil Rights than Whites	Low	Medium	High
Low	33%	46%	73%
Number	(75)	(57)	(22)
Medium	22%	21%	59%
Number	(59)	(53)	(22)
High	16%	18%	21%
Number	(61)	(84)	(43)

[a] Excludes those classified as upper class.

this aspect of Negro-Jewish relations, then impersonal economic contact is a potent source of prejudice. Among Negroes who do not identify the Jews as civil rights allies, 33 per cent who lack economic contact with Jews scored as anti-Semitic, while among those with a good deal of such contact 73 per cent exhibited anti-Semitism.

Ghetto Merchants

The sheer quantity of contact between two groups is one thing; the quality of these contacts is quite another. Because of their powerlessness and relative lack of sophistication, many Negroes in the ghetto find they are often taken advantage of in many impersonal economic situations. At least since the 1930s, ghetto landlords and businessmen have been frequently criticized for unethical behavior.

A recent study of the situation of the low-income consumer in several of New York City's most impoverished areas noted that he often faced misrepresentation of prices, substitution of reconditioned or inferior merchandise for new or high-quality goods, misleading advertising, high-pressure tactics, and exorbitant prices for generally shoddy products. In commenting on this situation, Caplovitz notes, "this marketing system is in many respects a deviant one, in which unethical and illegal practices abound."[37] It would indeed be surprising if such a system did not generate feelings of hostility on the part of many.[38]

Just how widespread dishonesty is among Jewish ghetto merchants or whether these merchants behave any differently from Italian, Irish, or Negro ghetto merchants was beyond the scope of our data to discover. However, when respondents were asked whether they felt that they had ever been treated unfairly by a Jewish merchant, from 7 per cent of those in Birmingham to 21 and 25 per cent of those in New York and Chicago reported that they had.

This measure must be used with caution. In some cases respondents may not have been able to differentiate a Jewish from a non-Jewish merchant, even though they may have thought they were able to do so. In some urban areas, ghetto Negroes use the word "Jew" to refer to all white men, just as in some rural areas whites use the word "Jew" to refer to all traveling salesmen. Although mistreatment at the hands of a Jewish merchant may lead to anti-Semitism, in some cases holding anti-Semitic attitudes may prompt the inference that, because he is unfair, the merchant must be Jewish or, if he is in fact Jewish, he must be engaging in unethical practices.

Perceived mistreatment at the hands of a Jewish merchant was strongly related to holding anti-Semitic beliefs. Among those who said they were treated unfairly, 50 per cent scored as anti-Semitic, in contrast with only 18 per cent of those who felt that they had never received unfair treatment (Tables 93 and 94).

---

[37] David Caplovitz, *The Poor Pay More,* New York, Free Press, 1965, p. 180.

[38] It should be noted that higher prices and inferior products are not necessarily due simply to merchant cupidity. Because of the financial risk involved in dealing with some slum dwellers (in part due to their lack of savings and the instability of the job market), prices may be higher than elsewhere. In addition, many ghetto stores are smaller and perhaps less efficiently run and have a smaller volume of business. Furthermore, because of limited income, the customer may demand the cheapest goods, which are in fact often inferior.

Because of such factors it may be relatively easy for corrupt merchants to justify their practices. The perspective of some ghetto merchants no doubt receives expression in the following statement: "Yes, pawnbroking thrives on people's woes. But what of that? Undertaking thrives on people's deaths, but it is not responsible for their dying" (Edward Wallant, *The Pawnbroker,* New York, MacFadden, 1965, p. 107).

Paul Jacobs has further catalogued the attitudes of some merchants. "The *schwartzes* steal me blind so I'm gonna charge them more." "The colored people don't make their payments, so we have to have a high rate of interest in order to make up for our losses." "In a way, I'm doing the niggers a favor selling them. No one else will go down there and if I didn't they wouldn't have anything." "Business is business" (Jacobs, *op. cit.,* p. 54).

Table 93. PERCEIVED UNFAIR TREATMENT BY A JEWISH MERCHANT BY REGION

	Metro.	N.Y.	Chic.	Atl.	Birm.	Total
*"Do you feel that Jewish store-owners have treated you unfairly?"*a						
Yes	17%	21%	25%	12%	7%	16%
No	79	76	73	88	92	82
Don't know	4	3	2	0	1	2
Total	100%	100%	100%	100%	100%	100%
Number	(293)	(177)	(117)	(189)	(181)	(873)

a Among those who have shopped at Jewish-owned stores.

Table 94. ANTI-SEMITISM BY PERCEIVED UNFAIR TREATMENT BY A JEWISH MERCHANT

	Per Cent Anti-Semitic	Number
*"Do you feel that Jewish store owners have treated you unfairly?"*a		
Yes	50%	(135)
No	18	(706)

a Among those who have shopped at Jewish-owned stores.

Respondents were asked how they had been treated unfairly; and comments ranged from cases of obvious fraud, to morally questionable but probably legal activities, to the expression of a general class resentment.

I have bought merchandise on credit, and picked it out in the store. I got seconds or damaged goods when it was delivered. They added more money to my bill than what I owed. When I send children to store, the Jew sends tainted meat, damaged milk containers and canned goods.

—Power machine operator, New York

I bought a car and paid fifteen hundred dollars and the Jew tried to gyp me . . . he put me through some funny finance company.

—Retired worker, Chicago

They cheated me out of my money. They just cheat you, they don't want you to have one penny.

—Housewife, Atlanta

I got taken by some of them. The clothes don't fit right because he was holding it in the back.

—Public utilities worker, New York

I got a rotten deal. He was pretty nasty about his money. I was behind in my payments $10 a week and I missed a week and he wanted to take stuff out. Furniture store. I told him I'd get a gun.

—Housewife, Buffalo, New York

They made me pay for goods twice. They didn't give receipts so I had to pay twice.

—Laborer in a paint factory, Atlanta

He charged me more money for a plain television. I could get a colored television for the $500 I paid for this small one. They charge too much for the products they sell you.

—Domestic, New York

Selling inferior merchandise for sky high prices.

—Hospital worker, Philadelphia

They charged more. A fair price system [should be] established by law . . . this would open the door for a few more Negroes to go into business. Well, I'm very concerned that my children will see some of our own people in business at least in our own neighborhoods.

—Unemployed clerk, New York

A Jew tricked my wife into signing a blank paper and charged her more for the cost and payments than he told her.

—Plastic molder, Chicago

The price is higher than in Harlem where I used to live because he puts his hand on the scale to make the number of pounds more to charge me more money.

—Housewife, Brooklyn

This old Jew across the street here. I bought some pig feet. I caught him taking some of them off after he'd weighed them. . . . One Sunday morning there was a lady in there. She bought a chicken. He put the chicken on the scales, she walked away to buy some greens. He had taken some sausage and put it on the scales to make the chicken weigh more and I seen him and I told the lady.

—Domestic worker, Brooklyn

I sold a car for a Jew once for $800. My share was to be $250. The guy paid the Jew with a thousand dollar bill. The Jew gave me $25. . . . I walked away to keep from shooting him.

—Auto mechanic, Atlanta

When my husband had a heart attack, unable to work and we owed a bill they were very nasty, and dirty people not to understand the condition of the poor Negro.

—Housewife, Pittsburgh

I bought some furniture from one and seem as if I never finished paying him for it. They cheat you with the law, call your job, get you fired from your job. They lie on you when someone calls to find out your reference.

—Garment industry worker, New York

I work at a store myself and I know the price of things. This Jew didn't put any price on his merchandise, and he charged me a higher price than it should of sold for. This happens lots of times.

—Warehouse worker, Atlanta

I think he overcharge me, but it was the only store I could get credit from at the time.

—Housewife, Detroit

Criticisms of Jewish merchants frequently involved questions of credit. The low-income consumer desires the same material splendor as everyone else. However, he must buy most things on credit, and he can receive this only from merchants who specialize in giving credit to those without resources. As a result of the high risk involved in such credit, merchant greed, and client unsophistication, excessive prices are no doubt often paid for frequently inferior merchandise. For some, bad credit experiences with Jewish merchants are no doubt a source of anti-Semitism.

Those interviewed were asked whether they thought credit was more easily obtained in a Jewish or in a non-Jewish store, and whether Jewish merchants were harder or easier than other white merchants on people who fall behind in their payments. Responses to these questions followed a pattern similar to that observed for the questions about Jewish support of civil rights, and Jews as landlords, merchants, and employers. Whatever their evaluation of Jews in an absolute sense, *Negroes see Jews in a more favorable light than they see non-Jewish whites.* The majority of those in each of the samples felt that Jews gave credit more easily than other whites. Almost a majority felt that Jews were easier on people who were behind in their credit payments. Only a small minority of each sample said that non-Jewish store owners were easier on Negroes than Jewish owners. The rest thought them the same or did not know. However, those treated unfairly by a Jewish merchant were twice as likely as those treated fairly to take a negative view of Jewish credit practices. Attitudes toward Jewish

Table 95. BELIEFS CONCERNING JEWISH CREDIT PRACTICES, BY REGION

	Metro.	N.Y.	Chic.	Atl.	Birm.	Total
Easier to get credit in Jewish or in non-Jewish, white-owned store?						
Jewish	63%	63%	67%	59%	61%	62%
Non-Jewish	9	8	8	13	7	9
Same	4	4	5	8	3	5
Don't know	24	25	20	20	29	24
Total	100%	100%	100%	100%	100%	100%
Are Jews harder or easier than other white store owners on people who fall behind in their payments?						
Jews easier	43%	45%	47%	52%	57%	49%
Jews harder	22	17	20	12	11	16
Same	15	16	17	17	16	16
Don't know	20	22	16	19	16	19
Total	100%	100%	100%	100%	100%	100%

credit practices help to predict anti-Semitism. When the two credit items are considered together, among those who felt Jewish credit practices were worse than those of other whites, 40 per cent scored as anti-Semitic against 18 per cent among those who felt they were better than or no different from those of other whites (Tables 95–97).

Table 96.   TREATMENT BY JEWISH MERCHANTS BY PERCEPTION OF BELIEFS ABOUT JEWISH CREDIT PRACTICES

| | Treated Unfairly? | |
	Yes	No
Think Jewish credit practices worse than those of other whites[a]	38%	17%
Number	(137)	(711)

[a] On either or both of the two questions about credit.

This discussion of the economic sources of anti-Semitism has not meant to suggest that all Jewish ghetto merchants are grasping Shylocks or that they are less honest than other businessmen in the ghetto. How widespread dishonesty is among ghetto merchants, whatever their race, religion, or ethnic background, is an important question beyond the present study. Nor has the dicussion meant to imply that the relationship of merchant to customer is always one of crass exploitation. The richness and complexity

Table 97.   ANTI-SEMITISM BY BELIEFS ABOUT JEWISH CREDIT PRACTICES

	Jewish Credit Practices Worse than Those of Other Whites	Jewish Credit Practices Not Worse than Those of Other Whites
Anti-Semitic	40%	18%
Number	(199)	(735)

of human relationships can hardly be captured by a question in an interview which asks whether an individual has ever been mistreated by a Jew or how many Jewish-owned stores he shops at. Almost of necessity, interview questions have an aura of unreality if for no other reason than that they often call upon the respondent to ignore ambiguity and complexity in favor of making broad generalizations. Quantitative studies are often usefully supplemented by case histories. Dick Gregory catches the essence of one merchant-customer relationship in describing how the local Jewish merchant treated his family; his account suggests feelings of ambivalence rather than simple hostility. He notes that this merchant sold them three-day-old bread because that was the only kind he sold to his credit book customers, that "the peaches were rotten . . . and sometimes the butter was green," and that he himself once broke into the store for petty thievery. However, he adds, "when it came down to the nitty-gritty you could always go to Mister Ben. Before a Jewish holiday he'd take all the food that was going to spoil while the store was shut and bring it over to our house. Before Christmas he'd send over some meat even though he knew it was going on the tablet and he might never see his money. When the push came to the shove and every hungry belly in the house was beginning to eat on itself, Momma could go to Mister Ben and always gets enough for some dinner."[39] Such relationships may help explain why anti-Semitism was not even higher among those who hold attitudes, and report having had experiences, which would seem to predispose them toward anti-Semitism.[40]

In spite of the complexity of the relationship of the ghetto merchant to his low-income customer, it is not surprising that, when Negroes accept anti-Jewish stereotypes, they should tend to accept economic stereotypes. The economic sources of some Negro hostility to Jews can hardly be denied. It has been observed that a high degree of impersonal economic contact, perceived mistreatment by a Jewish merchant, and negative beliefs about Jewish credit practices all relate positively to anti-Semitism. To some extent, these factors may be seen to be causally linked. As degree of contact increases, so does perceived mistreatment by a Jewish merchant and negative beliefs about Jewish credit practices. They can now be combined into an index of predisposition to economically based anti-Semitism.

This index is very powerfully related to anti-Semitism. Among those with seemingly no predisposition to economically based anti-Semitism (these people have little economic contact with Jews, have never been mistreated by a Jewish merchant, and do not think Jewish credit practices are worse than those of other white merchants), only 13 per cent scored as anti-Semitic. This figure consistently increases to a maximum of 70 per cent for those who scored highest on the index. Looking only at those scored as very high on anti-Semitism, the figures increase from 3 per cent to 31 per cent (Table 98).

A word of caution must be introduced into this discussion. No time order unequivocally can be established for these data. It is far from clear that negative economic experiences with Jews always precede feelings of anti-Semitism, or whether it is primarily anti-Semitic persons who interpret their economic experiences with Jews negatively. Indeed, it seems likely that both sequences occur in real life. Still, it would seem to be an overly psychologistic interpretation of the data to dismiss Negro perceptions of their economic experiences with Jews as totally deriving from their pre-existing anti-Semitic attitudes. To an important extent, attitudes are fashioned from experiences, from factors outside the psyche. The fact of widespread economic contact between Negroes and Jews is certain, and that

[39] Dick Gregory, *Nigger,* New York, Dutton Pocket Cardinal Edition, 1965, p. 35.
[40] In addition, Caplovitz suggests that the ghetto merchant performs an important function for his low-income customers. In his traditionalistic relationship, he offers them the consumer goods desired by all yet without the customer's feeling overwhelmed and bewildered by having to go through the impersonal bureaucratic maze of the large department store (if he could obtain credit there, which often he cannot).

some hostility may arise from these contacts seems entirely plausible. Thus, while we do not assume that these contacts are the sole source of Negro hostility, it would seem from the data that they are an important source.[41]

Table 98.   ANTI-SEMITISM BY PREDISPOSITION TO ECONOMICALLY BASED ANTI-SEMITISM

Score on Index of Predisposition to Economically Based Anti-Semitism[a]

	Low 0	1	2	3	4	5	High 6
Anti-Semitic (including those very high)	13%	16%	29%	36%	50%	67%	70%
Very high on anti-Semitism	3	2	7	16	12	24	31
Number	(279)	(231)	(200)	(81)	(52)	(21)	(13)

[a] Those low, medium, and high in impersonal economic contact were scored 0, 1, and 2, respectively. Those who felt that Jews compared unfavorably with other whites with respect to credit practices were scored 2, while those not feeling this way received a score of 0. Respondents who reported being treated unfairly by a Jewish merchant were scored 2, while those who had never shopped at a Jewish store or those who did shop and had not been treated unfairly were scored 0, as were those who said "don't know." This table excludes 55 respondents who, because of interviewer error, were not asked if they were ever treated unfairly by a Jewish merchant, and 25 who could not be scored because they failed to respond or were not asked one or more of the other items used in the index.

It seems instructive at this point to inquire into the extent to which Negro anti-Semitism has economic origins. Some rough estimates can be made by simply observing what percentage of the people who scored as anti-Semitic are in situations where an economic explanation seems a reasonable one. When this is done, 24 per cent of the anti-Semites were in positions where an economic explanation of the hostility they expressed toward

[41] To the extent that these economic factors operate to produce hostile feelings toward Jews, greater government regulation of ghetto credit practices and consumer training for the poor might have much relevance in curtailing this hostility.

Another study in this series demonstrates the connection between a certain type of religious outlook and anti-Semitism, and concludes that the eradication of this religious source of anti-Semitism is up to the leaders of the church and the Christian community. However, given the data observed here it would seem that responsibility for the eradication of Negro anti-Semitism does not primarily lie within the Negro community but rather with the community at large. The general social conditions which can in some cases give rise to such vitriolic hatred of both Jewish and non-Jewish whites must be changed.

In addition, our data suggest that greater support of the Negro cause on behalf of the Jewish community as a whole and publicizing of this support would be important factors in the curtailment of hostility. It may be recalled that, even among those who were strongly predisposed to economically based anti-Semitism, only a small minority were in fact anti-Semitic when they were aware of Jewish civil rights support. In addition, it is particularly relevant that, although only 3 per cent of the sample felt Jews to be *less* in favor of Negro rights, this small group was particularly likely to be anti-Semitic.

Jews seems likely (those with scores of four or more on the Predisposition Index) and another 42 per cent of the sample (those with scores of two and three) are in situations where economic factors could be relevant. Indeed, only 17 per cent of those scored as anti-Semitic seem to lack any economic basis for their prejudice.

Among Negroes, as among whites, beliefs about Jews are largely determined by contact with the prevailing stereotypes, and the acceptance of these beliefs is no doubt affected by psychological factors. However, for Negroes, anti-Semitic stereotypes appear to be much more related to actual experiences with Jews in the economic world. The white anti-Semite who is concerned about the supposed power of international Jewish bankers and Jewish control of the mass media probably does not work for, rent from, and purchase from Jews to the extent that many Negroes in metropolitan areas do.

The involvement of Negroes with Jewish employers, landlords, and merchants is one reason that activities on behalf of improvement in the Negro's situation, though not inspired by anti-Semitism, sometimes come to have an anti-Semitic tone. The aim of such programs is frequently to encourage Negroes to patronize Negro-owned establishments or to make white merchants or landlords stop their unfair practices. They thus differ markedly from the anti-Semitic activities of whites which have focused more on the supposed political and economic power of Jews or their rejection of Christ, and which have had much wider goals of political, economic, and social discrimination. While Negro anti-Semitism is deplorable, it certainly is more understandable than white anti-Semitism. It is worthy of note that, where Jews do not predominate in the ghetto, the particular ethnic group that does is likely to be the recipient of economically inspired hostility. In some West Coast communities, this seems to be the Chinese. Drake and Cayton note that in New Orleans, where Italians are predominant in Negro areas, they are targets of attack,[42] and in the past, when Negroes had disproportionate contact with the Irish, considerable hostility was felt toward them.[43] Hostility toward West Indians has similar roots.

Even in areas where Jews do predominate, an important factor in reducing anti-Semitism and one that clearly differentiates the attitudes of Negroes from those of whites is that Jews are perceived as a minority group which has also suffered at the hands of the dominant group and which is more committed to Negro rights than other whites. Differences between anti-Semitism among Negroes and among whites may be largely explained by the economic involvement of Negroes and Jews, the Jewish position as a fellow minority group, and the fact that Jews are, in addition, a white group.

[42] St. Clair Drake and Horace Cayton, *Black Metropolis,* New York, Harper & Row, 1962, p. 432.
[43] Berry, *op. cit.,* p. 449.

The White Man

I'd say kill all them white folks. . . . Look at what they done to my people.

—*Housewife, New York*

All colors are alike. . . . There is some good and some bad among all of them.

—*Retired man, Cleveland*

Negroes have traditionally been taught to hide their hostility toward whites, and this hostility has often been expressed indirectly, or redirected against other Negroes. Still one need not look far for examples of it. The existence of a large number of derogatory words such as crackers, rednecks, white trash, lynchers, paddies, pinks, ofays, grays, cotton tops, peckerwoods, devils, buckras, whitey, charley, honkeys, and the use made of the usual derogatory names for white ethnic groups, attest to this hostility. Hostility is more evident in the sporadic outpourings of violence toward whites and white-owned property, the angry tone in the writings of many Negro novelists and essayists, and the hate-filled statements of young slum dwellers to which the mass media give such prominence. Whites are said to lack "soul" and spontaneity, in some circles to have no ability to blow jazz or dance and to be inferior to Negroes in athletic and sexual prowess.

Past research has found that, although Negroes tend to express relatively less social distance toward whites than whites do toward Negroes, there are always some who indicate no desire to have contact with whites.[1] An analysis of the stereotypes of whites in fiction written by Negroes

[1] For example, Donald L. Noel and Alphonso Pinkney, "Correlates of Prejudice: Some Racial Differences and Similarities," *American Journal of Sociology*, May 1964. Nevertheless, using comparable measures of social distance, this study notes that 41 per cent of Negroes in four American cities expressed no social distance feelings toward whites, while only 5 per cent of whites who were questioned were without social distance feelings toward Negroes.

In spite of probably universal tendencies toward stereotyping and the suffering of

notes "a significant bias toward the sordid and unlovely side of white characters" and finds that whites were most frequently characterized as feeling superior, hating Negroes, and being brutish, impulsive, and mean.[2]

Other research has discovered equally unfavorable stereotypes of whites as "grasping, deceitful, cruel, and quick-tempered." Such research has also found positive stereotypes, such as that whites are "intelligent and industrious."[3] This ambivalence toward whites shows up very clearly in the case of the Muslims, who accuse whites of being the lowest form of man, yet constantly admonish their members to observe the white man and copy many of his ways.

In this chapter our concern will not be with giving a broad description of the positive and negative stereotypes which Negroes hold of whites or with analyzing overt expressions of hostility.[4] Rather, attention will be

---

Negroes at the hands of whites, it is significant that in every study I have come across where comparisons are possible, Negroes express less social distance feelings, hostility, and negative stereotypes toward whites than whites express toward Negroes, and often the differences are very pronounced. While for some Negroes, experience as a member of a persecuted minority has no doubt led to bitterness and hatred, for a great many others it has developed an increased appreciation of the need for tolerance and of the variation that exists within any particular out-group.

[2] Tilman C. Cothran, "White Stereotypes in Fiction by Negroes," *Phylon,* 1950, p. 252. This study also notes that whites were categorized into "social types," some of which were "crackers," "rich whites," and, as a counter to the "good nigrah" the "decent white man."

[3] J. A. Bayton, "Racial Stereotypes of Negro College Students," *Journal of Abnormal and Social Psychology,* 1947. Positive as well as negative stereotypes are also reported in Tilman C. Cothran, "Negro Conceptions of White People in a Northeastern City," *American Journal of Sociology,* March 1951; and P. McDaniel and N. Babchuk, "Negro Conceptions of White People," *Phylon,* Spring 1960.

Similar images emerge in the conception Mexican Americans hold of the Anglo majority. Simmons reports that Mexicans have positive (ambitious and industrious) as well as negative (cold, unkind, and mercenary) stereotypes of Anglos (Ozzie G. Simmons, "Anglo-Americans and Mexican-Americans: Images and Expectations," in Bernard E. Segal, ed., *Racial and Ethnic Relations,* New York, Thomas Y. Crowell, 1966, p. 201).

The consistency of stereotypes held by Mexicans and Negroes reflects their shared structural position relative to the dominant whites. Stereotypes, while undoubtedly distortions of reality, are not necessarily unrelated to it.

Some consistency also emerges in the stereotypes Anglos hold of Negroes and Mexicans. Simmons indicates that Mexicans are seen as "musical" and fun loving ("always ready for a fiesta"). Negroes have traditionally been seen as childlike and musical (although in at least one instance Mexicans are stereotyped in the same way as Japanese Americans). Note the view that Mexicans "love flowers and can grow them under the most adverse conditions."

[4] The assumption is again made that, other factors being equal, people who feel hostility toward whites will be more likely to act out this hostility than those who do not. It should again be stressed that the relation between attitudes and behavior is by no means always a clear one; hostile attitudes may never be expressed in behavior and hostile behavior toward whites need not be supported by an elaborate and consistent antiwhite ideology.

focused exclusively on negative beliefs and feelings about whites, although it is important to keep in mind that most of those questioned probably also hold at least some positive stereotypes as well. Antiwhite sentiment will be considered in relation to anti-Semitism and in light of many of the social and psychological factors observed in past chapters.

Beliefs About Whites

The belief about whites most universally accepted was that "most whites want to keep Negroes down as much as they can"; more than seven out of ten respondents in each of the samples agreed with this statement (Table 99).[5] In light of American history and the indifference and prejudice of many whites today, this finding is easily understood.

In addition to this question about whites in general, respondents were asked about several white groups in particular. In the first chapter, it was seen that a sizable percentage of respondents in each sample felt that the police treated Negroes badly, from 23 per cent in Chicago to 60 per cent in Birmingham.[6] In the preceding chapter the relation of the low-income consumer to the Jewish ghetto merchant was discussed. Those interviewed were also asked their feelings about white store owners in general, and about one in five felt that "almost all" white merchants take advantage of Negro customers. In addition, nearly one in five felt that "many" white merchants take advantage; not even one in ten felt that "almost" no white merchants take advantage of Negroes (Table 99).

Respondents were asked a question about another white group—the white liberal, in the person of the white civil rights demonstrator. One of the ironies of racial and ethnic liberation movements, which often explicitly speak the language of racial purity or define opponents along racial lines, is that success is rarely obtained without the cooperation of some members of the "enemy" group, and in spite of the efforts of some members of its own group. In the last century white abolitionists existed alongside of Negroes who betrayed planned slave uprisings.

In the beginning stages of a movement sympathetic members of the dominant group are freer to act and have greater resources. They may add an aura of legitimacy to protest and are likely to be closer to the centers of power. In addition some members of the oppressed group may have a vested interest in maintaining the status quo while many others, isolated from alternative definitions of the situation and sunk in despair and apathy, may never come to question actively the legitimacy of the system.

[5] Research by Cothran and by McDaniel and Babchuk, referred to earlier, also found that of twenty-six "conceptions of white people" a similar statement was one of the two or three most widely accepted.

[6] Of course, some may have interpreted the question to mean police in general, Negro as well as white. However, the comments of most respondents indicated that they interpreted the question to mean white police.

There can be little doubt that some whites have had an important role in helping bring about recent civil rights change. Recently, much attention has been directed to the white liberal and his involvement in the civil rights struggle. James Baldwin has stated: "There is no role for the white liberal, he is our affliction." As skilled and articulate Negro leaders emerge who are less dependent on white financial and political power for support, and as pride in blackness increases, the role of the white concerned with civil rights has been increasingly open to scrutiny.

Table 99. BELIEFS ABOUT WHITES BY REGION

	Metro.	N.Y.	Chic.	Atl.	Birm.	Total
"Most whites want to keep Negroes down as much as they can."						
Agree	72%	72%	72%	76%	71%	73%
Disagree	26	26	26	22	24	25
Don't know	2	2	2	2	5	2
Total	100%	100%	100%	100%	100%	100%

"Some people have told us that there are white store owners who take advantage of Negro customers. How many white store owners would you say are like this?"

	Metro.	N.Y.	Chic.	Atl.	Birm.	Total
Almost all of them	20%	19%	22%	21%	22%	20%
Many of them	14	20	20	15	12	16
A few of them	44	43	42	38	39	41
Almost none of them	12	12	8	18	13	13
Don't know	10	6	8	8	14	10
Total	100%	100%	100%	100%	100%	100%

"Most whites who take part in civil rights demonstrations aren't really interested in the problems of Negroes."

	Metro.	N.Y.	Chic.	Atl.	Birm.	Total
Agree	27%	29%	28%	31%	35%	30%
Disagree	66	64	68	64	60	64
Don't know	7	7	4	5	5	6
Total	100%	100%	100%	100%	100%	100%
Number	(330)	(190)	(133)	(198)	(200)	(957)[a]

[a] As noted in Table 1 those interviews from the metropolitan area sample which occurred in New York (44 cases) and Chicago (54 cases) have been reported in both the metropolitan sample and the New York and Chicago samples. Hence the total reported in this column, and throughout this chapter, is less than, the total number of respondents for the samples shown separately. In addition, here and in all subsequent tables in this chapter those 162 cases from the metroplitan area sample interviewed by whites are excluded.

It has been suggested that it is degrading and reminiscent of an earlier rather lengthy period in American history to have whites lead and play a dominant role in Negro civil rights organizations. Their "missionary complex" has also been criticized as has the fact that, although they go further than other whites, they still often do not go far enough and sometimes act inconsistently. The black nationalist press has been particularly critical of whites, often meaning Jewish whites, for supposedly subverting these organizations to their own ends.

The white liberal, partly as a result of Negro support, has had considerable political power in this country since 1960, particularly with respect to domestic issues. Yet radical change in the patterning of race relations has not occurred, and segregation in the North is even increasing. Some black leaders have wondered why they should cooperate with such "liberal" whites if only token gains are forthcoming.

In addition it has been suggested that whites cannot understand the anguish that can result from being born black in a white man's country. Even when they are concerned, whites rarely appreciate the urgency of the movement. Furthermore, they may have other racial, ethnic, or religious interests, and these can affect their commitment. Beyond this, the deeply committed white activist tends to receive more attention from the press and protection from the government than the black activist, and the martyrdom of a white arouses much greater national indignation. Many blacks resent this and see it as a subtle kind of racism.

The radicalism of involved whites, which is often based on Marxian or pacifist ideology, and which is likely to be less narrowly focused on racial matters and involve a broader concern with the problems of American society, may be a source of tension. Thus the white activist tends to be against the war in Vietnam because it is killing people, not because it is killing yellow people, and he opposes the draft because it is seen as a violation of individual liberty and not because it drafts black people who are otherwise not free.

The fact that whites could leave the struggle and attendant problems faced by black people anytime they chose has also been resented. Of course, part of the hostility felt toward white liberals stems from the fact that they are white; no matter how great the sincerity of whites, certain tensions are structured into the relationship.[7] Difficulty in communicating deeply will probably characterize Negro-white relationships for many years. In some cases it is possible that, as a readily accessible symbol (in some instances

[7] A Negro civil rights activist reports, "I've been in the Movement in North Carolina and there were whites in it too. We got arrested together and we were beaten together, but we were still divided because there was no real understanding between us. . . . Even in the cell, the whites were at one end of the cell and we were at the other end" (as quoted in Nat Hentoff, *The New Equality,* New York, Viking, 1965, pp. 16–17).

In light of the belief that whites dominate and control civil rights organizations it is interesting to note Powell's finding that "CORE groups are dominated—often numerically and almost always psychologically by the Negro members" (Ingeborg B. Powell, "Ideology and Strategy of Direct Action: A Study of the Congress of Racial Equality," Ph.D. dissertation, University of California in Berkeley, 1965, p. 308). In terms of the militancy of whites she notes ". . . in the Southern chapters whites are more radical than Negroes, and probably provide a radicalizing influence, while in the Northern chapters whites are more moderate than Negroes and exert a moderating influence" (*ibid.,* p. 327).

perhaps even wanting to suffer and feel guilty), the white liberal becomes a scapegoat for the hostility felt toward whites in general. At the same time, the white liberal is at least a friend, in contrast with the majority of bigoted or apathetic whites.

Feelings toward the white liberal are no doubt quite complex, and our questionnaire did not begin to tap the subtleties of this relationship. Respondents were asked whether they agreed or disagreed with the statement "Most whites who take part in civil rights demonstrations aren't really interested in the problems of Negroes." At the time this question was

Table 100. FEELINGS TOWARD WHITES, BY REGION

	Metro	N.Y.	Chic.	Atl.	Birm.	Total
"I am suspicious of whites who try to help Negroes."						
Yes, true	20%	23%	15%	16%	23%	19%
No, not true	78	74	83	79	74	78
Don't know	2	3	2	5	3	3
Total	100%	100%	100%	100%	100%	100%
"It bothers me to see immigrants succeeding more than Americans who were born here."						
Yes, true	51%	54%	55%	47%	45%	50%
No, not true	47	44	42	47	53	47
Don't know	2	2	3	6	2	3
Total	100%	100%	100%	100%	100%	100%

asked, the murder of the three young civil rights workers in Mississippi was still drawing much attention in the press. Although roughly three out of ten of those in each of the various samples indicated agreement with the statement, two-thirds of the sample rejected it out of hand.[8] While a substantial number of Negroes do reject the sincerity of white civil rights activists[9] the overwhelming majority accept them as genuine.

[8] In this regard it is interesting to note that in a study done in 1949, 55 per cent of the respondents agreed with the statement "White liberals give largely lip service" and 34 per cent agreed that "liberals are not sincere" (percentages recomputed from data presented in Cothran, "Negro Conceptions of White People").

[9] However, this suspiciousness is not necessarily directed only toward whites. Dick Gregory, in commenting on the suspiciousness found among Mississippi blacks when he came to march, notes, "What scared me most was when Negroes asked if it was true that I had gone down to Greenwood for publicity. And it dawned on me that anytime you help a Negro in America, even the Negroes will question your intentions. I could have quit show business and joined the Peace Corps and gone to Viet Nam and no one, white or black, would have questioned why I did it. But to help Negroes . . ." (*Nigger*, New York, Dutton Pocket Cardinal Edition, 1965, p. 177).

Furthermore, civil rights organizations are often extremely critical of each other behind the scenes. Jealousies and the desire to be independent go far beyond criticizing white liberals and lead to much in-fighting and name-calling of other civil rights workers who are black. Criticism of whites is one aspect of a pervasive desire for autonomy and independence.

The questionnaire also included several items to tap personal feelings toward whites in general. Although it was noted that more than seven out of ten believed that whites want to keep Negroes down as much as they can, only about one in five respondents said "yes" to the statement, "I am suspicious of whites who try to help Negroes" (Table 100).[10] That less suspiciousness is expressed in this question than in the one dealing with civil rights demonstrators may be attributed in part to the fact that white civil rights workers, often outside the mainstream of contemporary American life and somewhat unconventional in dress and behavior, have frequently been stigmatized by the mass media.

According to some observers, Negro hostility is particularly pronounced toward white immigrants.[11] Impoverished European immigrants were often drawn to the same slum areas as poor Southern Negroes, and they competed with each other in the unskilled labor market. In the past Negroes were said to be losing their jobs only to be replaced by white foreign workers.[12] It would be surprising if the preferential treatment and success of newly arrived immigrants, unable to speak English, did not arouse feelings of hostility among many native-born Negro Americans forced to remain mired in the ghetto. Almost one out of two of those in the different samples said "yes" to the statement "It bothers me to see immigrants succeeding more than Americans who were born here" (Table 100).[13]

[10] Although this is perhaps the "hardest" antiwhite item in the survey, it may seem surprising that only about one in five of those questioned accepted it. However, past research using similar "hard" items has found that the overwhelming majority of the black community does not indicate hatred of whites or a desire for revenge. For example, a study done in Elmira, New York, Bakersfield, California, and Savannah, Georgia, found that only about three respondents in ten said "yes" to the statement "Sometimes I hate white people" (Donald L. Noel, "Correlates of Anti-White Prejudice: Attitudes of Negroes in Four American Cities," Ph.D. dissertation, Cornell University, 1960, p. 161). Respondents in Elmira were asked their feelings about the statement, "I would like to get even with the white man for some of the things he has done to Negroes"; and one in four said "yes." In response to a question similar to that considered above, about one in four felt that "No matter how nicely he treats a Negro, a white man doesn't really mean it" (Robert B. Johnson, "Negro Reaction to Minority Group Status," in M. Barron, ed., *American Minorities,* New York, Alfred Knopf, 1957, p. 201).

[11] B. Berry, *Race and Ethnic Relations,* Boston, Houghton Mifflin, 1958, p. 416: "Negroes have traditionally manifested a bitter prejudice against foreigners." Another observer notes: "Often this hostility is deflected at specific groups, particularly the foreign born, who are resented as having greater privilege on their first day in America" (Johnson, *op. cit.,* p. 201). However, Johnson mentions that in the city he studied this hostility was not directed against Jews.

[12] St. Clair Drake and Horace Cayton, *Black Metropolis,* New York, Harper & Row, 1962, p. 83.

[13] Since this question did not specifically mention white immigrants, it is possible that some may have had Puerto Ricans or West Indians in mind as well. Conflict within the ghetto community between native-born Negroes and West Indians has often been noted, partly due perhaps to the greater success of the West Indians. Conflict between Negroes and Puerto Rican and Cuban immigrants has also been noted and seems to be increasing.

Respondents were asked an additional question which may to some extent be seen as a measure of social distance preference. This question involved the kind of neighborhood the individual would like to live in. It can be seen that the majority of those in each of the samples indicated that they preferred a "mostly Negro neighborhood" (Table 101).[14] While, by itself, the preference for a mostly Negro neighborhood cannot be taken as an indication of antiwhite sentiment, when it is coupled with the negative beliefs and feelings considered above it may serve as a rough indicator of social distance preference (one type of antiwhite attitude).

Each of the previously mentioned aspects of antiwhite sentiment (belief, feeling, and social distance) was positively related to the other, and they have been combined into an antiwhite index.[15]

Although all areas of the country are characterized by prejudice and discrimination against Negroes, these are most visible and receive the most

[14] This certainly does not mean that these people are satisfied with conditions in their present neighborhoods or that they would endorse legally enforced segregation. It should also be noted that when they were asked to express a preference for an *all-*Negro neighborhood as against one that is mostly Negro, a different pattern emerges. In this case only 20 per cent of a national survey preferred a *totally* Negro neighborhood. (W. Brink and L. Harris, *The Negro Revolution in America,* New York, Simon and Schuster, 1964, p. 159.)

Rather than viewing this pattern of response as a measure of social distance, Clark notes, "A most cruel and psychologically oppressive aspect and consequence of enforced segregation is that its victims can be made to accommodate to their victimized status and under certain circumstances to state that it is their desire to be set apart . . ." (Kenneth Clark, *Dark Ghetto,* New York, Harper & Row, 1965, p. 63).

[15] The belief items used were those which asked about white civil rights demonstrators and white merchants (thinking almost all white merchants take advantage of Negroes was scored as "antiwhite"). The feeling items used were those which asked about suspiciousness of whites "who try to help" and being bothered by the success of immigrants. An antiwhite response to any of the previously mentioned items was scored one, while those who said "don't know" or did not give the antiwhite response were scored zero. On the other hand, for the social distance item, those who preferred a Negro neighborhood received a score of two while those who preferred a more mixed neighborhood or who said "don't know" received a score of zero. Thus each of the several aspects of antiwhite sentiment considered is weighted equally.

It might be argued that, in accepting these various statements about whites, Negroes are not giving evidence of irrational prejudice or excessive stereotyping and that their responses to some extent approximate reality. Certainly this is true when beliefs Negroes hold about whites are compared with those whites hold about Negroes. However, despite the extreme treatment Negroes have received at the hands of some whites and the indifference of many others, it would seem that something more than recognition of reality is being expressed in acceptance of many of the items included in the index. In any case, the question of the extent to which hostility toward whites, as measured by the index, is justified is entirely independent of analyzing its social and psychological correlates.

Some evidence of the internal validity of the index is provided by the fact that only 12 per cent of those with scores of zero felt that the police treated Negroes very badly, and this figure steadily increases to a high of 54 per cent for those with scores of six on the Antiwhite Index.

support, both by custom and overt violence, in the South. Numerous studies have shown that white Southerners are more prejudiced toward Negroes than whites in other areas of the country. It might be expected that Southern Negroes would respond in kind. It is thus somewhat surprising to see that about one respondent in four scored as anti-white (score of four, five, or six) regardless of the area of the country (Table 102).[16]

Table 101. RESIDENTIAL PREFERENCE BY REGION

	Metro	N.Y.	Chic.	Atl.	Birm.	Total
Type of neighborhood preferred, if all equally well kept up:						
Mostly Negro	55%	52%	68%	74%	69%	62%
Mixed or no difference	38	35	25	18	27	31
Mostly white	4	9	5	5	1	4
Don't know	3	3	4	2	3	3
Total	100%	100%	100%	100%	100%	100%

However, those in the South were more likely than Negroes in New York or in the metropolitan area sample to show at least some antiwhite sentiment. They were less likely to score zero or one (least antiwhite feeling) on the index. In considering just the extremes of the index, those in New York have both the highest percentage very antiwhite and the highest percentage free of antiwhite sentiment.

It may seem surprising that antiwhite sentiment was not more widespread at the time of the study. However, these data are consistent with past research using interview techniques if not with the occasional pronounce-

[16] Since the present study did not make any social class or geographical distinctions in the wording of the questions, it must be assumed that respondents were answering with respect to whites in general. It is worthy of note that past research has found relatively greater feelings of social distance expressed toward Southern than toward Northern whites and toward whites of lower social position than toward those of higher social status (J. B. Edlefsen, "Social Distance Attitudes of Negro College Students," *Phylon*, 1956; and F. Westie and D. H. Howard "Social Status Differentials and Race Attitudes of Negroes," *American Sociological Review*, 1954).

Some evidence of regional bias can be seen in the fact that many Negroes prejudge whites on the basis of whether or not they come from the South. Carl Rowan notes: "It's only after considerable experience and the attaining of a degree of intellectual sophistication that a Negro is honestly able to say that he doesn't judge white men by where they come from" (as quoted in Robert Penn Warren, *Who Speaks for the Negro*, New York, Random House, 1965, p. 308). With respect to differential class hostility, Richard Wright states: "And rich white people were not so hard on Negroes; it was the poor whites who hated Negroes" (*Native Son*, New York, New American Library, 1964). This belief is no doubt related to the widespread notion among subordinates that the people at the top are noble and just creatures whose will is somehow subverted by evil intermediaries.

Table 102. SCORE ON ANTI-WHITE INDEX, BY REGION

Score on Antiwhite Index		Metro	N.Y.	Chic.	Atl.	Birm.	Total
Not antiwhite	0	14% } 32%	16% } 37%	7% } 21%	8% } 18%	11% } 20%	12% } 27%
	1	18	21	14	10	9	15
Low in antiwhite hostility	2	26	18	30	27	23	25
	3	19	20	23	32	32	25
Antiwhite	4	15	13	16	13	17	15
	5	7 } 23	8 } 25	10 } 26	9 } 23	7 } 25	7 } 23
	6	1	4	0	1	1	1
Total		100%	100%	100%	100%	100%	100%

ments of angry Negroes, journalists, and some psychiatrists.[17] It must be kept in mind, of course, that in an interview some people may be hesitant to express their true feelings about other groups. Negroes, in particular, as a matter of survival have been trained to conceal their real thoughts, often even from each other. To the extent that this occurs, the findings underestimate the extent of antiwhite sentiment. However, it is doubtful that the bias introduced in this fashion is a serious one, since on such an item as "Most whites want to keep Negroes down," the overwhelming majority of Negroes interviewed were perfectly willing to criticize whites. It might even be argued that, given the fervor of the civil rights struggle, the current norm is to express hostility toward whites, and hence a bias in the other direction may exist.

A more important factor reducing the amount of antiwhite sentiment found in surveys is that the interviews are usually carried out in the quiet of the respondents' homes, divorced from real-life incidents. Presumably most Negroes at some time feel aggression and hostility toward whites.[18] If people were to be questioned right after they had experienced a personal affront, or after the bombing of a Birmingham church, or after the governor of Mississippi shakes hands with the accused slayer of Medgar Evers, the

[17] For example, one interview study reports "Hatred of whites is amazingly rare in all three communities surveyed" (Noel, *op. cit.*, p. 169). And a recently completed University of California study of almost all junior and senior high school students in Richmond, California, a racially tense area, reports that in response to the question "How do you feel about whites?" of the Negro students, only 8 per cent said "dislike them," while 41 per cent said "like them" and 51 per cent responded don't especially like or dislike them." Alan B. Wilson, Travis Hirschi, Glen Elder, "Richmond Youth Project, Technical Report 1," Survey Research Center. Making use of social distance measures, a 1966 Howard University study of high school seniors and drop-outs in Washington, D.C., notes "a remarkably high willingness to associates with whites." Sophia F. McDowell, "Prejudice and Other Interracial Attitudes of Negro Youth," unpublished interim report.

In contrast, a psychiatrist writes, ". . . I have yet to see a Negro who did not unconsciously have a deep fear of and hostility toward white people" (Helen McLean, "The Emotional Health of Negroes," *Journal of Negro Education*, 1949, p. 286). Other psychiatrists, including Harry Stack Sullivan, have expressed similar ideas (see Thomas F. Pettigrew, *A Profile of the Negro American*, Princeton, N. J., Van Nostrand, 1964, p. 40). However, as is often the case in their remarks about homosexuality, the comments of psychiatrists tend to be based upon observations made in a clinical setting. It would seem doubtful that the experiences and attitudes of those under psychiatric care are necessarily representative.

[18] This seems to be Baldwin's point in qualifying what he considers earlier misinterpretations of his statements about categorical hatred of whites: "And as far as I know . . . I never said that all Negroes hate white people either. What I *have* said is that I cannot imagine any Negro in this country who has not for at least one of the twenty-four hours of a day hated all white people just because they were on his back" (James Baldwin, *Commentary*, March 1964, p. 36).

Even Martin Luther King has stated: "I just saw Malcolm X on television. I can't deny it. When he starts talking about all that's been done to us, I get a twinge of hate, of identification with him" (Hentoff, *op. cit.*, p. 47).

amount of hostility discovered would no doubt be much greater than it appears here.[19]

Even though the vast majority of Negroes do not consistently hate or feel hostility toward whites in general, this certainly does not mean that they have any undue love for them. In a study done in New York City, respondents were asked, "How do you think most Negroes feel about whites?" Consistent with the data observed above, only 7 per cent of the sample said "most Negroes hate whites."[20] However, what is of greater interest is the fact that *only 5 per cent* indicated "most Negroes like whites," while 63 per cent felt most Negroes "don't hate [whites] but don't like them either" (Table 103). Perhaps the mood of the majority is captured by one man who said, "White people have done us wrong for so many years, that's why we don't like them. But I can't say we really hate them. We have to live together, don't we?"

Antiwhite Attitudes and Anti-Semitism

In the previous chapter it was pointed out that Negro anti-Semitism may in fact be only one aspect of a more general hostility toward whites. Contrary to popular opinion, much Negro anti-Semitism may be directed not at Jews as Jews, but at Jews as whites. Indeed, the data showed that, to

[19] These data certainly do not mean that widespread hostility may not be felt toward certain whites. On the other hand, even those consistently antiwhite may still differentiate among whites, in spite of the image of categorical hatred created by the mass media. For example, in an article in the San Francisco *Chronicle* of July 19, 1966, about the arrest of two young men in a "near riot," entitled "Two Young Men Who Hate Whitey," one is quoted as saying, "Not all whiteys are bad, just most of them." Some, however, would no doubt go along with the following parable offered by Malcolm X to Robert Penn Warren before his attitudes changed as a result of his trip to Mecca and break with the Muslims:

Warren: What about the matter of nonselective reprisal?

Malcolm X: Well, I'll tell you, if I go home and my child has blood running down her leg and someone tells me a snake bit her, I'm going out and kill snakes, and when I find a snake I'm not going to look and see if he has blood on his jaws.

Warren: You mean you'd kill any snake you could find?

Malcolm X: I grew up in the country, on a farm. And whenever a snake was bothering the chickens, we'd kill snakes. We never knew which was the snake did it.

Warren: To read your parable, then, you would advocate nonselective reprisals?

Malcolm X: I'm just telling you about snakes.

(Warren, *op. cit.*, p. 261.)

[20] It is interesting to contrast the almost complete absence of the belief that "most Negroes hate whites" with the finding that, in both a Southern and a Northern city, more than six out of ten workingclass Negroes believe "white people hate Negroes" and roughly four out of ten of those high in status believe this (Cothran, *op. cit.*, and McDaniel and Babchuk, *op. cit.*).

the extent that Negroes distinguished between Jewish and non-Jewish whites as merchants, landlords, and employers, they overwhelmingly preferred Jews.

We may now pursue these findings in a more general context by relating the Index of Anti-Semitism to the Antiwhite Index. To what extent is anti-Semitism identical with antiwhite hostility; to what extent are Jews a special target, a scapegoat for Negro anger?

Table 103.   HOW DO YOU THINK MOST NEGROES FEEL ABOUT WHITES?[a]

Hate whites	6%
Some Negroes hate whites	13
Negroes hate some whites	7
Don't hate whites but don't like them either	63
Like whites	5
Don't know	6
Total	100%
Number	(190)

[a] Taken from *New York Times* survey of New York City Negroes, reported July 27, 1964.

As is evident in Table 104, antiwhite and anti-Semitic feelings are very strongly related. Among those with scores of zero on the Antiwhite Index, only 5 per cent scored as anti-Semitic and 58 per cent scored as non-anti-Semitic. As score on the Antiwhite Index increases, the percentage anti-Semitic increases to 69 per cent among the most antiwhite group. Furthermore, among the 13 respondents in the most antiwhite group, not a single one scored as non-anti-Semitic.

When these two measures are combined, an elaborate typology of attitudes toward Jewish whites and toward whites in general emerges. This typology permits an over-all description of the extensiveness of Negro hostility. In the total sample, 13 per cent gave almost no evidence of either antiwhite or anti-Jewish hostility, and another 29 per cent seem quite low on both (scoring as non-anti-Semitic, but low on the antiwhite index, or vice versa). At the other extreme, 9 per cent of the sample scored as high on both the Anti-Semitism Index and the Antiwhite Index, and another 29 per cent of the sample expressed considerable hostility on both, scoring as anti-Semitic and expressing a moderate amount of antiwhite sentiment or vice versa (Table 105). The cells of this typology with the fewest num-

Table 104. ANTI-SEMITISM BY INDEX OF ANTIWHITE ATTITUDES

Score on Anti-Semitism Index	Score on Antiwhite Index						
	Not Anti-white		Low in Antiwhite Attitudes			Antiwhite	
	0	1	2	3	4	5	6
Not anti-Semitic (0, 1)	58%	39%	41%	36%	23%	10%	0%
Low on anti-Semitism (2, 3, 4)	37	38	41	39	45	47	31
High on anti-Semitism (5, 6)	4 } 5%	19 } 23%	13 } 18%	20 } 25%	23 } 32%	25 } 43%	31 } 69%
Very high on anti-Semitism (7, 8, 9)	1	4	5	5	9	18	38
Total	100%	100%	100%	100%	100%	100%	100%
Number	(113)	(135)	(227)	(231)	(136)	(68)	(13)

ber of cases are those containing respondents with the most markedly inconsistent attitudes. Four per cent of the combined samples scored as high on the Anti-Semitism Index, yet gave no evidence of antiwhite sentiment, and the same percentage scored as antiwhite yet gave no indication of anti-Semitism. Combining closely related categories, about four in ten of those interviewed evidenced little or no hostility toward either Jews or whites in general (hostility was expressed toward neither group or moderate hostility was expressed toward only one group), two in ten expressed moderate hostility toward both groups (scoring in the middle categories of both indexes), and about three in ten expressed considerable hostility toward both groups (scoring as high on both indexes or high on one and moderate on the other).

Table 105. A TYPOLOGY OF NEGRO HOSTILITY TOWARD WHITES IN GENERAL AND TOWARD JEWS

Score on Anti-Semitism Index	Score on Antiwhite Index		
	Not antiwhite (0, 1)	Low on antiwhite hostility (2, 3)	Antiwhite (4, 5, 6)
Not anti-Semitic (0, 1)	13%	19%	4%
Low on anti-Semitism (2, 3, 4)	10	20	11
Anti-Semitic (5, 6, 7, 8, 9)	4	10	9
Total		100%	
Number		(923)	

Thus, pure anti-Semitism, not accompanied by antiwhite feelings, is to be found among only 4 per cent of the sample. Exactly the same proportion harbored antiwhite sentiments unaccompanied by anti-Semitism. For the vast majority of Negroes, the two are relatively indistinguishable, and more than half of our respondents expressed very little hostility on either index. Indeed, only 30 per cent showed much hostility toward both, and only 9 per cent could be called both definitely anti-Semitic and definitely antiwhite.

These patterns were virtually identical in all regions. The only slight deviation was that of New York Negroes and those in the metropolitan sample. These respondents were a bit more likely to be anti-Semitic but not antiwhite (8 and 6 per cent, respectively) than they were to be antiwhite but not anti-Semitic (4 and 3 per cent, respectively). In Chicago and the South, respondents were slightly more likely to be antiwhite but not anti-Semitic than to be the reverse. Thus, pure anti-Semitism is slightly more common, but still very rare, in New York and in Northern metropolitan areas, while pure antiwhite feelings are a bit more common, but still rare, elsewhere. It must be emphasized that these are very uncommon patterns anywhere, but they provide the only meaningful regional variations to be seen in Table 106.

For those few respondents in each sample (one in twenty-five of the combined samples) who scored as anti-Semitic yet gave no evidence of antiwhite sentiments, the scapegoat interpretation of hostility expressed toward Jews might be applied.[21] However, since for most respondents de-

Table 106.   HOSTILITY TO JEWISH WHITES AND WHITES IN GENERAL BY REGION

Hostility to Jewish Whites and Whites in General	Metro.	N.Y.	Chic.	Atl.	Birm.	Total
Not hostile to either[a]	42%	42%	45%	42%	41%	42%
Moderately hostile to both[b]	18	15	18	24	22	20
Hostile to both[c]	31	31	29	29	29	30
Anti-Semitic but not antiwhite	6	8	3	2	1	4
Antiwhite but not anti-Semitic	3	4	5	3	7	4
Total	100%	100%	100%	100%	100%	100%
Number	(320)	(186)	(131)	(195)	(190)	(923)

[a] Those who scored as neither antiwhite nor anti-Semitic and those who exhibited moderate hostility on one and no hostility on the other.
[b] Those who scored as moderately hostile on both measures.
[c] Those who scored as high in antiwhite attitudes and anti-Semitism, or as moderate in one and high in the other.

gree of hostility expressed toward Jews was roughly comparable to degree of hostility expressed toward whites, it appears that the scapegoat interpretation does not have widespread applicability, at least in the sense that hostility is expressed toward Jews but not toward whites in general. Even in New York City, where the data offer the most support for such an interpretation, the overwhelming majority of those scored as anti-Semites also expressed hostility toward whites. From observing the strong relation

21 Even here the scapegoat theory must be used with much more caution than in the case of white anti-Semitism. As was noted in the last chapter, because of the economic involvement of Negroes and Jews there may be some very concrete sources for hostility felt toward Jews, independent of attitudes toward whites in general. In addition, this "singling out of the Jews" for hostility must be considered in perspective by noting that an equal number of respondents (for the combined samples) singled them out by expressing no hostility toward them yet a great deal of hostility toward whites in general.

of these measures to each other it appears that, for many, "Negro anti-Semitism" is simply a reflection of the hostility felt toward all whites.[22]

This is not true for all Negroes. Four per cent were anti-Semitic but not anti-white. Another 4 per cent were antiwhite but not anti-Semitic. It is possible to distinguish these two groups, and thus partly account for the discrepancy in their attitudes, on the basis of their perceptions of and experiences with Jews (Table 107). Persons who were exclusively anti-

Table 107.   PERCEPTIONS OF JEWS BY ANTI-SEMITIC AND ANTIWHITE TYPOLOGY

	Anti-Semitic, but Not Antiwhite	Antiwhite, but Not Anti-Semitic	Others in Sample
Per cent who regard Jews as a minority group supportive of civil rights	33%	52%	41%
Number	(27)	(21)	(534)
Per cent high on predisposition to economically based anti Semitism	31%	13%	19%
Number	(35)	(37)	(789)

Semitic were less likely than others in the sample to perceive of Jews as belonging to a persecuted minority or to recognize their support of the civil rights movement. On the other hand, Negroes who are hostile toward whites but not toward Jews are more likely than the average to see Jews as allies and as also discriminated against.

Similarly, the extent to which Negroes have predispositions for economic hard feelings toward Jews is more widespread among exclusively anti-

[22] Of course, just because many of the people who are anti-Semitic are also anti-white, it does not follow that in all cases the sources of these attitudes are necessarily the same or that the same negative characteristics are assigned to both Jews and non-Jews, although this may often be the case. A notable exception may be seen in Claude Brown's report of a conversation with a younger brother:

"Sonny, what is crackers? They ain't the kinda crackers you buy in the candy store, is they?"

"No, the crackers down South is white people, real mean, white people."

"Is Mr. Goldman a cracker, Sonny?"

"No, he's a Jew."

"But he's white and look real mean."

"I know that, but some white people is crackers and some-a dem is Jews, and Mr. Goldman is a Jew. You see, Pimp, white people is all mean and stingy. If one-a dem is more stingy than he is mean, he's a Jew; and if he is more mean than he is stingy, then he's a cracker."

(Claude Brown, *Manchild in the Promised Land,* New York, Macmillan, 1965, p. 43.)

Semitic Negroes than among others in the sample—31 per cent versus 19. Conversely, Negroes who exclusively dislike whites are less likely to have these economic predispositions toward anti-Semitism (13 per cent).

In another study in this series, *Christian Beliefs and Anti-Semitism*,[23] the authors analyze the Christian roots of much contemporary anti-Semitism, making use of a fairly involved series of measures. One facet of their analysis involved the belief that Jews were guilty of rejecting Jesus, and hence were subject to God's wrath. When acceptance of this belief was examined in the present study, it was found that those who were anti-Semitic but not antiwhite were more likely than others in the sample to think that God is punishing the Jews for rejecting Jesus.

Thus these two groups may be distinguished from one another by the presence of factors working against anti-Semitism, and the absence of those working for it, among persons whose prejudice is limited to non-Jewish whites. The opposite is the case for persons who are anti-Semitic, but not antiwhite.

Some Sources of Anti-White Attitudes[24]

One important indication of the changing pattern of race relations in America may be seen in the effect of age on attitudes of racial tolerance. Many studies have shown that among white Americans, as age decreases, tolerances increases.[25] This is not only because the younger are better educated, but because they are more likely to be brought up in a milieu which encourages tolerance and respect for differences among people. It is somewhat ironic that, although the attitudes of white Americans toward Negroes may be becoming more favorable, the reverse is not necessarily true. While the differences are not large, as age decreases there is a tendency for antiwhite sentiment to increase from 14 to 27 per cent (Table 108). When the effect of education is held constant, this tendency becomes much more pronounced. Thus, among people with only a grammar school education, 47 per cent of those under 29 scored as antiwhite in contrast to 23 per cent of those 60 and over. Among the college educated, in the youngest group 20 per cent scored as antiwhite while none of the college educated over 60 did.

[23] Charles Y. Glock and Rodney Stark, New York, Harper and Row, 1966.

[24] Given the strong relation between anti-Semitism and antiwhite attitudes, in almost all cases the variables to be observed in this section relate to both in the same way. Data will therefore be presented only for the more general Antiwhite Index.

[25] For a recent example, see P. Sheatsley, "White Attitudes Toward the Negro," *Daedalus*, Winter 1966, p. 228. However, in the South younger whites who have reached maturity during the civil rights struggle seem somewhat more intolerant than those slightly older.

Differences between the sexes were less pronounced than for age, although in each sample there was a slight tendency for women to score higher than men in antiwhite attitudes (Table 108).

Table 108. ANTIWHITE ATTITUDES BY AGE AND BY SEX

	Age				
	Under 30	30–44	45–59	60–75	75+
High in antiwhite attitudes	27%	25%	23%	19%	14%
Number	(199)	(320)	(232)	(154)	(28)

	Sex	
	Men	Women
High in antiwhite attitudes	21%	25%
Number	(420)	(515)

In observing regional differences, those brought up in the deep South were the most hostile, while those raised within the United States, but outside the South, were somewhat less antiwhite. Among those few respondents raised outside of the United States only 5 per cent were antiwhite (Table 109).

Table 109. ANTIWHITE ATTITUDES BY AREA RAISED IN

State Where Most of Childhood Was Spent

	Deep South	Border States	Non-South	Outside U.S.
High in antiwhite attitudes	26%	24%	18%	5%
Number	(486)	(235)	(235)	(20)
High in antiwhite attitudes (among those now living in the North)	29%	24%	17%	
Number	(129)	(202)	(219)	

An earlier study of hostility among Negroes noted that "migrants from the South in particular, who have stored away memories of deep cutting offenses discreetly tolerated in the South, may reveal undue aggressiveness [in the North]."[26] In the present study, among those who were raised in the South and then moved to the North, 29 per cent were antiwhite, while for those raised in the North this figure drops to 17 per cent (Table 109).

[26] Charles S. Johnson, *Patterns of Negro Segregation*, New York, Harper and Row, 1943, p. 310.

The fact that many of those currently living in the North are migrants from the South may help explain why regional differences in antiwhite sentiment were not more pronounced. When migrants are excluded, differences in antiwhite hostility between the North and the South become more pronounced, although they are still not large. For example, among those in the metropolitan area sample 38 per cent gave almost no indication of antiwhite sentiment and 17 per cent scored high in such sentiment.

Table 110. ANTIWHITE ATTITUDES BY REGION (EXCLUDING SOUTH-NORTH AND NORTH-SOUTH MIGRANTS)

	Metro.	N.Y.	Chic.	Atl.	Birm.
Not antiwhite (0, 1)	38%	40%	24%	16%	19%
Low on antiwhite attitudes (2, 3)	45	41	54	60	56
Antiwhite (4, 5, 6)	17	19	22	24	25
Total	100%	100%	100%	100%	100%
Number	(133)	(74)	(49)	(190)	(179)

However, in Atlanta only 16 per cent were without antiwhite hostility and 24 per cent scored as high in antiwhite attitudes (Table 110). Those raised on farms and in small cities were slightly more antiwhite than those raised in big cities.

It may be recalled that, in Chapter 2, age, sex, type of community, and region were combined into an index of presumed exposure to values legitimating protest. This index was strongly related to civil rights concern. It might be thought that a measure which was useful in predicting militancy would also be useful in predicting antiwhite sentiment, and to some extent it is. However, the direction of the prediction is the opposite of that observed for militancy. As score on the Value Exposure Index increases, the percentage scoring as antiwhite remains about the same; however, the percentage scoring as not at all antiwhite increases from 18 and 15 per cent among those with scores of zero and one to 34 and 31 per cent among those with scores of six and seven (Table 111). The significant thing about this table is not that this inverse relation between presumed exposure to protest values and antiwhite attitudes is so pronounced but that it is the reverse of the relation noted for militancy. With the exception of age, each of the variables summarized in this index related positively to militancy but negatively to antiwhite hostility.

This pattern may be more understandable when it is realized that the variables summarized in the index are presumed to differentiate those largely exposed to the values of the traditional South from those more

Table 111.   ANTIWHITE ATTITUDES BY EXPOSURE TO VALUES LEGITIMIZING PROTEST

Score on Index of Exposure to Values Legitimizing Protest

	High on Presumed Exposure to Values of Traditional South				High on Presumed Exposure to Equalitarian Values		
	0	1	2	3	4	5	6	7
Not antiwhite (0, 1)	18%	15%	23%	23%	22%	35%	34%	31%
Low in antiwhite attitudes (2, 3)	64	58	55	48	56	46	47	47
Antiwhite (4, 5, 6)	18	27	22	29	22	19	19	22
Total	100%	100%	100%	100%	100%	100%	100%	100%
Number	(40)	(102)	(131)	(212)	(183)	(106)	(100)	(55)

exposed to the equalitarian values of the rest of the country. For many, removal from the normative patterns of the traditional South and the resultant greater sophistication may lead to greater appreciation of the need for tolerance (among whites as well as Negroes) which then may serve to inspire protest. Of course, for some, the intensity of protest may serve to diminish tolerance. However, the data suggest that hatred and suspiciousness of whites is much more a part of the Southern Negro's culture than the Northern; if this is true then it is not surprising that those most removed from Southern culture are the more tolerant.[27]

The social privilege variables examined earlier also relate inversely to

Table 112.   ANTIWHITE ATTITUDES BY SOCIAL CLASS

Social Class

	Lower 0	1	2	3	4	5	Upper 6
Not antiwhite	15%	23%	30%	29%	34%	35%	40%
Low on antiwhite attitudes	54	41	47	51	49	49	43
Antiwhite	31	26	23	20	17	16	17
Total	100%	100%	100%	100%	100%	100%	100%
Number	(156)	(207)	(233)	(181)	(91)	(37)	(30)

[27] Robin Williams reports similar findings in *Strangers Next Door,* Englewood Cliffs, N. J., Prentice-Hall, 1964, pp. 257–258.

antiwhite attitudes, although differences are not great. For example, 27 per cent of those with only a grammar school education scored as anti-white; this decrease to 14 per cent among those who have attended college. When education and age are observed together, the least hostility is shown by those over 60 who have attended college and the most by those under 29 with only a grammar school education. With each increase in education or age the percentage antiwhite decreases.

In like manner, as income and prestige of occupation increase, there is a slight tendency for antiwhite sentiment to decrease. However, when education is taken into account, differences by income and occupation tend to disappear. In contrast, the unemployed continue to have a higher per-centage scoring as antiwhite than the employed even when education is controlled.

When education, occupation, and income are combined into a measure of social privilege (the same as used in Chapter 2), again the pattern is the opposite of that observed for militancy. As class position increases,

Table 113. ANTIWHITE ATTITUDES BY SYMBOLIC SOCIAL PARTICIPATION

(Per cent high in antiwhite attitudes; number of respondents shown in parentheses)

Number of Negro *newspapers read*		
0	26%	(196)
1	24	(448)
2	20	(290)
Number of Negro *magazines read*		
0	30	(335)
1	20	(269)
2	19	(329)
Number of general *magazines read*		
0	30	(410)
1	26	(159)
2	15	(364)
How often read *other newspapers*		
Less than once a week	31	(151)
Once a week to several times a week	27	(178)
Every day	19	(600)

hostility toward whites decreases. The percentage scoring as not antiwhite increases from 15 among those lowest in social position to 40 for those highest. Likewise the percentage scoring as antiwhite decreases from 31 per cent among those lowest in social position to 17 per cent among those highest (Table 112).[28]

In Chapter 2 it was noted that those more involved in society, whether measured in terms of "symbolic" or "actual" participation, were more likely to be militant. For hostility toward whites, the opposite pattern again emerges. Although differences are often very slight, for six of the seven indicators of social participation shown in Tables 113 and 114, the greater

Table 114. ANTIWHITE ATTITUDES BY ACTUAL SOCIAL PARTICIPATION

(Per cent high in antiwhite attitudes; number of
respondents shown in parentheses)

Number of organizations belong to		
0	26%	(583)
1	21	(256)
2	16	(93)
Vote in 1960		
No	27	(305)
Yes	20	(525)
Socialize with friends		
Almost never	23	(186)
Often	23	(627)
Every day	28	(113)

the social participation, the lower the degree of hostility toward whites. For example, among those who read two or more general magazines, 15 per cent were antiwhite, and this figure increases to 30 per cent for those not reading any magazines. For those belonging to two or more voluntary organizations, 16 per cent were antiwhite, and for those belonging to none[29] this figure increases to 26 per cent.

When these items are combined into measures of symbolic participation and actual participation, the effect becomes somewhat stronger. Among those lowest in actual participation, the per cent giving no evidence of antiwhite sentiment is only 13, and this increases to 36 per cent for those highest on the index. Conversely, the per cent scoring as antiwhite decreases

[28] It may be recalled that our measure of antiwhite sentiment is composed of three dimensions—beliefs, feelings, and social distance. However, when considered separately, each of these dimensions was related to social privilege in the same way.

[29] Excluding church and civil rights organizations.

Table 115. ANTIWHITE ATTITUDES BY INDEX OF ACTUAL SOCIAL PARTICIPATION

	Score on Index of Actual Social Participation				
Antiwhite Attitudes	0	1	2	3	4, 5
Not antiwhite	13%	20%	30%	31%	36%
Low on antiwhite attitudes	52	59	45	51	42
Antiwhite	35	21	25	18	22
Total	100%	100%	100%	100%	100%
Number	(70)	(239)	(337)	(196)	(93)

from 35 to 22 (Table 115). The situation is similar for the measure of symbolic participation, although not so pronounced (Table 116).

That both these measures are strongly related to education and position in the class structure helps to explain their effect on antiwhite attitudes. Nevertheless, social participation has some slight effect independent of social class. When the two measures of social participation are combined,

Table 116. ANTIWHITE ATTITUDES BY INDEX OF SYMBOLIC SOCIAL PARTICIPATION

	Score on Index of Symbolic Social Particiaption				
Antiwhite Attitudes	0	1	2	3	4
Not antiwhite	19%	20%	22%	24%	35%
Low on antiwhite attitudes	49	46	49	57	47
Antiwhite	32	34	29	19	18
Total	100%	100%	100%	100%	100%
Number	(53)	(132)	(192)	(222)	(329)

as participation increases, there is a tendency for antiwhite hostility to decrease within each category of social class (Table 117). In the group high in both social participation and social class, only 12 per cent were antiwhite, and 39 per cent were almost without antiwhite sentiment. On the other hand, in the group low in both social participation and social class, 31 per cent were antiwhite and only 14 per cent were without antiwhite sentiment. Those high in social position, yet low in participation, show about the same level of antiwhite sentiment as those low in social position yet high in participation.

The effect of participation may be due to greater exposure to norms of tolerance or to the greater appreciation of diversity that may develop among those exposed to a wide variety of stimuli and experiences. In addition, the effect of participation may stem from the nature of many voluntary associations wherein race and ethnicity are transcended by whatever interests are the basis of the association.

Table 117. ANTIWHITE ATTITUDES BY SOCIAL CLASS AND SOCIAL PARTICIPATION

	Social class		
	Lower	Middle	Upper
Index of Social Participation[a]			
Low (0–3)			
Not antiwhite	14%	25%	23%
Low on antiwhite attitudes	55	49	54
Antiwhite	31	26	23
	100%	100%	100%
Number	(159)	(80)	(13)
Medium (4, 5)			
Not antiwhite	21	23	33
Low on antiwhite attitudes	53	52	44
Antiwhite	26	25	23
	100%	100%	100%
Number	(126)	(161)	(40)
High (6+)			
Not antiwhite	30	37	39
Low on antiwhite attitudes	44	46	49
Antiwhite	26	17	12
	100%	100%	100%
Number	(73)	(171)	(102)

[a] Scored as in Table 45.

The expression of generalized hostility among black Americans involves elements not found in the hostility and negative stereotyping that occurs among white Americans. Nevertheless both seem to be related to lack of sophistication. The less sophisticated are not as likely as the more sophisticated to be exposed to the "official" norms of tolerance or to perceive differences in the behavior of various outgroups. Their more insular perspective makes it more difficult for them to appreciate the existence of a broad range of values and approaches among whites. It is thus not surprising that most of the measures of intellectual sophistication developed in Chapter 3 are useful in predicting hostility toward whites. For example,

Table 118. ANTIWHITE ATTITUDES BY INTELLECTUAL SOPHISTICATION

(per cent high in antiwhite attitudes; number of respondents shown in parentheses)
Score on *F*-Scale

Broad Perspective 0	1	2	3	4	Narrow Perspective 5
9% (22)	18% (97)	13% (220)	25% (266)	30% (228)	36% (92)

Score on Acceptance of Intellectual Value Index

Intellectually Oriented 0	1	2	Nonintellectually Oriented 3
15% (150)	21% (320)	28% (425)	32% (34)

Number of Civil Rights Leaders Correctly Identified

4	3	2	1	0
17% (397)	25% (231)	27% (124)	30% (160)	50% (20)

Number of Writers Correctly Identified

3	2	1	0
14% (58)	18% (195)	22% (208)	28% (458)

"I am suspicious of people who try to be different from everybody else."

True	Not True
30% (494)	16% (416)

using the F-scale items, originally developed to analyze prejudice, the percentage antiwhite increases from a low of 9 per cent to a high of 36 per cent (Table 118). On the Index of Acceptance of Intellectual Values antiwhite sentiment increases from 15 per cent to 33 per cent. Similarly, when knowledge about Negro culture figures is considered, among those who could not identify any civil rights leaders, 50 per cent were hostile, while for those able correctly to identify all leaders this figure drops to 17 per cent.

It can be said that the unsophisticated tend to generalize about other groups partly because they often find it difficult to recognize and appreciate subtle forms of diversity. But the unsophisticated fail to appreciate diversity in still another sense of "appreciate." The unsophisticated are apt to denigrate and be suspicious and intolerant of diversity. Respondents were presented with the statement "I am suspicious of people who try to be different from everybody else," and were asked whether it was true or not true for them. Among those who agreed with this statement, 30 per cent were antiwhite while among those who disagreed this figure was 16 per cent (Table 118).[30]

Of course, more is involved in the acceptance of negative statements about other groups than simply degree of intellectual sophistication or tolerance of diversity. In the case of Negroes it would be particularly

Table 119. ANTIWHITE ATTITUDES BY FEELINGS OF FRUSTRATION

"I sometimes get so angry I feel like smashing things"

	Yes	No
High in antiwhite attitudes	32%	21%
Number	(318)	(613)

important to consider the experiences and contacts an individual has had with whites. It has often been stated that frustration plays an important role in the generation of prejudice. Black Americans besides having the usual reasons to be frustrated are further beset by the stigma of race. Unfortunately, the study did not ask about unpleasant experiences with whites in general,[31] although it did include an item which attempted to assess frustration. Those questioned were asked to agree or disagree with

[30] Rather than, or in addition to, being seen as a measure of tolerance for diversity, this item might be interpreted as a measure of a more deep-lying personality characteristic, suspiciousness. It has often been suggested that one characteristic of the prejudiced person is suspiciousness. When this table is considered in the opposite direction almost seven out of ten of those considered antiwhite responded "yes" to the above question.

[31] However, in the last chapter it was noted that, as degree of impersonal contact with Jews increased, so did anti-Semitism. Particularly important was the belief that one had been mistreated by a Jewish merchant. Presumably those who have had the most unpleasant experiences with whites would also be highest in antiwhite sentiment.

the statement "I sometimes get so angry I feel like smashing things."[32] It can be seen (Table 119) that those who agreed with this item were somewhat more likely to be antiwhite (32 per cent) than those who disagreed (21 per cent). Furthermore, the unemployed were more likely to be antiwhite than other groups. However, other measures of presumptive frustration showed no relation to antiwhite attitudes. For example, those who had been downwardly mobile, those in positions of structured strain (desiring but not expecting a promotion), and those in positions of marked status discrepancy (having a college education yet being in a workingclass occupation) were no more antiwhite, and often less so, than those not in such positions.

Although frustration, however defined, may be an important factor in predisposing some toward ethnic hostility, for others it may have the effect of spurring them on to greater personal achievement, antisocial behavior involving other Negroes, some type of religious involvement, and the like. No doubt there is a great deal of frustration in the Negro community, but there are outlets for this frustration other than generalized hostility toward whites. Conversely, there are reasons for Negroes to be antiwhite other than personal frustration. Finally, it should be noted that the measures of frustration used in the study were crude and inadequate.

Table 120. ANTIWHITE ATTITUDES BY MORALE

Score on Index of Morale

	High 3	2	1	Low 0
High on antiwhite attitudes	15%	18%	25%	33%
Number	(233)	(295)	(222)	(177)

The measure of morale (built up in Chapter 3) also was related to antiwhite hostility, although again in the opposite direction from the way it was related to militancy. Thus, among those considered to have the lowest morale, 33 per cent were antiwhite; this figure decreases to 15 per cent among those considered to have a high morale (Table 120). Srole, using similar items as a measure of "anomie," has found that those who feel most isolated and alone are those most likely to be prejudiced.[33]

[32] Psychoanalytically oriented discussions of frustration and prejudice often suggest that those whose intense frustration results in prejudice are pathological types. On the other hand, it has frequently been noted that frustration can lead to withdrawal and apathy. Those who "never feel like smashing things" may be at least as psychologically damaged as those who constantly feel like smashing things.

[33] Leo Srole, "Social Integration and Certain Corollaries: An Exploratory Study," *American Sociological Review*, December 1956. Srole further suggests that for his sample the relation of authoritarianism to prejudice is to an important extent a func-

Self-Image

There is some confusion in the literature about the connection between self-image and out-group hostility. Psychoanalysts such as Eric Fromm and Karen Horney have stressed the connection between acceptance of others and of oneself. Sociologists, more concerned with group conflict, have tended to see hatred of an out-group as a factor operating to build in-group morale.[34] Although hostility toward whites may have the effect of building in-group solidarity, it does not seem, from our data, to lead to a more favorable group image. Thus, among those lowest in antiwhite sentiment, only 10 per cent were considered to have an "unfavorable self-image" and this percentage steadily increases to 31 per cent for those who were the most antiwhite (Table 121).

Table 121. SELF-IMAGE BY ANTIWHITE ATTITUDES

Score on Antiwhite Index

| | Not Antiwhite | | | | | | Antiwhite |
	0	1	2	3	4	5	6
Have unfavorable self-image	10%	12%	16%	16%	18%	26%	31%
Number	(113)	(136)	(227)	(237)	(135)	(69)	(13)

In summary it may be noted that, although antiwhite hostility was related to the same set of variables as was militancy, in almost all cases the direction of this relation was the reverse of that noted for militancy. Thus, those lowest in exposure to the values of the traditional South were the least antiwhite, as were those higher in social participation and position. Similarly, the more sophisticated and those with a higher morale and a more positive self-image showed the least hostility toward whites. However, in some cases, the differences observed were not very pronounced. Unfortunately, our study did not ask about experiences and contact with whites in general, and it did not measure other relevant variables such as darkness of skin color.[35] If it had, differences might have been greater, particularly if

---

tion of the relation between anomie and prejudice. However, with respect to the data in the present study, both morale and the *F*-scale items were related to antiwhite hostility independent of their relation to each other.

[34] For example, Rose notes: "Negroes who never hate whites are the ones who soon come to hate Negroes" (A. Rose, *The Negro's Morale: Group Identification and Protest*, Minneapolis, University of Minnesota Press, 1948, p. 116). Simpson and Yinger note that hatred of whites is "among the factors working against self-devaluation" (George Simpson and Milton Yinger, *Racial and Cultural Minorities*, New York, Harper & Row, rev. ed., 1958, p. 215).

[35] A study of middle-class Negro women notes that the lighter the skin color the less the degree of antiwhite sentiment expressed (Howard Freeman, J. Michael Ross,

a factor such as perceived mistreatment at the hands of whites were to be combined with the social and psychological factors found here to relate to antiwhite sentiment. The present analysis suggests that variables which have proved useful in understanding intergroup hostilities of whites may not be as useful in understanding the intergroup hostilities of Negroes, although in many cases the relations reported were in the same direction as those often reported for whites. The relative weakness of the relation between antiwhite hostility and predisposing variables might be expected in view of the many realistic reasons for black Americans to be antiwhite.

David Armor, and Thomas Pettigrew, "Color Gradation and Attitudes Among Middle-Income Negroes," *American Sociological Review,* June 1966, p. 371).

Civil Rights and Tolerance

In the particular movement in which I am involved, hate doesn't have much function. Hope does. . . . None of us really have time to hate. It's too all-consuming.

—Civil rights worker, Cleveland

The human beast—the serpent, the dragon, the devil, and Satan—all mean one and the same: the people or race known as the white or Caucasian race. . . . By nature they were created liars and murderers, they are the enemies of truth and righteousness.

—Elijah Muhammad

Thus far the analysis has been divided into two parts: attitudes toward the civil rights struggle and attitudes toward whites, including Jews. Now these separate themes must be united. One of the questions with which this book began is how protest and attitudes toward whites are related. Is a high degree of civil rights concern compatible with tolerance toward whites?

Writing in the early 1920s Franklin Frazier noted that "if the masses of Negroes can save their self-respect and remain free of hate, so much the better but . . . I believe it would be better for the Negro's soul to be seared with hate than dwarfed by self-abasement."[1] Since that time, some radicals have assumed the necessity of hate for protest and consequently have welcomed the supposed increase in antiwhite sentiments. Others, who have not welcomed antiwhite feelings, have also seen them intimately tied to a degree of protest concern.[2] Indeed, one tradition in social theory has been that hatred of an out-group can serve to strengthen one's identification with the in-group and its cause.

Discussions of this issue are usually based on two assumptions: that there has been a marked increase in antiwhite hostility in recent years, and

[1] Lerone Bennet, *Confrontation: Black and White,* Chicago, Johnson Publishing Company, 1965, p. 185.

[2] For example, Handlin states: "The more concerned they are with integration, the more likely they are to see the whole society rigidly divided into blacks and whites" (Oscar Handlin, *Fire Bell in the Night,* Boston, Beacon Press, 1964, p. 62).

that this increased hostility results from, causes, or is a concomitant of recent increases in protest. Since the present study has no panel or trend data it cannot adequately address itself to the questions of whether there has or has not been an increase in antiwhite feelings among Negroes.[3] However, the relation between attitudes of protest and hostility toward whites can be analyzed.

Table 122. ANTIWHITE ATTITUDES BY CIVIL RIGHTS CONCERN[a]

Style of Response to Civil Rights Struggle

Score on Anti-white Index	Black Nationalist	Conservative	Moderate	Militant
Not antiwhite (0,1)	11%	16%	26%	39%
Low in antiwhite attitudes (2,3)	45	56	52	44
Antiwhite (4, 5, 6)	44	28	22	17
Total	100%	100%	100%	100%
Number	(36)	(168)	(459)	(237)

[a] Here and in the remaining tables in this chapter, those 162 cases from the metropolitan area sample interviewed by whites are excluded.

In contemplating the relation between protest and prejudice, important distinctions must be made between types of protest. It may be recalled that respondents in the study have been characterized by four possible styles of response to the civil rights struggle: black nationalists, conservative, moderate, and militant. Presumably the implications for antiwhite attitudes of the black nationalist perspective are different from those of a conventionally militant perspective. It is perhaps more difficult to foresee how the conventionally militant would differ from those who are moderate and conservative on civil rights issues. It is easy to project oneself into the situation of the militant Negro and see how strong civil rights concern might

[3] While the samples are very different, it is interesting to note that studies done in 1949, 1959, and 1964 show somewhat comparable percentages scoring as antiwhite. In 1949 Johnson, studying a smaller New York urban area, found that about one respondent in four agreed that "no matter how nicely he treats a Negro, a white man doesn't really mean it" while the present study found that in New York in 1964 roughly one respondent in four indicated that they were suspicious of whites who try to help Negroes. On similar items where comparisons were possible between the study done by P. McDaniel and N. Babchuk ("Negro Conceptions of White People," *Phylon*, Spring 1960), and the New York sample of the present study the percentage giving the antiwhite response was often about the same. It is also interesting to note that Tilman C. Cothran ("Negro Conceptions of White People in a Northeastern City," *American Journal of Sociology*, 1951) in 1949, studying a Southern community found roughly comparable levels of antiwhite sentiment as did McDaniel and Babchuk in their replication of this study ten years later.

lead to antiwhite sentiments. But it is equally easy to imagine that concern over the rights of one's own group would be related to an appreciation of the need for tolerance toward all groups.

In Table 122 it can be seen that, not surprisingly, the most antiwhite group are the black nationalists. Only 11 per cent of this group scored as not antiwhite, and 44 per cent scored as high in antiwhite sentiment. But what is perhaps of greater interest is that, as measured by the Index of Conventional Militancy, *as civil rights concern increases so does tolerance.* Only 16 per cent of the conservatives scored as not antiwhite, as against 39 per cent of the militants. Similarly, 28 per cent of the conservatives scored as high in antiwhite attitudes, as against 17 per cent of the militants.

Table 123.   ANTIWHITE ATTITUDES BY REPORTED MEMBERSHIP IN A CIVIL
RIGHTS ORGANIZATION

Belong to Civil Rights Organization?

Score on AntiWhite Index	Yes	No
Not antiwhite	41%	23%
Low in antiwhite attitudes	47	51
Antiwhite	12	26
Total	100%	100%
Number	(197)	(726)

When the relation is considered in the opposite direction, the least antiwhite group is the highest in conventional militancy. Of those judged least antiwhite, 38 per cent were militant. Of those judged most antiwhite, only 19 per cent were militant. (The percentage in sympathy with black nationalism was 2 per cent among the least antiwhite, 8 per cent among those most antiwhite.) This pattern—that those with the greatest civil rights concern are most apt to be tolerant and that the most tolerant are most apt to be highly concerned with civil rights—was observed for each of the separate samples and when numerous variables were controlled for.

In pursuing this relation further, it can be seen that those who belong to civil rights organizations are *less* antiwhite than those who do not. Furthermore, even within civil rights groups, the more militant an individual is, the less likely he is to be antiwhite (Tables 123 and 124).

The most militant members of civil rights organizations were thus the most tolerant Negroes in our sample. Almost half of this group expressed little or no antiwhite sentiment and only one in ten indicated strong antiwhite sentiment. In marked contrast, the least tolerant group (excluding the few black nationalist sympathizers) were those uninvolved in civil rights organizations and seemingly unconcerned with the civil rights struggle. Three in ten of these conservatives were strong in antiwhite sentiment while only slightly more than one in ten were without any antiwhite sentiment.

Table 124. INVERSE RELATIONSHIP BETWEEN MILITANCY AND ANTIWHITE ATTITUDES
WITHIN CIVIL RIGHTS ORGANIZATIONS

Style of Response to the Civil Rights Struggle[a]

Score on Antiwhite Index	Conservative	Moderate	Militant
Not antiwhite	28%	38%	47%
Low in antiwhite attitudes	55	51	44
Antiwhite	17	11	9
Number	(18)	(80)	(86)

[a] Only among those who report membership in a civil rights organization. Of four respondents whose style of response was Black Nationalist, two scored high on the Antiwhite Index.

When the measure of anti-Semitism and the combined measure of antiwhite attitudes and anti-Semitism are observed in relation to civil rights concern the results are essentially the same.[4] The black nationalist sympathizers are the most intolerant.[5] But within the limits of conventional militancy, the greater the degree of civil rights concern, the less intolerance. Conversely, the greater the intolerance, the less the likelihood that an individual will be militant. Members of civil rights organizations were again less likely to be anti-Semitic or to express hostility against both Jews and whites in general.

[4] In Atlanta the percentage scoring as militant was about the same irrespective of the score on the Anti-Semitism Index, while the percentage scoring as anti-Semitic was about the same independent of whether an individual was conservative, moderate, or militant. However, when only those who had opinions about Jews are considered, the relation is the same as that reported for the other samples. It may be recalled that, in building the Index of Anti-Semitism, those who gave the "don't know" response to an item, as well as those who did not give the anti-Semitic response, were scored zero. Thus, two kinds of respondents are considered non-anti-Semitic: those who consistently rejected the anti-Semitic response ("convinced non-anti-Semites") and those who consistently had no opinion ("unconvinced non-anti-Semites"). When this added distinction is made, for Atlanta as well as each of the other samples, the militant were much more likely to score as convinced non-anti-Semites. On the measures of conventional militancy and antiwhite attitudes very few respondents gave more than one or two "don't know" responses. With respect to the Antiwhite Index, 3 per cent of the sample gave the "don't know" response to two of the five items, and less than 1 per cent gave this response three or more times. With respect to the Militancy Index, only 1 per cent of the sample gave the "don't know" response to three or more of the eight items in the index.

[5] It has sometimes been suggested that the Muslims with their plea for economic self-sufficiency, occasional involvement with the Arab world, and criticisms of Jewish involvement in the civil rights struggle are an important source of Negro anti-Semitism. The few Muslim sympathizers in our sample were the most likely to be anti-Semitic, as well as antiwhite. However, it is a gross oversimplification to explain Negro anti-Semitism in terms of Muslim agitation. As noted in Chapter 4, there are factors in the Negro-Jewish relationship conducive to hostility far beyond an occasional Muslim harangue. Furthermore, in their public statements the Muslims sometimes speak favorably of Jews, at least relative to other whites (see Chapter 6, note 15). Negroes are often encouraged to copy the ways of the Jews, and the latter are sometimes referred to as Asiatics. The religious hostility expressed by the Muslims is primarily anti-Christian, not anti-Jewish.

Although past research on this subject is slight, several studies have reached similar conclusions about the militancy-tolerance relationship.[6]

A word of caution is perhaps in order with respect to these data. This material does not mean that the civil rights struggle has necessarily resulted in an over-all decrease in antiwhite hostility. Certainly the protest movement lowered Negro inhibitions about publicly expressing antiwhite sentiments. Without adequate panel data, there is no way of knowing whether antiwhite hostility has increased or decreased over-all. These data also say little about the intensity of hostility that some may feel. However, they conclusively show that antiwhite and anti-Jewish feelings are negatively related to militancy.

The finding that individuals most concerned with racial injustice are also most likely to be tolerant of whites seems readily understandable when considered in light of the analysis carried out in the book. The factors associated with militancy in the black community (excluding the tiny minority who are militants of the Muslim variety) are also in most cases the factors associated with tolerance. Those most removed from the value system of the traditional South, those highest in social position and participation, and those most likely to possess a positive self-image, high morale, and intellectual sophistication were the most militant. They were also the most tolerant.

People high in social involvement are more likely to have contact with whites, and while this factor no doubt helps explain their greater militancy it may also be relevant in explaining their lesser hostility. Numerous studies have shown that under certain conditions contact may reduce intergroup hostility.

This relation may reflect an ideological link between militancy and tolerance and not just an empirical association. Even when the factors related to both were held constant, in almost all cases the most militant were the least hostile. For some individuals, of course, support for the civil rights struggle may stem from or even lead to, hatred of whites and a desire for

[6] For research before the contemporary civil rights movement began, see Williams, *op. cit.*, pp. 281–282. Using the same data is Donald L. Noel, "Minority Group Identification and Societal Integration," paper presented at 1966 meetings of the American Sociological Association. Noel suggests that militant group pride can be an important factor in societal integration so long as minority group members perceive the larger system as supporting their efforts to achieve or maintain major group goals.

Another study reports that among Negro college students activists were more tolerant than nonactivists, Matthews and Prothro, *op. cit.*, p. 421.

In commenting on antiwhite sentiment among CORE activists, Powell notes that the largest number of negative statements were made about particular whites—active segregationists, white hecklers, and assailants and the police. Such people were seen as being "blind to reality, hypocritical and self-seeking, cowardly, and filled with hatred." However, Powell adds: "It is striking that these negative comments were never charged with strong emotion. Most were in the form of ridicule and mild mockery, accompanied by a tone of disbelief" (Ingeborg B. Powell, "Ideology and Strategy of Direct Action: A Study of the Congress of Racial Equality," Ph.D. dissertation, University of California in Berkeley, 1965, p. 160).

revenge. But for most, concern for the civil rights of Negroes may increase sensitivity to the injustices and distortions of reality that emerge when categorically negative attitudes and behavior are directed toward groups different from one's own. Militancy itself may be seen as a reaction against such categorical attitudes and behavior. In view of the greater sophistication of the militants, it is likely that many see the inconsistency which emerges when a black man attacking white racism is himself a racist. They may also be more aware of the positive (although not positive enough) efforts of many whites, from the President, the Supreme Court, and Congress down to the countless thousands of white supporters of civil rights. For many, the image of a monolithic racist white society may be shattered. In addition, it was noted that militants were much more tolerant of the civil liberties of religious dissenters and also more accepting of diverse points of view (as measured by the Index of Intellectual Values). It seems likely that for many militants their relative tolerance for whites is part of a generally more tolerant world view related to their greater sophistication and greater exposure to official values.

It is, of course, true that the current civil rights struggle draws upon profound frustration and discontent. However this frustration is mixed with hope and is more likely to be over the situation of one's group, rather than the kind of deep personal frustration characterized by Eric Hoffer's portrait of the True Believer. The militants in our sample were much more likely to have a high morale and not the sense of despair and hopelessness that is often thought to lead to prejudice.

In its beginning phase the conventional civil rights movement was a mixture of very deep Negro anger and Christian principles of love and forgiveness.[7] Not stooping to hate in a hate-filled society may offer feelings of self-worth and moral superiority to those otherwise deprived. In addition, civil rights leaders stress that they are attacking the system of evil rather than whites per se.[8] Anger and even hatred, where it existed, were directed toward bringing about change and not in attacking the enemy for the sake

[7] In discussing his speech given at a protest meeting during the Montgomery bus boycott, King writes, "With this ground work for militant action, I moved on to words of caution. . . . 'Love your enemies, bless them that curse you, and pray for them that despitefully use you'" (Martin Luther King, *Stride Toward Freedom*, p. 69).

This emphasis and a deep moral commitment to nonviolence are more characteristic of the movement in the South than in the North. However, even in the South, King's perspective characterizes only a minority. Among CORE activists there, Powell notes that 35 per cent were morally committed to nonviolence, while an additional 30 per cent accepted it simply as a pragmatic technique, and the remainder were uncertain or rejected it (*op. cit.*, p. 229).

[8] It was this very subtle and highly important distinction that Malcolm X eventually came to make. He notes ". . . it isn't the American white *man* who is a racist, but it's the American political, economic, and social *atmosphere* that automatically nourishes a racist psychology in the white man" and ". . . the white man is *not* inherently evil, but America's racist society influences him to act evilly" (Malcolm X, with the assistance of Alex Haley, *The Autobiography of Malcolm X*, New York, Grove Press, 1965, p. 377).

of attack. Furthermore as a result of historical exclusion and segregation the dominant thrust of the struggle has been toward integration and inclusion. Implicit in this emphasis would seem to be the notion that whites are worth mingling with. Had the dominant thrust of the movement been one of separatism, and to the extent that this theme becomes dominant, protest and hostility toward whites might be expected to be more closely linked. However, as things stood at the time of our study in 1964 the relationship between protest and tolerance noted in this chapter seems readily understandable.

The interesting possibility emerges that, although the civil rights struggle obviously increases overt conflict between Negroes and whites, it may decrease generalized intolerance of whites.[9] Ironically, those concerned with reducing prejudice among Negroes might best begin by encouraging the development of the very conditions which make for militancy. However, there is no doubt a point beyond which the militancy-tolerance relation would be reversed, although at the time of our study this point had not been reached for the majority of militants. As Rustin has pointed out, the continued frustration of Negro demands and the lack of marked improvement may lead many of those who originally favored integration and cooperation with whites to change their position.[10]

[9] Another interesting and unanticipated consequence (although perhaps foreseen by Durkheim) may be a reduction in Negro crime during periods of organized civil rights activity (Frederic Solomon et al., "Civil Rights Activity and Reduction in Crime Among Negroes," in R. Murphy and H. Elinson, eds., Problems and Prospects of the Negro Movement, Belmont, Cal., Wadsworth, 1966, p. 337). A reduction in conflict among Negro gangs has been suggested by many, and the Commissioner of the Federal Bureau of Narcotics, in noting the decline in addiction among Negroes, has even offered as one of the reasons "growing racial pride that has accompanied the fight for civil rights." (San Francisco Chronicle, March 7, 1967.)

[10] Bayard Rustin, " 'Black Power' and Coalition Politics," Commentary, September 1966, p. 38.

Other periods in American history show examples of Negro leaders who began strongly favoring integration and then, overwhelmed by a sense of futility, turned to separatist positions; for example, Paul Cuffee and Martin Robinson Delaney (see Charles E. Silberman, Crisis in Black and White, New York, Random House, 1964, p. 146).

As the case of the Jews in Europe clearly indicates, the type of orientation dominant within an ethnic minority group at any one time is to an important extent dependent on the receptiveness of the dominant group. When the dominant group seems receptive, emphasis is placed on inclusion and assimilation. When the dominant group is not receptive, or its supposed receptiveness is illusory, the minority group turns inward and in a separatist direction.

The "natural history" of social movements with special emphasis on the point at which tactics and goals may come to be radically altered has been little studied. However it would seem that continued frustration in obtaining goals (in the absence of an ideology explaining this failure) and efforts on the part of government or other institutions to suppress a movement would be particularly relevant factors.

SNNC members have lost faith in America's ability to integrate and at the same time have been subjected to increasing efforts of social control on the part of the government. In recent months SNCC has increasingly been under surveillance and its offices have been raided, in at least one case without a warrant.

Some Final Thoughts

The data observed in this study suggest that in late 1964 the collective mood of the Negro community was still a fairly moderate one, riots and impressionistic statements to the contrary.[11] Isolation from protest media and society generally, feelings of despair and helplessness, preoccupation with the problems of daily living, otherworldly religiosity, and remnants of an oppression mentality involving feelings of inferiority and the belief that the black man's plight is his own fault in part help explain why this is true.

But some of this moderation may stem from optimism over the many gains that have been made. Perhaps these gains have been more symbolic than actual. Still, they give many Negroes reason to hope,[12] even if to some their hope is naïve.

Some of the following major findings of this study are interesting in light of the sensational statements about the Negro mood played up by the mass media and the seeming evidence offered by riots:

—Only a third of the Negro community was consistently militant in outlook.

—In spite of what many would consider strong provocation, even fewer were strongly antiwhite.

[11] However, it is rare indeed that a social movement catches the interest of the entire mass in whose behalf it speaks and that more than a very small percentage of the total mass is ever motivated to sustained action.

[12] It is a specially delicate matter for a white to write about the progress that is being made, since he cannot know the wellsprings of anger that put this progress in perspective relative to the changes that must take place before "these rights" are in fact secured. My point here is to suggest not that equality of opportunity or of outcome is just around the corner or that in terms of social relations whites feel appreciably different now than in the past, but rather that some very vital changes have taken place, and the perception of these changes by many (whether in fact *their* lives have been materially altered) is relevant. The legal structure of segregation has been severely undermined and the Government has in principle committed itself to equal treatment for all citizens.

Moreover, beyond symbolic gains, some material gains have taken place, particularly in an absolute sense. These gains have been perceived, as well as exaggerated, by many. It is interesting to note that, although the year 1966 saw an increase in public expressions of disillusionment on the part of many articulate Negroes, it also saw an over-all increase in reported satisfaction with jobs, schools, and housing on the part of the black masses. For example, a Gallup poll done in 1963 revealed that 51 per cent of the black population was satisfied with their jobs, 43 per cent with the education received by their children, and 36 per cent with their housing. Moreover, by November of 1966 these figures had increased to 69, 64, and 51 per cent.

Another Gallup poll in August of 1963 reports that nine out of ten black people felt that they were treated badly or not very well in this country, while in May of 1965 this figure had decreased to seven out of ten. The August 22, 1966, *Newsweek* survey reports that the percentage of people noting improvement in areas such as employment, schools, public accommodations, and voter rights has increased since 1963.

—To the degree Negroes distinguish between Jewish and non-Jewish whites, they prefer Jews.

—Civil rights militancy was negatively related to antiwhite and anti-Jewish feelings.

—In spite of its importance to protest in some respects, religiosity is an important factor inhibiting militancy.

—Conventional civil rights groups and leaders enjoyed overwhelming popularity.

—Very few Negroes were strong supporters of the Muslims.

—The least-privileged Negroes, who are most likely to profit from social change, were the least likely to be militant.

But such findings offer no grounds for complacency. *The magnitude of moral injustice, the intensity of concern felt by many, and the ever-increasing potential for social disruption cannot be measured by a simple counting of the "yeas" and "nays."* A study such as this can paint a descriptive picture of what the collective mood of the Negro community was in 1964 and perhaps still is. It can observe factors that help explain these attitudes. But it would be a mistake to think that everyone's opinion counts the same or that opinions cannot change.

Many citizens hold the misconception that activists on behalf of "causes" such as the civil rights struggle are likely to be alienated misfits, rigid in their thought processes, who dislike themselves as well as out-groups, and who try to remake the world to compensate for their own failings. There is also a body of scholarly thought which argues for this perspective.[13] No doubt some such individuals may be found among those with the strongest civil rights concern and the greatest militancy. However, the data we have presented show that those militant over civil rights issues tend to be an elite within the black community.[14] They are better educated and more involved in voluntary organizations, more likely to vote, they have more friends, a more positive self-image, a higher morale, greater sophistication, and they are less hostile toward whites.[15] To reverse Yeats, it could almost be said that the best are filled with passionate intensity while the worst lack all concern. However, considering similar social movements, both here and in Europe, this finding is not surprising.

[13] Eric Hoffer, *The True Believer,* New York, New American Library, 1964; Edward Shils, "Authoritarianism: 'Right' and 'Left,'" in Richard Christie and Marie Jahoda, eds., *Studies in the Scope and Method of the Authoritarian Personality,* New York, Free Press, 1954.

[14] Similar findings are reported by R. Searles and J. A. Williams, Jr., "Negro College Students' Participation in Sit-ins," *Social Forces,* 1962. While in the present study data have been presented generally only for those who hold militant attitudes, when the same analysis is done on those who in fact have been mobilized to at least some degree of action, as measured by membership in a civil rights organization, the findings are the same.

[15] However, those few respondents who were classified as black nationalists of the Muslim variety tended to be characterized in a fashion opposite to this.

The course of racial change in the future will no doubt be uneven and will vary considerably from one region to another in tempo and types of change. Changes in the legal and political situation of the Negro, and to a lesser exent some changes in his economic situation, seem more likely than massive residential and school desegregation or meaningful changes in the over-all patterning of social relations. Nor will changes necessarily be linear. Some sudden setbacks, along with occasional rapid advances and the more usual slow, almost imperceptible improvement, are to be expected. The nature of this change will depend on a great many factors, one of the most important being the direction of the nation's economy. An equally important factor, perhaps, is the presence of an aroused Negro community which will no longer countenance the blatant injustice and humiliation which have been the fruits of its participation in the American harvest.[16] The role of moral persuasion in bringing about social change on behalf of a persecuted minority has been minimal here, as throughout much of history. There is much truth (particularly as it applies to the disprivileged) in the

[16] However, militant concern or sound and fury by itself is not likely to accomplish very much (see the excellent discussion in Clark, *Dark Ghetto,* New York, Harper & Row, 1965, p. 210). On the other hand, there may also be a point beyond which an increase in the intensity of the militancy expressed by some may inhibit group gains, as the setbacks in late 1966 would seem to indicate.

Some limitations on local political action among Negroes are discussed in James Q. Wilson, "The Changing Political Position of the Negro" in Arnold Rose, ed., *Assuring Freedom to the Free,* Detroit, Wayne University Press, 1964. Wilson notes two important constraints on political effectiveness, namely, that many cities have nonpartisan, at-large elections (with weak or nonexistent party organizations), making it difficult for Negroes to be elected to office, and that, in cities where partisan elections and strong party organizations exist, the price of election of a Negro may be racial moderation. However, I am referring to an organized Negro community able to exert pressure beyond that involved in the electoral process. Much of the power that developed out of the direct action movement was exercised outside of normal political channels. Pressure and coercion were brought to bear on particular targets, and demonstrations and boycotts (or the threat of them) were often sufficient to bring about limited change. However, even with respect to the electoral system, an aroused Negro community might be seen as a necessary, if by no means sufficient, condition for the occurrence of certain kinds of changes.

While this discussion refers to protest on the part of Negroes it does not mean to imply that the role of sympathetic whites in helping to bring about social change has been minimal. On the other hand the opposition of much of the white community should not be underestimated. Attitudes studies aside, even outside of the South, when asked to vote on matters directly related to civil rights, the white public has generally voted "no." It is surprising that this pattern has not yet led more militant Negroes to lose faith in traditional democraic forms. However, there is some evidence that civil rights activists tend to underestimate the extent of white resistance (just as segregationist whites underestimate the extent of Negro support of integration). See Matthews and Prothro, *op. cit.,* p. 422.

In stressing the importance of Negro militancy I do not mean to suggest that the answer to America's racial problem lies simply in attacking the discrimination and prejudice of white society. While the social forms found in many urban ghettoes developed in response to white oppression it is possible that to some extent these forms have now developed to a point where they are partially independent of that oppression. See Daniel P. Moynihan, "The President and the Negro," *Commentary,* February 1967.

statement of the father of Negro protest, Frederic Douglass, that "power concedes nothing without a demand, it never did and it never will . . . men may not get all they pay for in this world, but they must certainly pay for all they get."

Although predicting the future is more properly the business of prophets, gamblers, and weathermen, it seems reasonable that, as time passes, larger proportions of the Negro community will become aroused and militant. One impetus to militancy will stem from continued progress, particularly if it is coupled with deterioration in the relative situation of Negroes compared to whites.[17] An increase in militancy may also be inferred from certain demographic and social trends within the Negro community. The relations of region and type of community raised in, age, education, and social participation to civil rights concern, observed earlier in the book, all suggest this. Living in the North and being brought up in an urban area were positively related to militancy. The proportion of Negroes in rural areas and in the South has steadily been decreasing, and this trend shows no signs of reversing itself at the present.[18] There is a clearly discernible trend for Negroes to become concentrated in the central areas of cities. As this trend continues, the sense of separateness and related feelings of group identity should become more pronounced. Furthermore, this ever-increasing number of people with a shared problem gathered together in the same place may make the occurrence of mass action more likely.

Age also is related to militancy, and it was assumed that the effect of age was due to the nature of the social milieu in which an individual was raised rather than because of things associated with the aging process per se. If this is correct, then as the older, more conservative Negroes die and are replaced by today's young, the proportion of militant Negroes should also increase.[19] The situation is the same for education and social participation. The amount (and presumably the quality) of education received by Americans has steadily been increasing since the turn of the century.[20] As Negroes obtain more and better education, militancy should become more wide-

[17] Rashi Fein notes that although both whites and Negroes show improvement in education, health, and welfare, white progress has been so much faster than Negro progress that the differential between them is greater now than a generation ago ("An Economic and Social Profile of the Negro American," Daedalus, Fall 1965).

[18] Between 1950 and 1960 the net Negro migration from the South to the North was 1,457,000. Between 1940 and 1960 the number of Negroes living in standard metropolitan statistical areas more than doubled (Philip M. Hauser, "Demographic Factors in the Integration of the Negro," Daedalus, Fall 1965, pp. 851–852).

[19] But even if older, conservative Negroes did not die, militancy might still increase due to what Hauser has called "the striking rise in non-white urban fertility." If the nonwhite rate of population growth in 1960 continues, the Negro population will double in a little over thirty years (ibid., p. 849).

[20] Ibid., p. 855. For example, in 1940, nonwhite men 25 years of age and older had on the average only 5.4 years of schooling, and by 1960 this had increased to 7.9 years.

spread. Similar logic applies to social participation. As discriminatory barriers of various kinds are lowered (such as restrictions on membership in voluntary organizations, in the use of public facilities, and in voting, housing, and employment) and as Negroes participate more fully in society, militancy should again increase.[21] As was noted, as a result of these factors certain psychological perspectives conducive to militancy are likely to develop.

The above discussion refers to an increase (both absolute and relative) in the number of people that would be considered militant by the standard developed in Chapter 1.[22] However, in the future it seems probable that concern with integration, as opposed simply to opposition to discrimination, will be less relevant as a defining characteristic of militancy.

Increased awareness of, and frustration over, the massive obstacles to real integration and an increased pride in blackness (related to a questioning of the desirability of integration) are resulting in this important shift in one segment of the civil rights movement. For black power advocates the emphasis is increasingly put on equality[23] rather than integration and on

[21] Of course, increased involvement in integrated situations may produce what St. Clair Drake has referred to as the problem of reconciling "being a 'loyal Negro' or a 'Race Man' with new middle-class interracial or new occupational roles" ("The Social and Economic Status of the Negro in the United States," *Daedalus*, Fall 1965, p. 808).

[22] It should be noted that this statement refers to the existence of militant attitudes and says nothing about the strength of organized civil rights groups. The existence of an increased pool of militant individuals is somewhat independent of actual mobilization of these people into well-disciplined organizations concerned with social change. It is ironic to note that, although militancy is probably more widespread in 1966 than any time previously, the organized civil rights movement seems much weaker in 1966 than in 1964.

The draining off of civil rights workers by the war on poverty, the acceptance of many of the movement's goals as the official (if unenforced) policy of the United States government, the financial and spiritual retreat of many white liberals over the issue of black power, the increased factionalism among various rights groups over this issue and the war in Vietnam, and the decline in their membership and financial power all contribute to a weakening of organizational effectiveness.

Given the variation in ideology, emphasis, and sources of support, it is remarkable that the civil rights movement was able to demonstrate the unity it did up until the March on Washington. In a society as complex and diverse as the United States, it is rare that a social movement of national prominence is ever represented for long by a single unified organization. Those sharing many of the same goals may on occasion come together in the face of a crisis or to mount a single massive attack. Yet divisive factionalism is usually soon manifest.

[23] It is argued that emphasis on the token integration that has occurred only serves to focus attention away from the problems of millions still remaining in the ghetto. It has been suggested that those few Negro children in integrated Southern settings may have been psychically scared by having to face howling mobs and daily ostracism and humiliation from their fellow white students.

It is emphasized, and I think wrongly, that integration implies that there is nothing of worth within the black community. It is further suggested that integration must be a two-way street and will be meaningless until it is voluntarily initiated by whites. The white concerned with integration is welcomed to come live in Watts, yet few whites speaking the language of universal brotherhood have chosen this option.

developing a strong black community, rather than dispersing that community throughout the white community. The main issue is seen as poor schools, houses, and jobs, and not separate ones. The crucial goal then becomes obtaining equality in these areas and not integration. This is seen as politically more realistic as well as better for the black self-image.

The black power orientation within SNCC and CORE elaborates themes traditionally present (such as nondiscriminatory treatment and equality pursued through organizing the economic and political power of the Negro community and the right of self-defense). It also draws upon some new themes from the black nationalists (such as a more explicit orientation toward working-class Negroes[24] and rejection of the established Negro leadership, a strong concern with pride in blackness, an emphasis on developing the Negro community through self-help rather than cooperating with whites to pursue the goal of integration believed to be unobtainable, a lack of faith in nonviolence and often tacit support for urban uprisings, and an angrier more impatient tone and style.) Furthermore it also addresses itself to new problems and issues not traditionally the concern of civil rights groups. These have to do with pursuing the ethnic interests of black men rather than with questions of civil rights and discrimination per se.

Black power has raised the hopes of some and the fears of others, perhaps both unrealistically. Negroes must control their own communities and organizations and find means of making those in power locally and nationally more responsive to their needs. An unmatched sense of dignity and a positive self-image would no doubt arise, not only from the struggle for power and through self-help but from power used constructively. Yet as currently structured the black power movement seems far from obtaining such goals.[25]

As manifested by SNCC and CORE, the black power movement has been

---

For some the questioning of integration implies a broader critique of American society. Stokley Carmichael states, "I've never seen myself fighting to get into a country that's bombing hell out of Viet Nam or a country that sees money as its only raison d'être. The fight of the civil rights movement is to get white people off our backs."

[24] Marcus Garvey, in the 1920's, with his strong nationalist appeal, was able to reach a relatively larger segment of the black masses than has any non-nationalist organization. Whether the masses of Negroes can become truly involved in the absence of a nationalist and perhaps somewhat demogogic organization operating to a greater extent within what exists of working-class urban Negro culture is an open and relevant question.

[25] It lacks a well-developed ideology and its organizational structure is weak. It seeks to organize one of the least politically mobilizable groups in the country. It cries for unity where much disunity (based on social class, color, region, age, religion, and organizational and ideological rivalries) exists.

All democratic organizations face the problem of making leaders responsive to the needs and the interests of their members. In the case of minority groups this is likely to be particularly true, where, as Kurt Lewin noted, leaders are usually drawn from the periphery of their group. For Negroes the denial of opportunity in the

unduly labeled as proviolence and antiwhite. In a country that took its independence and its land in violence, with a strong frontier legacy, Negro talk
of self-defense and arming demonstrators and even veiled threats of future
uprisings if change is not forthcoming is hardly an American version of the
Mau Mau. To argue for the strengthening of Negro institutions is not
necessarily to be antiwhite, nor is it to support segregation. Although sometimes implying the contrary, Carmichael has repeatedly said that problack
does not mean antiwhite, unless whites make it that way. In a recent speech
in Puerto Rico, in language that could not be further from the rhetoric of
the white bigots, he called for the creation of "a new humanism in the
world" and then went on to quote Donne's sermon, "any man's death
diminishes me, because I am involved in mankind; and therefore, never
send to know for whom the bell tolls; it tolls for thee." McKissick has stated
"black power does not mean the exclusion of white Americans from the
Negro revolt, it means inclusion of all men in a common moral and political
struggle." Even in those instances where antiwhite sentiment is pronounced,

---

larger social structure results in intense competition for positions of leadership
within the black community. Traditions of Uncle Tom leadership have not entirely
died out, machine politics in cities such as Chicago may inhibit group demands. The
connection between the will of the voters nd public policy is by no means automatic.

Furthermore the solution to many problems faced by Negroes requires action at
the national and state level. The attainment of political power in local areas where
Negroes are a majority, while no doubt important to many issues, will not significantly
change the structure of power at a national or state level.

Being only ten per cent of the population hurts the Negro cause. In this sense the
powerful moral claim that Negroes have is interfered with by the workings of the
democratic political system, which tends to roughly give out shares of the spoils according to the amount of political power a group can mobilize. This is related to
the size of the group, its economic strength, its political skills, and the kinds of
coalitions it is willing to enter into. This system operates on the principle that in the
interests of social harmony there must be a give and take between various interests
groups, all of whom are acknowledged to have legitimate claims.

This system works well in mediating the conflicting claims of management and an
affluent working class, Catholics and Protestants, or rural and urban residents, whose
interests no longer fundamentally involve pursuing those things guaranteed to all
men by the Constitution and the Judaeo-Christian heritage. However for the impatient Negro this system presents many problems. "Negro interests" become partly
defined in terms of currently withheld rights of citizenship and the denial of equality.
Negroes find they must bargain for and enter into coalitions with respect to their basic
human rights. The workings of the political system force Negroes to make concessions of a morally and socially far more significant nature than in the case of the
labor union that must settle for only half of a wage increase it had asked for.

In spite of this, while the black power movement may gain something in independence and pride by being leary of white support and coalitions, outside the South
it no doubt stands to lose much more in expediency and the obtainment of short-term
minimal goals. The tragic question is not only how little has been gained from white
support and coalitions but to ask how much worse things might now be had this
minimal support not been forthcoming, and had coalitions not been entered into.

In addition many of the problems faced by Negroes are strictly speaking not civil
rights or "Negro" issues per se, but problems faced by the poor in general, the majority of whom are not Negro. While understandable, too exclusive a focus on ethnic
problems obscures this common interest.

as Rustin has noted, it is very different to say as some now do, "I don't want you because you don't want me," than to say what the white racist says, namely, "I don't want you no matter what you do."

For some black radicals any tolerance for whites is seen to indicate an Uncle Tom orientation and a lack of militancy. However, there is no reason why black anger need be connected with categorical antiwhite sentiment. The leader of a local Black Panther Party for Self-Defense states, "If I catch a cop brutalizing a black person, I'm going to kill him," but also adds, "We don't hate white men, we hate oppression." He stresses that whites should be grateful to his group because it offers organization and because it wants to prevent innocent persons from being hurt. And it is true that the disorganized and hopeless are a greater threat to white society than are organized Negroes. Here the legacy of Malcolm X works to produce anger as well as to channel it onto what is perceived as an oppressive system rather than onto whites per se.

Yet it would be wishful thinking to deny the antiwhite sentiment of an active minority and the increasing possibility of violent and self-destructive outbursts, where Negroes on a large scale would come to attack whites instead of white-owned buildings and would demonstrate their marksmanship by putting out the lives of policemen rather than by putting out automobile lights as in Watts. While such events may be encouraged by slogans and agitation, their ultimate source would be the inability of white society to change.

A popular protest song suggests that the coming battle will soon shake windows and rattle walls because the times are changing. It would appear that this battle is indeed likely to become more intense in the future. Although peace and justice may rank as equally important and compatible in the utopian imagination, in the more mundane world of bureaucratic ineptitude, white intransigence, and black militancy, they may not be compatible (nor to a great many equally important).

It is unrealistic to hope that further changes in the Negro's position will take place without intensified struggle and conflict. The extensiveness of white resistance in the North is now becoming clear to many, as is increasing Negro restiveness. The kinds of demands that Negroes will be making in the future are likely to have greater psychic and economic costs to the white community than granting the right to vote or curtailing police brutality, and hence will be met with greater resistance. The mobilization of Negroes can lead to increased mobilization of whites. Social analysts realize, moral platitudes aside, that the process through which racial injustice is eliminated is likely to be a slow one and to be incompatible with increased racial harmony, at least in the short run.[26]

[26] For example Lewis Killian and Charles Grigg, *Racial Crisis in America,* Englewood Cliffs, N. J., Prentice-Hall, 1964, pp. 130–144; and Tamotsu Shibutani and

It is similarly unrealistic to expect an aroused Negro community to love its enemies and "forgive them, for they know not what they do," except for the few who are masochists or saints or both.

However, an aroused black community can be asked that hatred and anger be addressed toward the system of evil, and those who support it, rather than toward all those who happen to have white skins. It can also be asked to reject indiscriminate terror.

Our data on the current civil rights struggle suggest that by and large the pursuit of justice with a vengeance need not involve the pursuit of vengeance. Whether this remains true in the future depends on many things, not the least of which is the extent to which this society can bridge the gap between its ideals and its practices. However, the continued failure to obtain meaningful integration or significant changes in the life situation of the average Negro may well relegate the findings reported here to a brief episode in a long historical struggle.

Kian M. Kwan,—*Ethnic Stratification: A Comparative Approach,* New York, Macmillan, 1965, pp. 341–402.

Even if equality of outcome, as well as of opportunity, is attained, tensions will exist as long as Negroes are clearly distinguishable as a group. Beyond the possible conflicts of interest that are relevant in the relations of ethnic, racial, and religious groups, men live in a symbolic world where memories of collective oppression may have relevance long after oppression has ceased. Malcolm X writes, "White people seem to think the black man ought to be shouting 'hallelujah!' Four hundred years the white man has had his foot-long knife in the black man's back—and now the white man starts to *wiggle* the knife out, maybe six inches! The black man's supposed to be grateful? Why, if the white man jerked the knife *out,* it's still going to leave a *scar!*" Malcolm X, *op. cit.,* p. 273.

Index

SURVEY RESEARCH SERVICE

National Opinion Research Center
University of Chicago

INTRODUCTION AT DWELLING UNIT:

Hello. I'm _____ from the National Opinion Research Center. We're con-
ducting a national survey and I'm here to interview a (man)(woman) who is (INSERT
QUOTA QUALIFICATION). Is there someone here who fits that description?

If Yes (PROCEED WITH INTERVIEW)

If No   (RECORD CALL ON SURS AND
        GO ON TO NEXT DU)

ENTER TIME INTERVIEW BEGAN: _____AM
                                          PM

INTRODUCTION TO INTERVIEW:

We're interested in finding out how people all over the country feel about some
important issues of the day, including how they feel about certain groups.

1. Do you think that in general things are getting better or getting worse for
   Negroes in this country?

   Better 1   8/_
   Worse 2
   Same 3
   Don't know X

2. Do you think Negroes are better off in the South, in the North, or isn't
   there any difference?

   In the South 1   9/_
   In the North 2
   No difference 3
   Don't know X

3. Where would you say things are improving faster for Negroes--in the South,
   in the North, or isn't there any difference?

   In the South 1   10/_
   In the North 2
   No difference 3
   Don't know X

4. What would you say about the civil rights demonstrations over the last few years—
that they have helped Negroes a great deal, helped a little, hurt a little, or
hurt a great deal?

Helped a great deal 1   11/
Helped a little 2
Hurt a little 3
Hurt a great deal 4
Don't know X

5. Would you like to see more demonstrations or less demonstrations?

More 1   12/
Less 2
Same 3
Don't know X

6. Some people say that no good can ever come from riots like those that happened
in Harlem this past summer. Other people say that such riots do some good because they make whites pay attention to the problems of Negroes. Which comes
closest to what you feel?

No good can ever come from riots . 1   13/
Riots do some good 2
Don't know X

7. In (name city or town), how would you say that the police treat Negroes--very
well, fairly well, fairly badly or very badly?

Very well 1   14/
Fairly well 2
Fairly badly 3
Very badly 4
Don't know X

8. If the United States got into a war today, would you personally feel this
country was worth fighting for, or not?

Yes 1   15/
No 2
Don't know X

9. In your opinion, is the government in Washington pushing integration too slow,
too fast, or about right?

Too slow 1   16/
Too fast 2
About right 3
Don't know X

10. Now I am going to read a list of statements to you and I would like to know whether you <u>agree</u> or <u>disagree</u> with each one.

		Agree	Disagree	Don't Know	
A.	An owner of property should not have to sell to Negroes if he doesn't want to.	1	2	X	17/
B.	A restaurant owner should not have to serve Negroes if he doesn't want to	1	2	X	18/
C.	Most whites want to keep Negroes down as much as they can.	1	2	X	19/
D	Negroes some day are going to rise to the leadership of the world.	1	2	X	20/
E.	It would be a good idea to give American Negroes their own country and let them set up their own nation.	1	2	X	21/
F.	Most whites who take part in civil rights demonstrations aren't really interested in the problems of Negroes.	1	2	X	22/
G.	Negroes should spend more time praying and less time demonstrating.	1	2	X	23/
H.	Negroes who want to work hard can get ahead just as easily as anyone else.	1	2	X	24/
I.	Violence will never help Negroes get equal rights.	1	2	X	25/
J.	Negroes blame too many of their problems on whites.	1	2	X	26/
K.	Generally speaking, Negroes are lazy and don't like to work hard.	1	2	X	27/
L.	Before Negroes are given equal rights, they have to show that they deserve them.	1	2	X	28/
M.	The day will come when Negroes will be fully accepted by whites.	1	2	X	29/

11. In general, do you think that Negroes are as intelligent as white people--that is, can they learn things just as well if they are given the same education and training?

Yes 1   30/
No 2
Don't know X

12. Do you think white children and Negro children should go to the same schools or to separate but equal schools?

Same schools 1   31/
Separate but equal schools . 2
Don't know X

13. If both neighborhoods were equally well kept up, would you rather live in a neighborhood that was mostly Negro or mostly white?

Mostly negro	. . 1	32/
Mostly white	. . 2	
Half and half	. . 3	
Don't know	. . . X	
No difference	. . **4**	

14. (HAND RESPONDENT CARD A) Please look at this card and tell me whether each of the people I mention is someone in civil rights, someone in sports, an entertainer, or a writer. Very few people would know all the names, so if you don't know some, just say so.

		Civil Rights	Sports	Entertainer	Writer	Don't Know	
A.	Martin Luther King . . .	1	2	**3**	4	X	33/
B.	Clarence Williams . . .	1	2	3	4	X	34/
C.	James Farmer	1	2	3	4	X	35/
D.	Ralph Ellison	1	2	3	4	X	36/
E.	Ray Charles	1	2	3	4	X	37/
F.	Floyd Patterson	1	2	3	4	X	38/
G.	Langston Hughes	1	2	3	4	X	39/
H.	Roy Wilkins	1	2	3	4	X	40/
I.	Medgar Evers	1	2	3	4	X	41/
J.	Percy Mayfield	1	2	3	4	X	42/
K.	Richard Wright	1	2	3	4	X	43/
L.	Lionel Hampton	1	2	3	4	X	44/
M.	Maury Wills	1	2	3	4	X	45/

15. (HAND RESPONDENT CARD B) Looking at this card, please tell me . . . .

A. Which of the groups on this card you have heard of? (CIRCLE AS MANY AS APPLY)

B. Are you a member of any of these groups? Which? (CIRCLE AS MANY AS APPLY) **A member of any others? Which?**

C. Which <u>one</u> do you think is doing most at the present time to help the Negro? (CIRCLE ONLY ONE)

D. Are there any groups on the card you don't like or disapprove of? (CIRCLE AS MANY AS APPLY)

Name of Group	A. 46/ Heard of Group	B. 47/ Member of Group	C. 48/ Helps Most	D. 49/ Don't Like
NAACP	1	1	1	1
CORE	2	2	2	2
Muslims . . .	3	3	3	3
None of these	0	0	0	0
Don't know .	-	-	X	X

16. (HAND RESPONDENT CARD C) Here is another card. This one has the names of some Negro leaders on it.

    A. Which person on the card do you think has done most to help Negroes? (CIRCLE ONLY ONE)

    B. Are there any you don't like or disapprove of? (CIRCLE AS MANY AS APPLY)

	A. 50/ Helped Most	B. 51/ Don't Like
Malcolm X	1	1
James Farmer	2	2
Martin Luther King	3	3
Roy Wilkins	4	4
Don't know	X	X

Now I would like to change the subject and ask you some questions about Jews.

17. Do you usually think of Jews as a race, a religion, or something else?

        Race 1   52/

        Religion 2

        Something else (SPECIFY)   3

        _____

        Don't know X

18. And do you usually think of Jews as Americans or as foreigners?

        Americans 1   53/

        Foreigners 2

        Don't know X

19. Do you think Christmas is a Jewish holiday or is it just a Christian holiday?

        Jewish holiday too 1   54/

        Just a Christian holiday 2

        Don't know X

20. The Ten Commandments are part of the Christian religion. As far as you know, are the Ten Commandments also part of the Jewish religion?

        Yes 1   55/

        No 2

        Don't know . . X

21. Do you think that on the average Jews have more money than other white people, less money, or about the same?

        More money . . . . . (ASK A) . . 1   56/

        Less money 2

        About the same 3

        Don't know X

    A. IF MORE MONEY: Some people have told us that it bothers them that Jews have more money. Does it bother you at all? In what way? (WRITE OUT FULL RESPONSE)

        Yes 1   57/

        No 2

        Don't know . . X

22. Do you think the Jews have too much power in the United States?

Yes . . (ASK Q. 23 AND Q. 24) . . 1 58/___
No 2
Don't know X

---

23. How about the business world--do you think the Jews have too much power in the business world?

Yes . . . . (ASK Q. 24) . . 1 59/___
No 2
Don't know X

IF YES ON EITHER Q. 22 OR Q. 23:

24. Do you think something should be done to take some power away from the Jews?

Yes . . . . (ASK A) . . 1 60/___
No 2
Don't know X

A. IF YES: What do you think should be done? (PROBE: Why do you think so?)

---

25. Now I am going to read a number of statements about Jews. In each case please tell me whether you think the statement is probably true or probably false.

		True	False	Don't Know	
A.	Jews are more willing than others to use shady practices to get what they want	1	2	X	61/___
B.	Jews don't care what happens to anyone but their own kind	1	2	X	62/___
C.	Jews stick together too much	1	2	X	63/___
D.	Jews are warm and friendly people	1	2	X	64/___
E.	You can usually tell whether or not a person is Jewish just by the way he looks	1	2	X	65/___
F.	Jews are better than other white people when it comes to hiring Negroes	1	2	X	66/___
G.	The trouble with Jewish businessmen is that they are so shrewd and tricky that other people don't have a fair chance in competition	1	2	X	67/___
H.	The more contact a person has with Jewish people, the more he gets to like them	1	2	X	68/___
I.	Jews still think of themselves as God's Chosen People	1	2	X	69/___
J.	Jews are just as honest as other businessmen . . .	1	2	X	70/___

002

26. How many stores where you shop are owned by whites--most of them, some of them, only a few of them, or none of them?

Most 1	8/
Some 2	
Only a few 3	
None 4	
Don't know X	

27. Some people have told us that there are white store owners who take advantage of Negro customers. How many white store owners would you say are like this-- almost all of them, many of them, a few of them, or almost none of them?

Almost all of them . . . 1	9/
Many of them 2	
A few of them 3	
Almost none of them . . . 4	
Don't know X	

28. Compared to other white store owners, do you think Jewish store owners are better, worse, or about the same?

Better (ASK A AND B) . . 1	10/
Worse . (ASK A AND B) . . 2	
About the same 3	
Don't know X	

A. IF BETTER OR WORSE: In what ways are they (better)(worse)?

11/

12/

B. ASK THE OPPOSITE OF ANSWER CODED IN Q. 28: Are there any ways they are (worse)(better) than other white store owners?

13/

14/

29. Do you think it is easier to get credit in a store owned by a Jew or in a store owned by a white person who is not Jewish?

Jew 1   15/
White person who is not Jewish . 2
Don't know X

30. From what you know or have heard, are Jewish store owners who give credit easier or harder than other white store owners on people who fall behind in their payments?

Easier 1   16/
Harder 2
Same 3
Don't know X

31. Are any of the stores in the area where you live or do your shopping owned by Jews?

Yes . . . . (ASK A) . . 1   17/
No . . . . (ASK B) . . 2
Don't know X

A.   IF YES: Do you shop in any of these stores?

Yes . . . . . (ASK C AND D) . . 1   18/
No . . . . (ASK B) . . 2
Don't know X

B.   IF NO: Have you ever shopped at a store owned by a Jew?

Yes . . . . . (ASK C AND D) . . 1   19/
No . . . . .⌐(SKIP TO Q. 32) . 2
Don't know⌐. X

IF NOW SHOP OR EVER SHOPPED AT JEWISH STORES:

C.   Have you ever bought anything on credit or on the installment plan from a store that was owned by a Jew?

Yes 1   20/
No 2
Don't know X

D.   Do you feel that Jewish store owners have ever treated you unfairly in any way?

Yes . . . . . (ASK E) . . 1   21/
No 2
Don't know X

E.   IF YES TO D: In what way were you treated unfairly?

22/
23/

32. Some Negroes say that Negro store keepers take advantage of Negroes just as much as white store owners do. Do you agree or disagree with this?

Agree 1   24/
Disagree 2
Don't know X

33. Would you say that Jewish landlords are better or worse than white landlords who are not Jewish?

Better . . . . (ASK A) . 1   25/___

Worse . . . . (ASK A) . 2

About the same 3

Don't know X

A. IF BETTER OR WORSE: How are they (better) (worse)?

26/___

27/___

34. Do you think it is better to work for a Jewish person or for a white person who is not Jewish?

Jewish person . . . . . . (ASK A) . 1   28/___

Someone who is not Jewish. (ASK A) . 2

Don't know X

A. IF JEWISH PERSON OR SOMEONE WHO IS NOT JEWISH: In what ways is it better?

29/___

30/___

35. Have you ever worked for someone who is Jewish?

                    Yes, in the past . . (ASK A) . . 1   31/___
                    Yes, I work now . . (ASK A) . . 2
                    No 3
                    Don't know X

A. IF YES: Compared to other white people you have worked for, do you
             feel these Jewish people (are)(were) better or worse people
             to work for?
                    Better . . . . (ASK B) . . 1   32/___
                    Worse . . . . (ASK B) . . 2
                    Same 3
                    Don't know X

B. IF BETTER OR WORSE: In what ways (are)(were) they (better)(worse)?

                                                              33/___

                                                              34/___

36. Has anyone (else) in your family ever worked for a Jewish person?

                    Yes, in the past 1   35/___
                    Yes, works now 2
                    No 3
                    Don't know X

37. On the whole, do you think that Jews are more in favor of civil rights for
    Negroes than other white people are, less in favor, or is there no differ-
    ence?
                    More in favor 1   36/___
                    Less in favor 2
                    No difference 3
                    Don't know X

38. Thinking of Jews as a group, would you say you feel more friendly toward
    them now than you used to, less friendly, or have you always felt as you
    do now?
                    More friendly (ASK A ON P. 11). . 1   37/___
                    Less friendly (ASK A ON P. 11). . 2
                    Same 3
                    Don't know X

38. Continued

   A. IF MORE OR LESS FRIENDLY: What would you say are the reasons that you
       feel (more)(less) friendly? (PROBE: Any
       other reasons?)

38/___

39/___

---

39. Do you think that <u>Jews</u> have changed in some ways during recent years?

Yes . . . (ASK A) . . 1   40/___
No 2
Don't know X

   A. IF YES: In what ways do you think Jews have changed? (PROBE: Any other
       ways?)

41/___

42/___

---

40. Some people say that Jews have suffered a great deal in the past. Which of
    these statements comes closest to your own feelings about this? (HAND RESPOND-
    ENT CARD D)

   The Jews have suffered no more than anybody else 1   43/___

   The Jews have suffered but they generally brought it on themselves. 2

   The Jews have suffered through no fault of their own 3

   Don't know X

---

41. As you may know, Jews have been discriminated against in the past. Would
    you say they are being discriminated against at the present time in this
    country?

Yes 1   44/___
No 2
Don't know X

42. At the present time, do you come into contact with Jews in any of the following ways?

		Yes	No	Don't Know	
A.	At your work or business?	1	2	X	45/
B.	In clubs or organizations you belong to?	1	2	X	46/
C.	Is your doctor or dentist Jewish?	1	2	X	47/
D.	Have you ever had a close friend who was Jewish? . . .	1	2	X	48/
E.	Are there any Jews living in this neighborhood? . . .	1	2	X	49/

43. Are there any ways that I have not mentioned that you come into contact with Jews? How?

1. _____ 50/

2. _____ 51/

3. _____ 52/

4. _____ 53/

003

44. I'd like to change the subject now and ask you whether you read any Negro newspapers.

Yes . . . (ASK A AND B) . . 1   8/
No 2
Don't know X

IF YES:
A. What paper is it?

Chicago Defender 1   9/
Pittsburgh Courier 2
Other _____ 3

B. How often do you read this paper--every day, several days a week, about once a week, or less often than that?

Every day 1   10/
Several days a week 2
About once a week 3
Less often than that . . . 4

45. How often do you read some other kind of newspaper--every day, several days a week, about once a week, or less often than that?

Every day 1   11/
Several days a week 2
About once a week 3
Less often than that . . . 4

46. Are there any magazines, including Negro magazines, that you read fairly regularly?

Yes . . . . (ASK A) . . 1 12/

No 2

A. IF YES: Which ones are they? (CIRCLE AS MANY AS APPLY)

Life 1 13/

Look 1 14/

Newsweek 1 15/

New Yorker 1 16/

Reader's Digest 1 17/

Saturday Evening Post 1 18/

Time 1 19/

U.S. News and World Report 1 20/

Negro magazines: Ebony 1 21/

Jet 1 22/

Negro Digest . . 1 23/

Sepia 1 24/

1 other 1 25/

2 others 2 25/

3 or more others 3 25/

47. On the average, how many hours a day do you watch television?

_____ 26/

48. (HAND RESPONDENT CARD E) Would you use this card and tell me which answer comes closest to how often you do the following things--

	Almost Every Day	Once or Twice a Week	Several Times a Month	About Once a Month	Several Times a Year	About Once a Year	Never	Don't Know
A. Spend a social evening with relatives? .	1	2	3	4	5	6	7	X 27/
B. Spend a social evening with someone who lives in your neighborhood? . .	1	2	3	4	5	6	7	X 28/
C. Spend a social evening with someone who lives outside the neighborhood? . . .	1	2	3	4	5	6	7	X 29/
D. Go to a bar or tavern? .	1	2	3	4	5	6	7	X 30/
E. Listen to the news on radio or television? . . .	1	2	3	4	5	6	7	X 31/

49. Do you belong to any organization or clubs, such as a union, lodge, church group, political organization, or social club?

Yes . . (ASK A) . . 1 32/
No 2

    A. IF YES: Could you tell me what these are? (PROBE FOR FULL DESCRIPTION OF ANY LOCAL ORGANIZATION OR GROUP WHICH IS NOT GENERALLY KNOWN)

    _____

    _____

    _____

    _____ 33/

    _____ 34/

50. I am going to read you some things that some people believe and some people don't. For each statement, please tell me whether you agree or disagree?

		Agree	Disagree	Don't Know	
A.	No weakness or difficulty can hold us back if we have enough will power	1	2	X	35/
B.	Sex crimes, such as rape and attacks on children deserve more than mere imprisonment; such criminals ought to be publicly whipped, or worse .	1	2	X	36/
C.	Much of our lives are controlled by plots hatched in secret places	1	2	X	37/
D.	Most people in welfare could take care of themselves if they really wanted to	1	2	X	38/
E.	Reading the stars can tell us a great deal about the future	1	2	X	39/
F.	People can be divided into two distinct classes-- the weak and the strong	1	2	X	40/
G.	A little practical experience is worth all the books put together	1	2	X	41/
H.	Getting to the top is more a matter of luck than ability	1	2	X	42/
I.	Poor people have no one to blame but themselves.	1	2	X	43/
J.	Most people will go out of their way to help someone else	1	2	X	44/
K.	You sometimes can't help wondering whether anything is worthwhile anymore	1	2	X	45/
L.	Nowadays a person has to live pretty much for today and let tomorrow take care of itself . . .	1	2	X	46/
M.	If you try hard enough, you can usually get what you want	1	2	X	47/

51. Do you think that having a death penalty for the worst crimes is a good idea or are you against the death penalty?

A good idea 1 48/
Against 2
Don't know X

52. What is your religion?

Protestant . (ASK A) . . 1 49/__
Catholic . . (ASK B) . . 2
Jewish . . . (ASK C) . . 3
Other (SPECIFY)   4

_____

None 5

A. IF PROTESTANT: What denomination is that?

Presbyterian . . . . . (ASK [1]) .   50/__
Lutheran . . . . (ASK [2]) .
Baptist . . . . (ASK [3]) .
United Church of Christ (ASK [4]) .
Other Denomination (SPECIFY)

_____   51/__

[1] Is that the . . . . . United Presbyterian Church or   1
                           Presbyterian Church, USA? 2

[2] Is that the . . . . . Missouri Lutheran Church 3
                           American Lutheran Church or   4
                           Lutheran Church in America   5

[3] Is that the . . . . . American Baptist 6
                           Southern Baptist 7
                           or some other Baptist Church 8

[4] Was your church originally . . . Congregationalist 9
                           or was it . . . Evangelical Reform 0

B. IF CATHOLIC: Have you ever attended a parochial school?

Yes: How many years? _____ . . 1 52/__
No 2

C. IF JEWISH: Are you a member of a synagogue?

Yes . . . . 1 53/__
No 2

_____

53. (HAND RESPONDENT CARD F) Please look at this card and tell me which statement comes closest to expressing what you believe about God.

I don't believe in God . . . . 1 54/__

I don't know whether there is a God and I don't believe there is any
way to find out 2

I don't believe in a personal God, but I do believe in a higher power
of some kind 3

I find myself believing in God some of the time, but not at other
times 4

While I have doubts, I feel that I do believe in God 5

I know God really exists and I have no doubts about it 6

Don't know X

54. Do you think that a person who doesn't accept Jesus can be saved?

                        Yes 1   55/
                        No 2
                        Other (SPECIFY)   3
                        _____
                        Don't know X

55. What about the belief that the Devil actually exists? Are you absolutely
    sure or are you pretty sure that the Devil exists or are you absolutely sure
    or pretty sure that the Devil does not exist?

                        Absolutely sure there is a Devil . 1   56/
                        Pretty sure there is a Devil . . . 2
                        Absolutely sure there is no Devil . 3
                        Pretty sure there is no Devil . . . 4
                        Don't know X

56. How sure are you that there is a life beyond death? Are you absolutely sure
    or pretty sure there is a life beyond death or are you absolutely or pretty
    sure there is no life beyond death?

                        Absolutely sure there is a life beyond death . 1 57/
                        Pretty sure there is a life beyond death . . ?
                        Absolutely sure there is no life beyond death . 3
                        Pretty sure there is no life beyond death . . . 4
                        Don't know X

57. All in all, how important would you say that religion is to you--extremely
    important, quite important, fairly important, not too important, or not
    important at all?

                        Extremely important 1   58/
                        Quite important 2
                        Fairly important 3
                        Not too important 4
                        Not important at all 5
                        Don't know X

58. About how often do you attend worship services? (CIRCLE CODE FOR CATEGORY
    THAT COMES CLOSEST)

                        Several times a week 1   59/
                        Every week 2
                        Nearly every week 3
                        2-3 times a month 4
                        About once a month 5
                        Several times a year 6
                        About once or twice a year 7
                        Less than once a year 8
                        Never 9
                        Don't know X

59. The Old Testament tells that God picked a certain group to be his Chosen People. Can you tell me what group this was--the Romans, the Greeks, the Jews, the Christians, or who?

The Romans 1   60/
The Greeks 2
The Jews 3
The Christians 4
Some other group (SPECIFY)   5

_____

Don't know X

60. Who do you think are God's Chosen People today?   (DO NOT READ CATEGORIES)

No one 1   61/
Christians 2
Protestants 3
Catholics 4
Jews 5
Other (SPECIFY) 6

_____

Don't know X

61. Who do you think was most responsible for crucifying Christ--the Romans, the Greeks, the Jews, the Christians, or who?

The Romans 1   62/
The Greeks 2
The Jews 3
The Christians 4
Some other group (SPECIFY)   5

_____

Don't know . . . . : . . X

62. Some people believe that the reason Jews have so much trouble is because God is punishing them for rejecting Jesus. Do you agree with this?

Yes 1   63/
No 2
Don't know X

63. Suppose a man admitted in public that he did not believe in God.
    A. Do you think he should be allowed to teach in a public high school?

Yes 1   64/
No 2
Don't know X

    B. Should he be allowed to hold public office?

Yes 1   65/
No 2
Don't know X

    C. Do you think that a book he wrote should be removed from a public library?

Yes 1   66/
No 2
Don't know X

64. How do you feel about prayers being said in the public schools--are you strongly in favor, somewhat in favor, somewhat opposed, or strongly opposed?

Strongly in favor 1   67/___
Somewhat in favor 2
Somewhat opposed 3
Strongly opposed 4
Don't know X

65. Now I'm going to read you another list of statements. For each statement, please tell me whether it's true for you or not.

004

		Yes True	No Not True	Don't Know	
A.	I worry quite a bit about what people think of me	1	2	X	8/___
B.	I don't like to hear a lot of arguments I disagree with	1	2	X	9/___
C.	It bothers me to see immigrants succeeding more than Americans who were born here	1	2	X	10/___
D.	Sometimes I feel so angry I feel like smashing things	1	2	X	11/___
E.	I like to hear all sides of an argument before I make up my mind	1	2	X	12/___
F.	I am suspicious of people who try to be different from everybody else	1	2	X	13/___
G.	I often feel quite lonely	1	2	X	14/___
H.	To tell the truth I would be afraid to take part in civil rights demonstrations	1	2	X	15/___
I.	I am suspicious of whites who try to help Negroes	1	2	X	16/___

Now I'd like to ask some questions about your own background.

66. What was the last grade you completed in school?

No formal schooling . . . .┐ 1   17/___
Grammar school: 1 . . . . . │ 2
                  2 . . . . . │ 3
                  3 . . . . . │ 4
                  4 . . . . . │ 5
                  5 . . . . . │ 6
                  6 . . . . . │ 7
                  7 . . . . . ├>(ASK A) . . 8
8 (finished grammar school . │ 9
High school: 9 . . . . . │ 1   18/___
              10 . . . . . │ 2
              11 . . . . . │ 3
12 (graduated from high school 4

1 year college 5
2 years college 6
3 years college 7
4 years college (graduated) 8
Postgraduate 9

A.   IF NO COLLEGE: Have you ever attended a trade school, a business or commercial school, or some other special school of this kind?

Yes 1   19/___
No 2

67. Compared to other Negroes who have had the same amount of education, would you say that you have been more successful, less successful, or would you say that you have had about the same amount of success?

More successful . . 1 20/__
Less successful . . 2
Same amount 3
Don't know X

---

68. Are you working at the present time, are you in your own business, are you unemployed, or something else? (PROBE)

Self-employed . . . . . . ┐ . . . . 1 21/__
Employed full-time . . . │ 2
Employed part-time . . . │ . . 3
Laid off temporarily . . │>(ASK A AND B) . . 4
Out of a job . . . . . . │ 5
Retired . . . . ┘ 6
Housewife . . . . . (SKIP TO QUESTION 71) . . 7
Student . . . . . . (SKIP TO QUESTION 71) . . 8
Military . . . . . (SKIP TO QUESTION 69) . . 9

IF SELF-EMPLOYED, EMPLOYED, UNEMPLOYED, OR RETIRED:

A. What kind of work (do you)(did you normally) do? (PROBE FOR EXACT DESCRIPTION OF OCCUPATION

22/__
23/__
24/__
25/__
26/__
27/__
28/__

B. In what kind of business or industry (is)(was) that?

29/__
30/__
31/__
32/__
33/__

FOR PRESENTLY WORKING RESPONDENTS, ASK Q. 69 AND Q. 70. ALL OTHERS SKIP TO Q. 71.

69. All in all, how satisfied are you with your present job--very satisfied, fairly satisfied, or not too satisfied?

Very satisfied . . . 1 34/__
Fairly satisfied . . 2
Not too satisfied . 3
Don't know X

DO NOT ASK Q. 70 FOR SELF-EMPLOYED RESPONDENTS.

70. A. Do you supervise anyone as part of your job?

Yes . . . . 1 35/__
No 2

B. How important is it to you to get a promotion on your job--very important, somewhat important, not very important, or not important at all?

Very important . . . 1 36/__
Somewhat important . 2
Not very important . 3
Not important at all 4
Don't know X

70. Continued

C. Would you say your chances of promotion in the next few years are excellent, good, fair, or poor?

Excellent 1   37/___
Good 2
Fair 3
Poor 4
Don't know X

71. Taken altogether, how would you say things are these days--would you say that you are very happy, pretty happy, or not too happy?

Very happy 1   38/___
Pretty happy 2
Not too happy . . . 3

72. What year were you born? (CIRCLE LAST TWO DIGITS OF YEAR)

    0 1 2 3 4 5 6 7 8 9 X   39/___

                  (IF DON'T KNOW, CIRCLE X AND ASK A)   40/___

    0 1 2 3 4 5 6 7 8 9 X   41/___

A. IF DON'T KNOW: Can you tell me about how old you are? _____   42/___

73. Would you say your health is usually excellent, good, fair, or poor?

Excellent 1   43/___
Good 2
Fair 3
Poor 4
Don't know X

74. Were you born in the United States?

Yes (ASK A TO D) . . 1   44/___
No .(ASK E AND F) . 2

IF YES:

A. In what state were you born? _____   45/___
                                                 46/___

B. In what state did you spend most of your childhood?

                                               47/___
                                             48/___

C. In what state was your father born? _____   49/___
                           Born outside U.S. (SPECIFY)   50/___
                                    _____ 1

D. In what state was your mother born? _____   51/___
                           Born outside U.S. (SPECIFY)   52/___
                                    _____ 1

IF NO:

E. In what country were you born? _____   67/___
                                                   68/___

F. About how old were you when you came to the U. S. _____   69/___
                                                   70/___

75. For the most part, were you raised on a farm, in a small town, in a small city, a medium-sized city, a big city, or a suburb of a big city?

```
                                Farm  . . . . . . . . 1    53/
                                Small town  . . . . . 2
                                Small city  . . . . . 3
                                Medium-sized city . . 4
                                Big city  . . . . . . 5
                                Suburb to a big city. 6
                                Don't know  . . . . . X
```

76. A. What was the last grade your father completed in school?

B. And your mother--what was the last grade in school she completed?

		A. Father	B. Mother
		54/	55/
Never attended school	. . . .	1	1
Grammar school:	1 - 4 years	2	2
	5 - 7 years	3	3
	8 years	4	4
High school:	9 - 11 years	5	5
	12 years (finished high school) .	6	6
College:	1 to 3 years college	7	7
	4 years college (finished college)	8	8
	Postgraduate	9	9
Don't know	. . . .	X	X

77. A. What kind of work did your father do when you were about 16 years old?
(PROBE FOR EXACT DESCRIPTION OF OCCUPATION)

```
                                                            56/
                                                            57/
                                                            58/
                                                            59/
B   In what kind of business or industry (is)(was) that?    60/
                                                            61/
                                                            62/
                                                            63/
C.  Was he self-employed at that time?   Yes . . . . . . . . 1   64/
                                         No  . . . . . . . . 2
```

78. Generally speaking, were your parents more religious than you are, less religious, or about the same?

```
                                More religious  . . . 1    65/
                                Less religious  . . . 2
                                About the same  . . . 3
                                Don't know  . . . . . X
```

79. I would like to ask you to compare your parents' feelings toward Jews around the time you were growing up with the way you yourself feel now. Would you say your parents felt more friendly toward Jews than you do now, less friendly, or about the same?

```
                                More friendly . . . . 1    66/
                                Less friendly . . . . 2
                                About the same  . . . 3
                                Don't know  . . . . . X
```

80. Are you single, married, divorced, separated, or widowed?

                    Single . . . . (SKIP TO QUESTION 85) . . 1   8/__
                    Presently married and living with spouse . . .⌐. 2
                    Separated . . . . ⎞   . . 3
                    Divorced . . . . ⎬(ASK A)   . . 4
                    Widowed . . . . ⌐   . . 5

A.   IF EVER MARRIED: How many children do you have?

                    None 1   9/__
                    One . . . . ⌐. 2
                    Two . . . . │. 3
                    Three . . . . ⎬(ASK B AND C) . . 4
                    Four . . . . │. 5
                    Five . . . . │. 6
                    Six or more . . . .⌐. 7

IF ANY CHILDREN:

B.   How many of them under twenty-one?   _____   10/__

C.   How many of them under twelve?   _____   11/__

FOR <u>PRESENTLY MARRIED</u>, ASK Q's. 81 TO 83.

FOR <u>WIDOWED, DIVORCED, OR SEPARATED WOMEN</u>, SKIP TO Q. 84.

FOR <u>ALL OTHERS</u>, SKIP TO Q. 85.

81. What was the last grade your (husband)(wife) completed in school?

                    Never attended school 1   12/__
                    1 - 4 years 2
                    5 - 7 years 3
                    8 years 4
                    9 - 11 years 5
                    12 years (finished high school) 6
                    1 - 3 years college 7
                    4 years college (finished college) . . . 8
                    Postgraduate 9
                    Don't know X

82. Is your (husband)(wife) working at the present time, does (he)(she) have (his)
    (her) own business, is (he)(she) unemployed, or what?

                    Self-employed . . .⌐. 1   13/__
                    Employed full-time . .│. 2
                    Employed part-time . .│. 3
                    Laid off temporarily .⎬(ASK A AND B) . . 4
                    Out of a job . . . . .│. 5
                    Retired . . . .⌐. 6
                    Housewife .⌐. 7
                    Student . . .⎬(SKIP TO QUESTION 85) . . 8
                    Military . .⌐. 9

IF <u>SELF-EMPLOYED, EMPLOYED, UNEMPLOYED, OR RETIRED</u>:

A.   What kind of work (does he/she)(did he/she normally) do? (PROBE FOR   14/__
     EXACT DESCRIPTION OF OCCUPATION)   15/__
                                                                             16/__
                                                                             17/__
                                                                             18/__
B.   In what kind of business or industry (is)(was) that?   19/__
                                                                             20/__
                                                                             21/__
                                                                             22/__
                                                                             23/__

IF SPOUSE IS PRESENTLY WORKING, ASK Q. 83:

83. How satisfied would you say (he)(she) is with (his)(her) present job--very satisfied, fairly satisfied, or not too satisfied?

Very satisfied . . . 1	24/__
Fairly satisfied . . 2	
Not too satisfied . 3	
Don't know X	

FOR WIDOWED, DIVORCED, OR SEPARATED WOMEN, ASK Q. 84:

84. A. What kind of work did your husband do during most of the time that you
were living together? (PROBE FOR EXACT DESCRIPTION OF OCCUPATION) 25/__
26/__
27/__
28/__
29/__
   B. What kind of business or industry was that? 30/__
31/__
32/__
33/__
34/__

ASK EVERYONE:

85. And how many years have you lived in this house?

Less than 1 year . 1	35/__
1 up to 2 years . 2	
2 up to 3 years . 3	
3 up to 6 years . 4	
6 up to 10 years . 5	
10 up to 20 years. 6	
20 up to 30 years. 7	
More than 30 years 8	
Don't know X	

---

86. About how many years have you lived in (name city or town)?

Less than 1 year . 1	36/__
1 up to 2 years . 2	
2 up to 3 years . 3	
3 up to 6 years . 4	
6 up to 10 years . 5	
10 up to 20 years. 6	
20 up to 30 years. 7	
More than 30 years 8	
Don't know X	

---

87. Is this the kind of neighborhood you would like to continue living in?

Yes 1	37/__
No 2	
Don't know X	

---

88. Do you own your own home or do you rent?

Own 1	38/__
Rent 2	
Other 3	

89. (HAND RESPONDENT CARD G) Will you please look at this card and tell me which figure comes closest to your total family income for the past year--before taxes, that is? Just tell me the letter next to the figure that fits you best.

A.	Less than $ 1,000	. . . 1	39/__
B.	$ 1,000 to $ 1,999	. . . 2	
C.	$ 2,000 to $ 2,999	. . . 3	
D.	$ 3,000 to $ 3,999	. . . 4	
E.	$ 4,000 to $ 4,999	. . . 5	
F.	$ 5,000 to $ 5,999	. . . 6	
G.	$ 6,000 to $ 6,999	. . . 7	
H.	$ 7,000 to $ 7,999	. . . 8	
I.	$ 8,000 to $ 8,999	. . . 9	
J.	$ 9,000 to $ 9,999	. . . 1	40/__
K.	$10,000 to $11,999	. . . 2	
L.	$12,000 to $14,999	. . . 3	
M.	$15,000 to $19,999	. . . 4	
N.	$20,000 to $24,999	. . . 5	
O.	$25,000 or more	 6	
P.	Don't know	 X	

90. How satisfied would you say that you are with your present income--very satisfied, fairly satisfied, or not too satisfied?

Very satisfied . . . . 1 41/__
Fairly satisfied . . . 2
Not too satisfied . . . 3
Don't know X

91. By and large, do you think of yourself as being of the upper class, upper middle class, middle class, working class, or lower class?

Upper . . . . 1 42/__
Upper middle 2
Middle 3
Working 4
Lower 5
Don't know X

92. Thinking back to the time you were growing up, would you say that your family was of the upper class, upper middle class, middle class, working class, or lower class?

Upper . . . . 1 43/__
Upper middle 2
Middle 3
Working 4
Lower 5
Don't know X

I have only a few more questions to ask you.

93. Do you usually think of yourself as a Republican, a Democrat, an Independent, or what?

Republican	1	44/
Democrat	2	
Independent . (ASK A) . .	3	
Other _____	4	
Don't know	X	

A. IF INDEPENDENT: Even though you think of yourself as an Independent, do you usually lean more toward the Republicans or more toward the Democrats?

Republicans 1

Democrats 2

Won't choose . . . . y

94. As things stand now, which candidate do you prefer in this coming election--the Democrat, Johnson, or the Republican, Goldwater?

Johnson	1	45/
Goldwater	2	
Don't know . . (ASK A) . .	X	

A. IF DON'T KNOW: The way it looks now, if you had to choose who would you prefer--Johnson or Goldwater?

Johnson 1

Goldwater 2

Can't choose . . . . y

95. Do you think you will certainly vote, probably vote, or aren't you sure yet?

Certainly	1	46/
Probably	2	
Not sure	3	
Probably not	4	
Certainly not	5	
Don't know	X	

96. Did you vote in the last presidential election in 1960 when Kennedy ran against Nixon, or did something happen to keep you from voting?

Did vote . . . (ASK A) . .	1	47/
Did not vote	2	

A. IF DID VOTE: Who did you vote for--Kennedy or Nixon?

Kennedy	1	48/
Nixon	2	

97. Is there anyone in your immediate family who is blind?

Yes . (ASK A AND B) . . 1	49/

No 2

IF YES:
A. How is that person related to you?

Self 1   50/

Parent or parent-in-law 2

Sibling or sibling in-law 3

Spouse 4

Child or grandchild . . 5

Other relative

_____ 6

B. Could we have his name and address? (We may be planning a study of the blind sometine im the future, and it would be helpful to have his/her name and address.)

Name _____

Address _____

City and State _____

98. May I have your name and telephone number in case my office wants to verify this interview?

NAME _____

TELEPHONE NUMBER _____ AREA CODE _____

Thank you very much for your time and cooperation. (You have been very helpful.)

===

FILL IN THE FOLLOWING ITEMS IMMEDIATELY AFTER LEAVING RESPONDENT.

TIME INTERVIEW ENDED: _____ AM
                                PM

1. Respondent's Sex:

Male 1   51/
Female 2

2. Respondent's Race:

White 1   52/
Negro 2
Oriental 3
Other   4

_____

53/
3. Respondent's Address: _____   54/
                          Street or Rural Route   55/
                                                           56/
              _____   57/
                    City or Town and State   58/

59/
4. Date of Interview: _____ 5. S.U. Number _____   60/
                                                                    61/
                                                                    62/
6. Interviewer's Signature: _____   63/
                                                              64/

Interviewer's Observation Sheet

7. Would you say the respondent was unusually tall, somewhere in the normal
    range, or unusually short?

    Unusually tall 1   65/___

    Normal range 2

    Unusually short 3

---

8. Would you say that the respondent was unusually fat, somewhere in the normal
    range, or unusually thin?

    Unusually fat 1   66/___

    Normal range 2

    Unusually thin 3

---

9. Generally speaking, would you say that the respondent was unusually attractive,
    somewhere in the normal range, or unusually unattractive?

    Unusually attractive . . 1   67/___

    Normal range 2

    Unusually unattractive . 3

---

10. The respondent seemed:

    Truthful 1   68/___

    Evasive 2

    Untruthful 3

    Can't be determined . . X

---

11. Standard of living of neighborhood:

    Upper class 1   69/___

    Middle class 2

    Upper middle 3

    Lower middle 4

    Working class 5

    Lower class 6

---

12. Racial composition of neighborhood:

    All white 1   70/___

    All Negro 2

    Mixed 3

    Can't tell X

---

13. How did the respondent's home compare to others in the neighborhood?

    Much better 1   71/___

    Slightly better 2

    Slightly worse 3

    Much worse 4

    About the same 5

This book may be kept

FOURTEEN DAYS

A fine will be charged for each day the book is kept over time.

NOV 21 '69			
JUN 29			
MAR 13			
DEC 13 1989			
DEC 0 3 1997			
OCT 2 2 1998			

bd   CAT. NO. 23 159   PRINTED IN U.S.A.